ITALIAN CULTURE

John Hely-Hutchinson LLD, Provost, 1774–94, is here reproduced
by permission of the Board of Trinity College. The original hangs in the
Provost's house, and is attributed to J. Peacock, after Joshua Reynolds.

ITALIAN CULTURE
Interactions, Transpositions, Translations

Cormac Ó Cuilleanáin, Corinna Salvadori
and John Scattergood

EDITORS

Per Maggie
ricordando le ore
a lezione, e con stima
per il suo coraggio nel
dolore —
Con affetto, Corinna
aprile
2006

FOUR COURTS PRESS

Set in 10.5 pt on 13.5 pt Bembo for
FOUR COURTS PRESS LTD
7 Malpas Street, Dublin 8, Ireland
e-mail: info@four-courts-press.ie
http://www.four-courts-press.ie
and in North America by
FOUR COURTS PRESS
c/o ISBS, 920 N.E. 58th Avenue, Suite 300, Portland, OR 97213.

A catalogue record for this title
is available from the British Library.

ISBN 1–84682–025–1

Printed in England
by MPG Books, Bodmin, Cornwall.

Contents

Acknowledgments

The editors gratefully acknowledge the financial contribution of the Faculty of Arts (Letters) of Trinity College Dublin that has made this publication possible, and the kind permission of the Board of Trinity College for the use of the reproduction of the portrait of John Hely-Hutchinson LLD, Provost, 1774–94, and of the 1755 drawing of the Baptistery in Florence, by Ferdinando Ruggieri. Permission was also generously granted by Mondadori and Garzanti to reproduce the texts by Piero Bigongiari and Mario Luzi, respectively, and by *Translation Ireland* and *Poetry Ireland* to reproduce some of the translations by Mark Hutcheson.

The editors are extremely grateful to all the contributors for their work on this volume, and they also wish to thank the following for their generous assistance at various stages: John Barnes, Michael Cronin, Jane Everson, Phyllis Gaffney, Jennifer Lorch, Duncan McDonnell, Brian McGing, Edward McParland, Catherine O'Brien, Daragh O'Connell, Eithne O'Connell, Cathal Ó Háinle and John Took. The editorial assistance of Francesca Bernardis at the outset was invaluable, as were the organizational skills of Eithne Healy, Mary Keating and Daragh O'Connell in making the events of April 2002 so successful.

Preface*

At a seminar in April 2002 at Trinity College Dublin, marking the retirement of Corinna Salvadori Lonergan, former students, recent graduates, colleagues and friends contributed papers on a variety of subjects. The occasion was both sombre and celebratory. On the one hand it remembered the recent deaths of two scholars – Harry McWilliam and Tom O'Neill – both of whom had contributed significantly to the Italian department in the latter half of the twentieth century. On the other it marked nearly two hundred and thirty years of teaching Italian in Trinity College, despite a variety of vicissitudes described in the opening historical essay by Corinna Salvadori.

Common themes among the papers presented on that day determined the choice of essays for the present collection, and were subsequently reinforced by the addition of further contributions. The resulting volume celebrates friendship, communication, performance, influence and transmission, as they apply not only to the academic study of Italian culture, but also to the creation of that culture.

Translation, both as practice and metaphor, provides a unifying thread. Contributors have been broadly concerned with the way in which Italian culture, particularly Italian literary culture, has interacted with other cultures and with itself, and so it was perhaps inevitable that many of the papers would be about transmission and especially about translation – partly because it is the activity which most firmly brings languages and cultures into relationship with one another, and partly because it is an activity in which several of the past and present members of the Italian department have excelled. Thus Cormac Ó Cuilleanáin's essay analyzes the contribution of Harry McWilliam, in the context of both translation criticism and theory, while Brian Moloney writes on Tom O'Neill who, fine revealer of allusiveness in both prose and poetry as he was, translated Piero Bigongiari. This task is taken up here by Mark Hutcheson who both translates and recreates poems by Piero Bigongiari and Mario Luzi, while reflecting on right and wrong turnings taken during the transmission process, and on the interaction between translation and new poetry. These efforts

* The present Preface is written by two of the editors. They would have liked to use their privileged position to pay tribute to the outstanding qualities of the third editor – the energy, commitment and style that she has brought to Italian studies in Trinity College over the past forty years – but their admiration for her qualities is exceeded only by their fear of her disapproval, so they will refrain from attempting any such tribute.

to convey Italian texts into English meet Dante Gabriel Rossetti's touchstone of translation quality, 'that a good poem shall not be turned into a bad one', while other instances of cultural transmission studied in the present volume exemplify, *mutatis mutandis*, Rossetti's further contention that 'the only true motive for putting poetry into a fresh language must be to endow a fresh nation, as far as possible, with one more possession of beauty'. Several essays address ways in which the beauties of Italian culture have been transmitted to fresh nations: George Talbot does this in relation to film, while John Scattergood looks at the way European humanist writings, including Machiavelli, came to be known in Ireland. Other essays deal with particular authors and texts: Eiléan Ní Chuilleanáin looks at the complex ways in which Thomas More related to Pico della Mirandola's life and works as he rendered them in English, Richard Andrews explores the absorption of features of the *commedia dell'arte* in Molière's *L'Avare*, while Doug Thompson looks at the Dantean echoes in T.S. Eliot's 'Burnt Norton', searching not only for obvious quotations but also for the rationale that creates a 'pattern behind the pattern'. Carol O'Sullivan shows how a proper consideration of what is involved in the translation (including self-translation) of James Joyce's *Anna Livia Plurabelle* can lead us to a broader appreciation of the creative status of translation as a language activity.

Translation emerges unambiguously in Rosangela Barone's essay as she takes us on a tour of creative responses and translations across four languages: from *Waiting for Godot* (Beckett's self-translation of his original *En attendant Godot*) to Alan Titley's *Tagann Godot* and her own Italian rendering of that text as *Arriva Godot*, while offering another example of the self-reflexive process that all translators must undertake. In both Titley's work and hers, we see the living process of creation as reaction. As we read her choices in the light of the staging of Titley's play, we find that we have strayed into the crossfire between language, literature and performance, a nexus continued in the essays by Richard Andrews and George Talbot, who show us how cultural and technical challenges and constraints are played out creatively on the stage and in the cinema, in ways which may be hidden from the audience though performed in full view of the auditorium.

Joseph Farrell, in his study of the *teatro grottesco*, is also concerned with performance arts, and with a group of dramatists who were never a school in the formal sense. What divided them was as deep as what united them, yet their interactions show another vital aspect of collegiality: the nexus of culture, companionship and professional practice in literary movements across the centuries. This is obvious, in the present volume, from Dante's fellow-poets to the actors of the *commedia dell'arte*, from the *teatro grottesco* to *mitomodernismo*, and much can be learned by reflecting on these interactions. They show us the personal and social context in which cultural works come into being, and although it is customary to look back afterwards and discern 'major' from 'minor' figures, it is well to remember that the development of even the greatest artists is nurtured by their peers, friends and rivals, who serve as their first critical readers. In the case of *mitomodernismo*, as described by Roberto Bertoni, the backward glance is not yet possible; this is a report from the front line of contemporary literature. In the case of Dante's Florence, Peter Armour shows how doctrines of *amicizia* underpin the complex doctrines of *amore* which are now seen as Dante's hallmark.

The book reflects something of the range of Italian culture covered by the Italian Department in Trinity College, from its most recent development – its contribution to a postgraduate degree in literary translation – to the long standing inclusion of Dante, Boccaccio, Machiavelli, and Ariosto in its undergraduate core course. These authors are here studied from various angles, and some are shown as living influences on major modern writers: another form of creative *amicizia*. Daragh O'Connell's study of the transmutations of Angelica shows how the myths that artists create can have an afterlife reaching far beyond their original maker's intentions. University teachers hope that a similar process of stimulation and reaction may apply in their profession.

Reading through these essays, with their major and minor overlaps of theme and approach, we see that literary culture is itself the product of traditions revived and extended, of friends, patrons, imitators, emulators, translators, adaptors, exporters and importers of cultural ideas and practices. Whether it is the poets of Florence testing and developing their art, English writers learning from their Italian models, or French comedy picking up rhythms and routines from a vernacular Italian tradition, the reader can find in these pages the living record of the transmission and development of European culture. The Italian Studies profession may be relatively small in the English-speaking world, yet it is highly productive and cohesive. It is our hope that some of the enjoyment that went into the making of this collection may be transmitted to the reader, and that, in its own way, this collaborative venture may stand as an example of the worldwide enterprise of Italian studies, *legato con amore in un volume*.

Dove 'l sì sona: two hundred and thirty years of Italian in Trinity College Dublin*

Corinna Salvadori

PART I: FROM THE BEGINNING IN 1776

Trinity College is unique in these islands in having had teachers of French, German, Italian and Spanish uninterruptedly for over two hundred years, although the nature, scope and aim of the teaching have changed radically.

The first intimation of this momentous development is to be found in the minutes of a meeting of the Board of Trinity College held on 4 August 1774. One of the suggestions put to the seven Senior Fellows by the newly appointed provost, the controversial John Hely-Hutchinson, was: 'that it would be highly useful to have Professors of modern languages established in the College'.[1] The outcome was the foundation of two chairs, one of Italian and Spanish and one of French and German, ratified by a letter despatched by King George III to the lord lieutenant on 29 October 1776. The king made financial provision for the foundation, thus relieving the provost of his altruistic determination to pay the salaries of the professors (£100 each) out of his own stipend (£800).

Provost Hely-Hutchinson's far-seeing decision, while applauded by posterity, was strongly criticized at the time. A Senior Fellow described it as 'pernicious'; would the next step be a professor of Horsemanship?[2] Languages, like horsemanship, were 'polite accomplishments' and 'teachers of modern languages, fencing and dancing masters, and horse-riders, are not always the most eligible companions for youth'.[3] The decision was taken, however, in a climate most propitious to it. It was customary for the sons of the Irish nobility and landed gentry, after their studies in Trinity, to complete their education by travelling on the Continent. That the University's graduates should have a knowledge of

---

* This brief history is dedicated to all students of Italian in Trinity College Dublin, past, present and future. The substance of Part I of this history appeared in the *Bulletin of the Society for Italian Studies*, 9 (1976), 8–16, and, in Italian, in *Il veltro*, 21, 1–2 (1977), 134–40. I am grateful for permission to re-use the material. **1** Minutes of the meetings of the Board of Trinity College will be referred to in the notes as BM and followed by the relevant date. **2** Patrick Duigenan, *Lachrymae Academicae: or, The Present Deplorable State of the College* (Dublin: printed for the author, and sold by all the booksellers, 1777), pp. 225–7. **3** Ibid.

the necessary foreign languages before they set out on their travels was an obvious advantage. But, aside from this practical consideration, one must remember that interest in continental literature flourished in the second half of the eighteenth century, and a number of Irishmen played an important part in the pre-romantic revival of British interest in Italian culture.[4] Some of these were graduates and Fellows of Trinity College, such as Philip Boyne who translated the *Gerusalemme liberata* (1761) and Henry Boyd who gave English readers the first entire translations of Dante's *Commedia* (1802) and of Petrarch's *Triumphs* (1807). Two Trinity Fellows, Thomas Wilson and Matthew Young, sponsored a highly laudable project whose floundering is much to be regretted: a handsome edition of Boiardo's *Orlando innamorato*, which had not been printed for over two hundred years. Not a Trinity man, but certainly a friend of the College, was the Dublin born James Caulfeild, earl of Charlemont (1728–99), who was an influential patron of Italian studies. This first president of the Royal Irish Academy had a scholarly knowledge of Italian poetry of which he wrote a three volume history illustrated with translations of the best poets.[5] He seems to have advised the College to invite as its first professor of Italian or of 'any other modern language he may chuse' (*sic*) his friend Giuseppe Baretti, who had dedicated to him his *Account of the Manners and Customs of Italy*.[6] Sadly for Trinity, Baretti declined: 'Were I thirty years younger [...],' he wrote to the Senior Fellow who had tendered the invitation on behalf of the provost.[7]

The College could have done a lot worse, however, than to secure instead, as professor of Italian and Spanish, the linguist Antonio Vieyra who had published in 1773 his Portuguese/English dictionary. According to procedure that was to last nearly a century, he was elected and recommended by the Board of the College and appointed by the crown in 1776. Though we have no evidence of Vieyra's work as a teacher of languages in the University, nor for that matter of Antonio Desca's who was appointed to the chair of French and German, the Board must have been suitably impressed by Vieyra's scholarship to give financial assistance to the publication of his work on the affinities between

4 See G.H. McWilliam, 'Some notes on the Irish contribution (1761–1812) to the Pre-Romantic Rediscovery of Italian Literature' in *Italian Presence in Ireland* (Dublin: Italian Cultural Institute, 1964), pp. 51–77. 5 Lord Charlemont, *History of Italian Poetry from Dante to Metastasio: A Critical Edition from the Autograph Manuscript*, ed. by George Talbot, 3 vols (Lampeter: Edwin Mellen Press, 2000). 6 The invitation written by the Senior Fellow, Thomas Leland, and Baretti's reply are reproduced by Lacy Collison-Morley in *Giuseppe Baretti: with an account of his literary friendships and feuds in Italy and in England in the days of Dr Johnson* (London: J. Murray, 1909), pp. 275–7. I am indebted to my former colleague, the late Professor W.B. Stanford, for a reference that led to my discovering this correspondence. 7 Ibid.

Arabic, Persian, Latin, and the Romance tongues. While at Trinity, he also published a volume of philological notes on the *Koran*. His bequeathing his library to the College must be indicative of his gratitude.

Of the existence of his successor, Alfonso Pellegrini, professor of Italian and Spanish from 1799 to 1824, we have only one outward sign: he published a laudatory sonnet on the election of Provost John Kearney. The limitations imposed on his imagination by the acrostic nature of the composition may be to blame for its dullness.

The teaching of languages seems to have been marginal to the studies of the University, where for a BA degree one read Greek and Latin, logic, ethics, mathematics, and Natural Philosophy. The appointment of Evasio Antioco Radice in 1824 brought some change. This patriot, who had escaped from Italy under sentence of death for his part in the Piedmontese rising of 1821, found his first home in exile in Spain, where he may have obtained the necessary knowledge of the language to enable him to secure the position of professor of Italian and Spanish in the University of Dublin. Though not an academic by vocation, nor a scholar like Vieyra – and the Trinity library had much to offer to an Italianist having secured by then the Fagel collection and the precious Italian incunabula of the Quin collection – Radice stands out for his seriousness of attitude as a teacher of languages. We learn from the Board minutes and the University calendars of the time that he volunteered to deliver lectures in Spanish and Italian literature without fee,[8] that he established the practice that the professors of modern languages should be in their chambers three days every week in order to receive pupils; that one day a week he delivered 'a prelection of the literature of some of the southern nations of Europe',[9] that he taught not just Italian and Spanish but also invaded the territory of his colleague, Charles Williomier, professor of French and German, without any recorded objection on the latter's part. Students were privileged to attend Radice's classes 'under advantages not afforded to others',[10] this mysterious clause being changed subsequently to the more mundane 'on the payment of a small fee to the Professor'.[11] The fee was truly small: two guineas to be paid at entrance for two years' tuition. Radice took his work so seriously that he introduced examinations in modern languages and convinced the Board in 1834 to award silver medals to those who performed with excellence. His measure of fairness is seen in the ruling that those who had already travelled on the continent were excluded from competing for prizes. The merit of candidates was to be ascer-

---

8 BM 11/2/1832.   **9** BM 15/12/1838.   **10** *Dublin University Calendar*, 1834, p. lvii.   **11** *Dublin University Calendar*, 1835, p. 27.

tained by the translation of English passages into the foreign language and by
conversation, two still extant features of lingustic assessment. From a letter he
wrote to the Board in March 1839, complaining that students were not attend-
ing classes, we can deduce that much of his Herculean effort may have moved
molehills rather than mountains, and one cannot but smile at the terse and practical reply sent by the Senior Fellows: 'the Professor be informed, that the Board
wishes him to repeat the trial next term, varying the hours of attendance'.[12]
(Was he, perhaps, lecturing at 8 a.m. as some of us were to do?)

Seriously though Radice took his work in Trinity, it is obvious that his commitment was primarily to the patriotic cause. He strove incessantly to return to
his native country and eventually achieved this, aided possibly by Mazzini with
whom he associated in London. In 1848 Radice was abroad on political matters
but left a deputy, Augusto Cesare Marani, who was a teacher of Italian in Dublin.
Radice resigned from his professorship formally with a letter from Brussels dated
23 January 1849, in which he expressed 'feelings of the deepest regret' at being
compelled to sever his Irish connection – not entirely, for he had married an
Irishwoman – to take up 'new and important duties'.[13] He returned to Turin,
to military honours and parliamentary duties undertaken with zeal and ability,
and it is sad to reflect that after a long Irish exile preparing for a fruitful return
in patria, this was to be short lived. He died of cholera in 1855.[14]

In his latter years in Trinity, and precisely since 1842 when the Reverend
Ignatius George Abeltshauser was appointed professor of French and German,
Radice had a colleague who shared his seriousness of approach to his duties in
the College. Indeed, so teutonically serious was Abeltshauser that he prevailed
at once upon the Board to substitute prizes, to consist of books in the language,
for the silver medals – beautiful, useless Italian things, no doubt. 'With
Abeltshauser's arrival', writes an historian of the chair of German in Trinity
College, 'the period of dilettantism was finished and the teaching of German as
a serious discipline had begun'.[15] But with the departure of Radice, Italian was
to enjoy dubious notoriety.

There were six applicants for the vacant chair of Italian and Spanish. They
included Radice's deputy of four years' standing, Marani, and a teacher of Italian

---

12 BM 23/3/1839.   13 BM 26/1/1849. It is more reasonable to assume that the date of
Radice's letter was transcribed incorrectly (3 rather than 23 January?) than that it travelled
from Brussels to Dublin in three days.   14 I was honoured to meet the grandson of Evasio
Radice, Fulke R. Radice, CBE, MA (Oxon.) who in 1982 founded the Evasio Radice Prize,
which is awarded annually in Italian in the two-subject moderatorship. See Fulke Rosavo
Radice, *The Radice Family* (Ilkely: The Scolar Press, 1979).   15 M.M. Raraty, 'The Chair
of German at Trinity College, Dublin 1775–1866' in *Hermathena*, 102 (spring 1966), 53–72
(p. 63).

in Dublin named Basilio Angeli, once a *figurista* in England, a painter of figures in landscapes by others, or so it was alleged in the notorious court cases of summer and autumn 1856. It is likely that the Senior Fellows chose Angeli because of political pressure; one of his referees was James Corry Connellan, private secretary to the lord lieutenant, whose testimonial was dispatched, impressively, from the viceregal lodge. As Angeli's defence stated in a densely crowded court room: 'when one man is appointed, another man is *dis*appointed – and disappointed gentlemen generally have friends'.[16] The three distinguished Trinity Fellows and professors who sponsored the cause of the disappointed Marani were Joseph Galbraith, John Kells Ingram and Samuel Haughton. They did not rest until they had a body of evidence to put before the Board to support their contention that Angeli had been less than honest in presenting his credentials and, more seriously, that being neither a scholar nor a gentleman he was incompetent and unfit to be professor of Italian and Spanish in the University of Dublin. Angeli took legal proceedings against Galbraith for libel; there were two court cases and the final result was that the crown acceded to the Board's request that Angeli be dismissed. The Board had already acted on this assumption and in April of that year Marani had been appointed 'Lecturer and Examiner in Italian and Spanish' with the security of a fixed salary so that he should not have to rely entirely on fees from the students. In fairness to the Board, one must add that it gave Angeli a pension and paid for a one-way ticket to Italy.

From the transcript of the court cases one well believes that Angeli had presented to the Board a much enhanced picture of himself. At Pisa, for example, he was an *uditore* and not a matriculated student. The lengthy discussion of the precise nature of an *uditore* was terminated humourously by the chief justice with the question: 'What sort of a 'tory' is as '*auditore*' – (laughter)'.[17] Galbraith's self-rightousness (vindication of justice, triumph of truth etc.) also gave rise to mirth which was duly recorded by the clerk. The cases were, indeed, most entertaining. Much was made of the fact that Trinity men intending to be 'candidates for appointments to the Civil Service in India feel it to be their interest to acquire a knowledge of the language and literature of Italy',[18] a knowledge which Angeli was considered unfit to impart. In truth there was nothing charismatic about Italian for India; it was allegedly easier to score marks for Italian than for other languages in the competitive examinations for the civil service.

One cannot but feel a certain sympathy for Angeli who was more sinned against than sinning. While Marani had a case in arguing that the professor was

---

16 W.R. Furlong, *Action for Libel*, Report of the case of *Angeli v. Galbraith* (Dublin: M.H. Gill at the UP, 1857), p. 7. 17 Ibid., p. 28. 18 Ibid., p. 14.

unfit to teach Spanish, there was less of a case where Italian was concerned though
Angeli was, to be sure, no scholar. Many of the faults found in his translation of
Sir Robert Kane's rhetorical and woolly inaugural address on his election as president of the Queen's College, in Cork, were more inelegant renderings and
printer's mistakes than downright linguistic errors. One cannot entirely blame
Angeli for failing occasionally to grasp the meaning of the English original. His
phrase 'Signori d'ambo i sessi', which was much bandied through both court
cases, and gave rise to the quoting in court of Cardinal Antonelli's comment that
'he was surprised to learn that there was any city in the world that could furnish
one thousand hermaphrodites',[19] could be said to find a parallel in Manzoni's
'Signori d'ogni età e d'ogni sesso', as an anonymous correspondent to a newspa-
per pointed out.[20] What really destroyed Angeli, however, was the evidence of
Antonio Panizzi, then director of the British Museum, whose unflinchingly arro-
gant remarks, delivered with utmost authority, not only silenced the nicer if lesser
man, Angeli, but even his much more famous defence counsel, Isaac Butt.

The difficulties the Board had encountered in requesting Angeli's dismissal
by the crown, may be responsible for the fact that it sought, shortly after, to
have the right of appointment of the professors of languages vested in itself, and
a letter was despatched in September 1858 by Queen Victoria repealing the letters patent of King George III. It was the Board therefore who appointed A.C.
Marani professor of Italian and Spanish in 1862. He was the last to hold the title
and was not given the honorary LLD that it had been customary to give the
professors in languages since the first appointment in the previous century. He
served the College conscientiously if unremarkably, teaching and examining
the limited number of students who presented themselves for Italian and Spanish.
The examination papers he set compare unfavourably with our modern ones
in that the questions test mnemonic rather than critical ability (for example,
'What is the early author's name mentioned by Dante in the fifteenth canto of
his *Inferno* and what work did he write?'), or are so generic that a candidate
could not possibly have answered in any depth (for example, 'Compare Ariosto
with Tasso and say to whom you would give the preference, and why?'). Yet,
one can expect that the prizemen, and there were some nearly every year, knew
their Italian grammar well in order to cope with the tricky questions on it and
with the stiff passages of translation. They must also have had a detailed knowledge of both the history and the literature of Italy of the periods prescribed.
These, however, very much reflect the fashion of the time; few if any undergraduates now could answer 'Qual è la storia scritta da Caterino Davila che gli

19 Ibid., p. 125.   20 Ibid., p. 507.

ha meritata l'immortalità?',[21] especially as the book concerned the French wars, nor (one hopes) would they now make that particular grammatical agreement.

Since 1834 Trinity had examinations for degrees with honor, or moderatorships, which enabled an undergraduate to specialize. Languages were not included among the moderatorships until 1873, although a formal qualification in either Italian or German or French (listed in that order) had been required for the degree in Music since 1863. For a moderatorship in modern literature, a student had to read two languages, one of them being English and the other either French, German, Italian or Spanish. Although the calendars from 1873 to 1876 give full honor and moderatorship courses for Italian and Spanish, it is doubtful that these courses were given. Did students not present themselves or was the polyglot Robert Atkinson channelling into French all those interested in a Romance language? He had succeeded Marani with the title of lecturer in Italian in 1867 and was elected professor of Romance Languages in 1869. In May of that year, by a decree of the provost and Senior Fellows with the consent of the Visitors, the professorship of Italian and Spanish had become one in Romance Languages, to include French. It was a case of the job changing to fit the man, but it was a sad change for Italian as no chair of it has been re-established since in the University of Dublin.

Atkinson, in 1871, was elected also professor of Sanskrit and Comparative Philology. This encyclopædic man, with numerous publications to reflect the range of his languages, taught and examined in Italian but his commitment to it must have been less strong than to French. Two other professors catered for the needs of those interested in Italian: the professor of Modern History, James Barlow, author of, *inter alia*, *Lectures on the History of Italy in the Middle Ages*, lectured on Dante; and the professor of Ancient History, John P. Mahaffy, who was to become one of Trinity's most famous provosts, taught language. However, moderatorships in Italian and Spanish were abandoned though reasons for this decision are not recorded in either Council or Board minutes. Teaching in these languages was to continue, as were the annual examinations for prizes which lasted until 1919, attracting candidates regularly though more for Italian than for Spanish. The Italian course was: Alfieri, *Saul*, *Bruto minore*, *Agide*; Manzoni, *Promessi sposi*, chapters 1–12; Dante, *Purgatorio*, Cantos 1–20. The list of prizemen, as they are styled, though some in latter years were female,

---

21 These three questions feature in the Examination papers in Italian for the years 1862, 1859 and 1863 respectively. Caterino Enrico Davila (1576–1631), was born in Padua; named by his parents after the king and queen of France, he is famous for his *Storia delle guerre civili di Francia*, a work of some thousand pages covering the period 1559–98. There are three copies in the Trinity collection, in English, French and Italian.

includes as first rank prizeman in Italian in 1884, Douglas Hyde, who was to become first president of Ireland.

In 1906 English as a compulsory component of the moderatorship in Modern Literature was dropped and a student could take any two of English, French and German. Italian and Spanish were added to that meagre list in 1920 when moderatorship courses were introduced together with courses leading to an ordinary (that is, pass) degree in these languages. By 1976, when the bicentenary of languages in Trinity College was celebrated, the moderatorship had been restyled as one in Modern Languages and Literature, with two languages studied together for three years, and only one of these in the fourth year, but both this moderatorship and the pass degree would soon be phased out.

A characteristic of the School of Modern Languages in Trinity in the early part of the twentieth century was the inter-disciplinary nature of the teaching and the lack of departmentalization where staff was concerned. Thomas Rudmose-Brown who became professor of Romance Languages in 1909, after Maurice Gerothwohl who had held the chair for only two years on the retirement of Atkinson, taught philology and history of the language to students in at least three departments. He became the University's first professor of French in 1937 and this restyling reflects a slight shift towards single disciplines since the time of the appointment of Atkinson. Breadth is giving way to depth. Walter Starkie, who for many years lectured, like Radice, on the literature 'of some of the southern nations of Europe', was to become professor of Spanish in 1926, but in 1930 he was given also the title 'Lecturer in Italian Literature', a position he held well into the 1940s.[22] The person responsible for the teaching of languages, including Italian, was Sir Robert Tate, reputed to have possessed extraordinary gifts as a grammarian. He had come to Trinity from Cambridge as lecturer in Classical Composition in 1908, and he was to be Public Orator for more than three decades (1914–50).[23]

The moderatorship course in Italian introduced in 1920 includes some thirty authors; alongside the usual familiar names are those who have fallen into different shades of oblivion, for such is the fickleness of fashion. Giacosa and Gozzano are hardly read nowadays, and one wonders how many students have heard of Bonarelli's *Filli di Sciro* – pastoral drama, once so important a feature of Italian university courses, now has virtually no place at undergraduate level. Methods of assessment have also been subject to radical change: students in those days were

---

22 Walter Starkie is most renowned for his writing on Spanish literature and culture, as well as his amusing personal reminiscences, but among his writings of Italian interest there is an important book, often reprinted: *Luigi Pirandello* (London: John Murray, 1937). 23 The elegance of his Latin can be enjoyed in Sir Robert William Tate, *Orationes et epistolae Dublinenses (1914–40)* (Dublin: Hodges, Figgis, London: Longmans, Green, 1941).

required to sit a formal examination each term, and to take six written papers and a *viva voce* examination for moderatorship, with no independent submitted work.

Board and Council minutes tell us that the moderatorship in Italian was introduced because there was a demand for it and, with the regular number of students the subject has attracted since, there can be no cause for regret.[24] While it would be invidious to mention 'distinguished' graduates one must be forgiven for pandering to human vanity and mentioning one, Samuel Beckett, First class Moderator, double gold medallist in Italian and French in 1927.

No history of Italian in Trinity, no matter how brief, would be complete without a few words on the legendary Sir Robert Tate, still remembered as one of Trinity's greatest 'characters', though some of the antics of this handsome socializer are best forgotten. He was a much loved Junior Dean who closed as many eyes as a gentleman could to all forms of indiscipline and, as an examiner, was an embarrassment to his colleagues for reducing female examinees to tears and awarding absurdly generous marks. He formed a truly gentlemanly team with Count Edoardo Tomacelli (later Duca della Torre) who joined the Trinity staff in 1944. With Sir Robert died the world of the men of letters; rigorous disciplined scholarship was heralded resonantly and harmoniously by a Welshman who is dearly remembered by his colleagues in Trinity, the Oxonian T.G. Griffith who came as lecturer in charge of the School of Italian in 1952 ('school' was changed to 'department' in the following year). The complete change can best be seen by looking at the moderatorship course and the examination papers: while language remains an unchanging and determining feature, the study of literature becomes analytical. In the mid-1940s few works were read in their entirety (although texts were specified for Dante, Petrarch, and Boccaccio), and there was much use of representative anthologies of both prose and poetry, as well as concentration on literary history; by the mid-1950s there are no more broadly-based anthologies, the number of authors to be read has increased dramatically – an appropriate word as Goldoni appears, as well as 'Drama after 1880' to include Verga, Pirandello and, a little later, Betti – and precise critical understanding of their work is required. Gwyn Griffith put in position a challenging course that is to this day, albeit modified, the foundation of Italian in the two-subject moderatorship. It was the good fortune of Trinity to secure as Griffith's successor in 1958 a scholar remembered not alone for his valuable work for the Department, but for his involvement in the College as a whole, G.H. McWilliam, under whose guidance the writer of this brief history had the honour and privilege to begin her service to Trinity.

---

24 Council Minutes 4/2/1920, BM 10/6/1920.

PART II: FROM 1961

A substantial change in numbers admitted to Italian was responsible for my appointment in 1961. While in the early to mid-1950s entrants annually numbered about five, this figure suddenly trebled, increasing further so that in Michaelmas 1959 eighteen Junior Freshmen presented for examination, and nineteen in the following year. (Not all were good: a couple of first class results are balanced by half a dozen failures.) Clearly, the department was getting too numerous for two lecturers to teach unaided; there was some additional teaching for language (and Italian has always been taught *ab initio*), but course coverage presented a problem as well as, more importantly, methodology. Edoardo Tomacelli's academic training was in jurisprudence, and his perception of literature was bellelettrist, rather than seeing it as a discipline for professional study. While students undoubtedly benefited from Tomacelli's style, Harry McWilliam clearly needed someone closer to him in training and rigour; this the College was to acquire despite my youth and lack of experience, although I had already taught language at the Italian Cultural Institute for four years.

The buoyancy of the numbers was not to continue; a largish proportion of the students of Italian in the early 1960s came from the United Kingdom,[25] were English rather than British, and Trinity was perceived as being a good option for those who were not offered a place in Oxford and Cambridge. University expansion in the neighbouring island, and the putting in position of a quota for non-Irish students in Trinity, followed by a policy, introduced in 1971 whereby students with home residences outside the thirty-two counties (unless Irish) were required to pay a surcharge of 60 per cent on already substantial fees, led to a dramatic drop in our numbers over some years which proved quite critical for the department. It was precisely the foundation of the University of Kent at Canterbury that lost us Harry McWilliam in 1966, with, as a contributing factor, his personal annoyance with the College for not establishing a chair of Italian. The professorship of the Romance Languages had become one simply of French in 1937, and this chair has been filled uninterruptedly to this day; German, a strong subject with good intake of mainly Protestant students from Northern Ireland, had a separate chair from 1932 to 1958 when a Reader (Lionel Thomas) was put in charge of the department; Spanish was in a similar position

25 The overall figure given for the University as a whole was not, of course, evenly distributed. John V. Luce, on p. 153 of the chapter 'Change from within: modernisation and reform 1952–1967' in his *Trinity College Dublin: The First 400 Years* (Dublin: Trinity College Dublin Press, 1992) writes: 'The percentage of students from Britain remained high during the 1960s, reaching a peak of 34 per cent in 1963.' This chapter chronicles very clearly, and supports with statistics, an important period of change in the history of the College.

with E.C. Riley promoted to Reader in charge of Spanish from 1957, and Harry McWilliam was promoted to the same grade for Italian in 1961. However, in 1965 it was decided that German and Spanish were to have chairs, to which the incumbent readers were promoted, and this left Italian as the only one of the four collateral subjects without a professor – a situation that has remained unchanged, although I became an associate professor in 1997.[26] McWilliam took this as a slight on our discipline, possibly less than correctly (he was younger than his colleagues) but, retrospectively, it could indeed be read as the beginning of an ambivalent attitude to Italian on the part of the College – *legato ma non troppo* – that was to last for two decades.

The College's reaction when McWilliam tendered his resignation was a proposal to close the department of Italian. It remained a source of bitterness for him that the College he much loved (as late as 1999 he wished Penguin Classics to describe him in print as a former Fellow of Trinity College Dublin) required of him as a last administrative task to submit a paper in justification of keeping Italian as a University subject. The motion to close Italian was defeated by a majority of one at the University Council. I was not to know then that the closure of Italian would, for twenty years, be an undulant solution offered by varying configurations of College officers to the serious financial problems of the University; that I too would repeatedly have to justify its presence; and that the waters would only be stilled finally by Provost W.A. Watts.

There were curious similarities between the first and the last threat: in both cases the debate whether to close Italian sprang from the resignation of a member of what was a tiny staff. In 1985 Tom O'Neill who, like McWilliam, was a Fellow of the College, and much committed to it, left Trinity because disappointed that he had not been promoted to a chair (a position he was to fill in the University of Melbourne). Provost Watts informed me that, Italian being so cheap, closure of the Department would make no significant financial saving; there would also have been strong opposition from one of the College officers who was to remain, in changing roles, vigilant of the interests and rights of small departments. When your whole life has been dedicated to studying authors like Dante and Boccaccio – McWilliam's case and mine – it is difficult to believe that academics can doubt the importance of your discipline, but without Philistines Samson could never have shown her strength. It is only right and just that it be recorded that while there were aberrant officers then (and now) swayed by no more than 'Paudeen's pence [and] Biddy's halfpennies', daily life

---

26 The chair of Spanish has been vacant since 1999, representative of a regrettable recent tendency not to fill chairs in the humanities.

had nought else than respect and support from colleagues, especially those in
Modern Languages. It was possibly that personal respect for the person whose
lifetime's work was the Italian Department that ultimately won the day.

How did the Italian Department survive in those twenty years? Remarkably
well. The situation in autumn 1966 was, as recorded in the *Calendar*, that there
were two lecturers in Italian: Edoardo Tomacelli and I, and that there were two
degree courses: one honor Moderatorship and one General Studies; the range of
authors prescribed stretched from Frederick II to Ugo Betti, from Alcamo to *Zeno*.
No one was in charge, but as I did what was required, I was subsequently formally
appointed 'in charge of the Department of Italian', a definition that accompanied
me for some thirty-five years, and was, in later years, distinctly unique and more
accurate, in my opinion, than the generally used 'head'. A decision of principle
had to be taken but, given what I was and the training I had received from Harry
McWilliam – our subject was too noble to be cheapened – the decision took itself.
The quality of our graduates, not their quantity, would be our hallmark. All efforts
would be made to train rigorously our undergraduates to enable them to attain
the highest standards in both language and literature. Resonantly though that may
sound, it would have been impossible had invaluable help not been at hand. An
energetic, versatile and effective teacher, who was ready to take on any course, so
wide was her knowledge of Italian literature, was appointed as Junior Lecturer:
Clotilde Soave Bowe.[27] She was to become a stalwart colleague and an invaluable
asset to our Department until her retirement, in her seventy-first year, in September
1994. Her appointment made us, uniquely in Modern Languages, a 'trinitarian'
deparment of native speakers, truly one *dove 'l sì sona*, and the use of our language
in our daily exchanges has remained one of our features; there has never been
more than one non-native Italian on our permanent staff.

Clotilde and I shared the most difficult years for the Department. We carried a teaching load in both language and literature that no one would under-

---

27 Clotilde Soave Bowe (MA, NUI) had interrupted her studies at Ca' Foscari (Venice)
when moving to Ireland in the mid-1940s; had taught at the Italian Cultural Institute since
its foundation in 1954, and had done some language teaching for our Italian Department
prior to her appointment. While her energies were channelled mainly into teaching, she also
wrote good academic articles of which two in particular should be mentioned: 'The Narrative
Strategy of Natalia Ginzburg', *Modern Language Review*, 68, 4 (1973), 788–95; 'Dante and the
Hohenstaufen: From Chronicle to Poetry', in *Dante and the Middle Ages*, ed. by John Barnes
and Cormac Ó Cuilleanáin (Dublin: Irish Academic Press, 1995), pp. 181–210. She died in
October 2003, and in February 2004 the Department honoured her memory and celebrated
her contribution with a Requiem in College Chapel, and a lecture on Carlo Levi by Brian
Moloney. On that occasion memorial addresses were given by Ester Tossi (Mod., 1984),
Professor Catherine O'Brien of NUI Galway, and myself.

take nowadays, and while our *ab initio* course was very successful the labour intensity of it (for the students as well as ourselves) would now be unacceptable. A strong similarity of purpose drove us: we were exacting teachers with a high intolerance of error; motivated by what we perceived as best for our subject and our students, we wanted them educated to standards comparable to the best in these islands, despite the many limitations of our small department; we valued, and demanded, ability in spoken Italian, not just written. Obvious though all this may be now, it was not quite so in the late 1960s, especially in relation to language. Our aims were as similar as our teaching styles were different, and our complementarity was good for our students, but we were ever conscious that they needed to hear different voices from ours, and that we badly needed contact with colleagues for whom it was possible to engage in research in a way that our day-to-day survival was making impossible. Isolation from other Italianists was, in academic terms, a most negative factor, much though I drew support from the Society for Italian Studies, and from external examiners whose invaluable advice resulted in regular improvement of our courses, while their praise renewed vigour against surrender. It must be recorded also with much gratitude that we received regular help from the Italian Cultural Institute, and a succession of directors responded always with the utmost generosity to our requests, thus enabling us to invite distinguished scholars from Great Britain and Italy. Their visits sustained us in what felt like a long great hunger.

Contrary to what we both taught (Dante's works, major and minor, featured always in our degree course), our state of 'sanza speme vivemo in disio' was not to last forever, nor were we to regret that we resisted all persuasion to increase our student numbers by lowering our standards. Numbers in Italian rose, albeit never dramatically, as they rose all over College in the 1970s: Trinity's 2266 full-time students recorded for 1959 had risen to slightly more than 4700 in 1974. Political attitudes towards the College were changing, and of great significance was the appointment of the first Chaplain for Roman Catholic Students in autumn 1970, an appointment that in effect removed the ecclesiastical 'ban' on Catholics entering Trinity.[28] This resulted in major changes in the composition of the student body; a difference noted in Italian was the arrival in 1971, possibly for the first time in the department's history, of Northern Irish Catholic students wishing to read a subject that was little taught in their part of the island, having been associated, historically, with popery. Those first students from Belfast

---

28 Catholics, first excluded from Trinity until 1793, were to be excuded by their own hierarchy from 1875. See James Lydon, 'The silent sister: Trinity College and Catholic Ireland' in *Trinity College Dublin and the Idea of a University*, ed. by C.H. Holland (Dublin: Trinity College Dublin Press, 1992), pp. 29–53.

stand out in one's memory for how passionately they engaged with the strug-
gles between White and Black Guelfs in Dante's Florence. The increase in student numbers in Modern Languages was also related to Ireland's joining the
European Economic Community (1973).

A change in the moderatorship programme strengthened our department. In
1978 'the old moderatorship in modern languages and literature and the (paradoxically) more recent, moderatorship in ancient and modern languages were
dissolved into the new two-subject moderatorship programme, covering the
entire range of Arts subjects, together with a selection of other subjects from the
natural and social sciences';[29] it meant also the discontinuing of the popular three-
subject General Studies degree which was absorbed in the new moderatorship.
The seeds of the two-subject moderatorship were first sown in 1972 by History
of Art and Italian when they sought permission to combine their degree courses
for a most obvious academically compatible study. History of Art, like Russian,[30]
was previously available only in the General Studies combination, but the new
degree enabled both subjects to be read for moderatorship.

By 1978 Italian was gaining strength: not only were its numbers buoyant but
the appointment in 1972 of a promising young scholar, Tom O'Neill, had heralded
a new phase. Never before had there been three lecturers of similar academic for-
mation, and students were enriched by a greater variety of critical approaches that
reflected the fruitful relationship between research and teaching. Individual teaching loads lessened, and that formerly elusive research became a real possibility. More
was to come. 1981 saw the appointment of an Italian Government-
sponsored *lettore di ruolo*, Roberto Bertoni. That the activity of the deparment could
expand as it did subsequently, and that it still can engage at a high level of produc-
tivity, is in part due to the fact that a member of its full-time staff has been provided uninterruptedly by the Italian Government since then, and that our *lettori di
ruolo* have been of such academic calibre that the department was proud to add to
its permanent ranks that very first *lettore*, now a senior lecturer and head (not just
in charge) of the Department. Recognition for this saving gift is due to the late
Italian ambassador Goffredo Biondi Morra who responded always with much generosity to all my requests for help (whether for the library or for visiting lecturers),
and who successfully negotiated the appointment with his government.[31]

---

29 Richard Cox, 'A curious history: two hundred years of modern languages', in *Trinity College
Dublin and the Idea of a University*, ed. Holland, 255–69 (p. 262). **30** Russian became available
as a subject in the General Studies Degree, with a first intake of Junior Freshmen in 1962; in
1974 the first honor students were admitted to read for Moderatorship. **31** *Hermathena*, 121
(winter 1976) was dedicated entirely to the celebration of the bi-centenary of Modern
Languages. The 'Premessa da S.E. Goffredo Biondi Morra' (pp.8–9) recalls Italy's cultural con

The resignation of Tom O'Neill, as mentioned, shook the department but stability was restored in January 1986 with the appointment of Cormac Ó Cuilleanáin. Retrospectively, one can see this as a new beginning as since then the department has been an equal to others in its cognate area, developing, changing and sharing in both good and bad fortunes as Trinity, like all universities, experiences cyclically frugal feasts and whittling famines (the latter being the situation as this history is being concluded).[32] It has been enabled to develop academically better than ever. On a personal level, we four permanent members shared a common vision, and we worked in unison with mutual respect; on a level beyond the department, no small thanks for our achievement is due to the support of successive deans of the Faculty of Arts (Letters), and their recognition of our worth. Our research could come to fruition; I enjoyed my first leave of absence after twenty-seven years of uninterrupted service in Hilary Term 1988, and the many years of work on Lorenzo de' Medici could hope to appear as a book.[33] Student intake both increased and improved, and with now two new lecturers willing to implement much needed changes, we were able to offer, in addition to our core courses, a remarkably wide range of options for so small a department, to collaborate with the Centre for Language and Communication Studies, and – a most important new beginning – to offer Italian in the Moderatorship in European Studies in 1991. This degree has regularly attracted high calibre students.

With staff too few and, therefore, with limitations in range, for many years it was not wise to accept research students, and our best graduates were encouraged to acquire new experience in larger departments, but from the later 1980s we seemed to have the resources to develop postgraduate studies. The department is strong

tribution to Europe, praises the University for its commitment to Modern Languages and ends with words of perennial validity: 'La necessità dello studio delle lingue moderne è diventata ai nostri giorni ancor più imperativa, non solo perché i legami economici e sociali si sono fatti più complessi, ma anche perché è proprio sui valori della cultura e dello spirito che la costruzione europea e di un mondo migliore può far leva e svilupparsi organicamente. / A tale costruzione intende prender parte anche l'Italia ed il Governo italiano, tramite l'Ambasciata e l'Istituto di Cultura, sarà lieto di dare in campo culturale tutto l'aiuto concreto possibile in modo che la collaborazione tra le istituzioni universitarie irlandesi ed italiane divenga sempre più stretta e feconda di risultati.' Ambassador Biondi Morra was also responsible for obtaining scholarships to Italy for members of the Association of Teachers of Italian in Ireland, which I had recently formed.   **32** In the academic year 2005–6, the Italian Department in addition to its two senior members, Cormac Ó Cuilleanáin and Roberto Bertoni, has only one other permanent member of staff, Giuliana Adamo, author of *Metro e ritmo del primo Palazzeschi* (Roma: Salerno, 2003). But other language departments are equally having their vacant posts left unfilled. **33** Lorenzo de' Medici, *Selected Writings*, with an English verse translation of the *Rappresentazione di San Giovanni e Paolo*, edited by Corinna Salvadori (Dublin: Belfield Italian Library, 1992). Promotion was to follow with my election to Fellowship in 1994.

both in modern poetry and in literary translation, and it was with justified confidence that we accepted our first doctoral postgraduate, George Talbot, now an accomplished Italianist; that early research of his was not only a major contribution to Montale scholarship, but also to translation studies, as it related the poet's translation work to his creative writing.[34] The department now contributes to a Master's in Literary Translation. Equally, we are strong in *Trecento* studies, and we are also contributing to a Master's degree in Medieval Language, Literature and Culture. It is to be hoped that the current staff's expertise in comparative studies will be channelled into a graduate course in this area. Some of this has seen the light in the department's publication series, *Quaderni di cultura italiana*,[35] edited by Roberto Bertoni, the principal organizer of the recent triennial exchange between Irish and Ligurian poets, thus bridging poetic cultures in contemporary Italy and Ireland, and, continuing the department's long standing commitment to cultural exchange.[36]

In April 2002, when my active service for the department and the College had officially ended, the department felt it could afford to be mildly triumphalistic about its success. The then head of department, Cormac Ó Cuilleanáin, together with Daragh O'Connell, hosted a celebratory study day attended by colleagues from Trinity and other universities and, what I found particularly gratifying, by graduates representative of the five decades of my teaching. The occasion will be a lasting one as many of the papers delivered on that day are being published in this book, and the generosity towards me by students, graduates, colleagues and friends will benefit future students of Dante. Dante's works are studied in detail by all students in the two-subject moderatorship, and convinced as ever, in my forty-fifth year of teaching his work, that there is no more rewarding author known to me, it seemed only appropriate that the generous gifting should go towards the creation of the Dante Alighieri Prize to be awarded annually. Dante, at the end of the first book of *Convivio*, expresses the wish that his very own *(questo mio) volgare illustre fiorentino* become 'luce nuova, sole nuovo, lo quale surgerà là dove l'usato tramonterà, e darà luce a coloro che sono in tenebre e in oscuritade per usato sole che a loro non luce'. May that sun continue to shine strongly in Trinity College Dublin.

---

34 George Talbot, *Montale's 'Mestiere vile'. The Elective Translations from English of the 1930s and 1940s* (Dublin: Irish Academic Press, 1995). **35** *L'ultimo orizzonte ... Giacomo Leopardi: A Cosmic Poet and His Testament* (1999), *Minuetto con Bonaviri* (2001), *Echi danteschi/Dantean Echoes* (2003), *Sei poeti liguri* (2004), *Narrativa italiana recente / Recent Italian Fiction* (2005). (In all cases: Dublin: Italian Department Trinity College, and Turin: Trauben.) **36** Fruitful links, in Italian universities, with colleagues working on Irish literature in English, have been maintained since a lecture tour I undertook in 1969, at the request of the Cultural Relations Committee of the then Department of External Affairs. I lectured in five universities, mainly promoting two poets not then widely known, Seamus Heaney and Brendan Kennelly.

De amicitia: poet-friends in Dante's Florence*

Peter Armour

Unlike in English where 'love', 'friend', and 'enemy' all have different etymo-logical roots, in Italian, of course, 'amico' – and its opposite 'nimico' ('nemico') – are clearly derived from 'amor'. Thus 'amico' and 'amica' have a wide range of reference, from that of the lover as a sexual partner (the 'amante') – thus, in the *Comedy*, the incestuous Mirra is called the 'amica' of her father (*Inferno*, XXX. 39) – to that of heavenly love, such as of two early Franciscans 'che nel capestro a Dio si fero amici', and of the blessed in Paradise as 'l'anime che Dio s'ha fatte amiche' (*Paradiso*, III. 66; XII. 132; XXV. 90). Between the two extremes, above illicit sexual 'friendships' but below the love owed to God, the supreme 'Friend', was the human *amicitia* which was a bond of goodwill and common purpose between fellow-citizens and, in a particular way, as we will see, fellow-poets writing of Love in the Florence (and Tuscany) of Dante's younger days.

The theme of human *amicizia* is one of the most conspicuous in Duecento culture, and it occurs in several contexts: civic, moral, and amorous. Several of Guittone's letters are addressed to a 'dolce amico', a 'caro amico bono', a 'bel dolce amico' (similar to the 'biaus dous amis' to whom Brunetto Latini addressed his *Tresor*).[1] Guittone also uses friendship as a metaphor for general moral and civic values when he bewails its disappearance in corrupt Arezzo: '[...] amistà lì è morta / e moneta è in suo loco' ('Gente noiosa e villana', 25–6).[2] Clearly, in such cases *amicizia* included 'amor patriae' and love of virtue.

* Editor's note: It was a mark of how deeply Peter Armour valued friendship that, although extremely ill, he nonetheless travelled to Dublin to deliver this paper which he dedicated to me and our sharing a love of friendship, poetry and Florence. It was his last public appear-ance as an academic. I reconstructed the text easily from his notes, partly manuscript partly typed, but there were no references, and these are my main contribution; any errors are mine. As I could not find a source for some of the translations, I have assumed that, unless other-wise stated, these were the author's own. I have done this work with deep sadness at the loss of *un bel dolce e caro amico bono*. I wish to thank Jane Everson and John Took, of London University, for generously allowing me access to Peter Armour's papers. [CS]

1 For the letters of Guittone see *Lettere*, edizione critica a cura di Claude Margueron (Bologna: Commissione per i testi di lingua, 1990); letters I, III, XXV, XXIX are particularly rich in exam-ples. For Brunetto Latini, see *Li Livres dou tresor de Brunetto Latini*, édition critique par Francis J. Carmody (Berkeley and Los Angeles: University of California Press, 1948), I. i. 4. 2 In *Poeti del Duecento*, ed. by Gianfranco Contini, 2 vols (Milan and Naples: Classici Ricciardi-Mondadori, 1995 [1960]), I, 200.

Before looking in detail at Dante and his poet friends, it is necessary to fill in some background. There were two main sources for the doctrine of friendship towards the end of the Duecento in Florence and Tuscany, and these were Aristotle's *Nicomachean Ethics,* Books VIII and IX, and Cicero's *Lælius de amicitia*. In the case of the first, Dante himself turns to the full Aristotelian philosophy of friendship only in the *Convivio*, on numerous occasions, including his friendship (love) for his mother-tongue and for Lady Philosophy. In earlier days he may have known only the relevant passages in Brunetto Latini's *Tresor*, and above all those ideas contained in Cicero's *Lælius de amicitia*, which, Dante tells us (*Convivio*, II. xii. 3), was one of the books he read to console himself on the death of Beatrice (the other being Boethius's *De consolatione philosophiae*). Cicero's account is set a few days after the death of Scipio Africanus, as a dialogue between Gaius Lælius and his two sons-in-law, one of whom, Scævola, later transmitted it to Cicero. It inherits numerous aspects of Aristotle's doctrine: true friendship can exist only between good, virtuous men (*in bonis*); natural friendship, the bond of cities and families, is based on *benevolentia*: 'For friendship is in fact nothing other than a community of views on all matters human and divine, together with goodwill and affection (*cum benevolentia et caritate*).'[3] True friendship is enjoyed in good fortune, shared in misfortune; it is altruistic, and its greatest enemies are competition for office and greed for money. Whilst the gifts of Fortune are mutable, those of true friendship are permanent, stable and sure. True friendship is not for profit but to assist in virtue, and it relies on truth itself. Thus a man must rebuke his friend gently when necessary, and friends should accept advice and rebukes when they are given in goodwill – even though the truth may compromise friendship since friends are more usually won by flattery. As Terence put it in the *Andria*, 'Obsequiousness produces friends, the truth hatred.'[4]

Cicero's dialogue was widely known in the Middle Ages, often alongside Ælred of Rievaulx, *De spiritali amicitia*, which absorbs Ciceronian ideas into that of monastic friendship that leads to the love of God, the Friend who loves the whole human race. Certainly parallels to this Christianized version of Cicero can be found in the Bible: friendship in vice is no friendship (compare *Ecclesiasticus*, XXII. 27); while the false friend will abandon you in times of trouble or need, the true friend is a faithful counsellor, a friend in adversity and in poverty (*Proverbs*, XVII. 17; *Ecclesiasticus*, XXII. 28–9); and the supreme model of friendship is Christ: 'Greater love than this has no man, that he should lay down his life for his friends' (*John*, XV. 13).

3 Cicero, *Lælius de amicitia*, 17–18, 20.   4 Ibid., 88–9; at 98 Cicero again quotes Terence on the subject of flattery (*Eunuch*, III, i. 1), and this was very likely Dante's source for the final lines of *Inferno* XVIII.

Alongside the classical and biblical concepts of true friendship, there was also a specific Florentine version represented by Brunetto Latini's *Tresor*, dedicated to a 'fair, sweet friend':[5] 'friends are very necessary [...] in all the sufferings and adversities that one can have, in that a good friend is a very good refuge and a safe harbour' (II. xliii. 2). Friendship for profit or pleasure is not true friendship, which can exist only between good men: 'And each of the friends loves his good, and one does favours for the other out of his goodwill [...]' (II. xliii. 5). True friendship survives in adversity and poverty, and it has a moral and social dimension in that a friend should chastise his friend secretly and praise him in public (II. civ. 2; here Brunetto is citing Seneca). Friendship for profit does not survive adversity, for the so-called friend 'acts like a nightingale which, in spring-time when the sun becomes strong and the flowers arrive and trees grow green, stays with us and sings and often consoles itself; but when the cold returns, it flies away and hurriedly leaves us'. Similarly, friendship for pleasure (most common among the young) is exemplified by foolish love (*Tresor*, II. cv and cvi).

In his Italian allegorical poem, the *Tesoretto*,[6] Brunetto mentions two personal friends, the 'caro amico' to whom he sent a 'prosimetrum' which was later lost (99–108), and a 'fino amico caro' (2421, etc.) to whom he addresses the entire episode of his confession – *La Penetenza* – as a disquisition and moral exhortation to reform. The *Favolello*, deriving some of its ideas from Boncompagno da Signa's *Amicitia* of 1205, was written in answer to a doctrine of friendship put forward in a work, now lost, by the Florentine comic poet, Rustico Filippi. Friendship starts with 'benvoglienza' and constantly increases in love; it consists in mutual assent and agreement; and true friendship not only survives but is tested by separation and adversity. False friends include the fair-weather friends ('amico di ventura', 72) who abandon you in misfortune, like a bird that sings in spring but disappears in winter – an image he used also in the *Tresor*, II. cv, as cited earlier. The true friend, always loyal, will rebuke you when necessary but defend and praise you in public:

> e se fallir ti vede,
> unque non se ne ride,
> ma te stesso riprende
> e d'altrui ti difende:
> se fai cosa valente,
> la spande fra la gente

5 Brunetto repeats his dedication at III. lxxiii. 1 and 6; the sections of the *Tresor* entirely on *amistié* are II. cii to cvi.   6 See Contini, II, i, pp. 175–277 for *Il tesoretto*, and pp. 278–84 for *Il favolello*.

> e 'l tuo pregio radoppia.
> Cotal è buona coppia. (*Il Favolello*, 123–30)

(and if he sees you at fault, he never makes fun of it, but he rebukes you
and defends you publicly; if you do something noble, he spreads it abroad
and redoubles your renown. Such is a good pair [of friends].)

Bondie Dietaiuti's 'Amor, quando mi membra' is a poem of consolation ('conforto') sent to a friend in Florence after the city's disastrous defeat at Montaperti
in 1260.

> Ma lo 'ncharnato amore
> di voi, che m'à distretto,
> fidato amico aletto,
> mi sforza ch' io mi deg[g]ia ·rallegrare [...]
> guardando al tuo trovato,
> amico, che d'er[r]anza mi dispoglia.[7]

(But the embodied love that has taken hold of me for you, my trusty,
chosen friend, compels me to rejoice [...] when I look at your poem,
which divests me of error.)

Bondie, devastated by the defeat, has received a poem of consolation and Stoic
resignation from a close friend – a poem which brings him some happiness and
frees him from 'eranza' (error or confusion). If Brunetto, then exiled in France,
had been the sender of the poem, it was an expression of friendship in adversity and separation, and its principal theme was the duty of friends and fellow-
citizens to give each other moral and civic 'conforto' – consolation and advice
– in a world of violent political and social crisis.

   Very different is the Amis of the *Roman de la rose*: although he fulfils (like
Amico in the *Fiore*) one Aristotelian and Ciceronian function – to comfort and
counsel – he is the exact opposite of the Ciceronian ideal in that he encourages
and advises Guillaume, the Lover, to do everything to serve, flatter, deceive,
and seduce the lady so as to obtain the Rose. (And Jean de Meun, in his con-
tinuation of the *Roman de la rose,* would have known Cicero's *De amicitia*, though
perhaps indirectly.)

   The doctrine of friendship is important to the *Convivio*, written after Dante's
exile in 1301; indeed, the whole work is presented as having been inspired by
that natural friendship which exists between all humans who naturally desire

---

7 See Contini, I, i, pp. 385–8.

knowledge but who are, for various reasons, deprived of it (I. i. 1–7). It is part of Dante's concept of friendship that a man should communicate his defects to his friend (I. ii. 5), that friends should spread the fame of their friends (I. iii. 7–8), that generosity is inherent to true friendship and that 'Amistade' pertains to 'soavità', one of the virtues of Adolescenzia (IV. xxiv. 11). As already said, Dante expounds the doctrine of friendship more fully when he applies it to two chief objects of his love: his own language, to which he dedicates most of Book I, and Lady Philosophy, for love of wisdom ('Filosofia') is a form of friendship based on the goodwill that comes from 'lo studio e la sollicitudine', from 'bontade' (not profit or pleasure), and the love of wisdom means also to be a friend of the truth.

Let us now focus on the years before Dante's exile, when he belonged to a circle of Florentine and other friends, including some fellow-poets and their ladies. In this period, the context of the poems is relatively secular, concerned with love and making oneself known to other poets – a form of 'networking' really.

Among Dante's earliest *rime* is a series of sonnets exchanged with another Dante, Dante da Maiano, who circulated a sonnet generally to any intelligent person ('saggio') asking him to uncover the true meaning of a vision in which a beautiful lady gave him a garland and clothed him in her shift:

Dante da Maiano:

> Provedi, saggio, ad esta visione [...].
> Allor di tanto, amico, mi francai,
> che dolcemente presila abbracciare:
> non si contese, ma ridea la bella.
> Così ridendo, molto la baciai:
> del più non dico, ché mi fé giurare.
> E morta, ch'è mia madre, era con ella.

(You who are intelligent, consider this vision [...]. Then I made so bold as gently to embrace her. The fair one did not resist, but smiled; and as she smiled I kissed her repeatedly. I will not say what followed – she made me swear not to. And a dead woman – my mother – was with her.)[8]

In reply to this overtly erotic imagining, the young Dante Alighieri first praised the other Dante's wisdom and ability to carry out his own interpreting

---

8 *Dante's Lyric Poetry*, ed. by Kenelm Foster and Patrick Boyde, 2 vols (Oxford: Clarendon Press, 1967), I, 2–3. Whenever it is certain that the author used the texts and translations from this edition of the lyrics, this is acknowledged. The sonnet was the form that most lent itself to poetic correspondence.

– 'Savete giudicar vostra ragione, / o om che pregio di saver portate …' (You know how to interpret your theme, intelligent as you are …) – and then offered his own 'amica oppiniöne' on the meaning of the symbols: the gift of the garland represents desire, the garment love, and the dead mother the lady's future constancy. Addressing each other as 'amico', paying fulsome tributes to the other's intelligence and wisdom, and replying to these compliments with modest disclaimers, the two Dantes continued to correspond in sonnet form on questions concerning Love: the suffering caused by unrequited love and the remedies for 'lo mal d'amore'. Despite these explicit expressions of friendship and respect, however, one of the Dantes was circulating his poems anonymously, for two of the replies begin: 'Qual che voi siate, amico …' and 'Non canoscendo, amico, vostro nomo, / donde che mova chi con meco parla …'.

> Qual che voi siate, amico, vostro manto
> di scienza parmi tal, che non è gioco; […]
> Sacciate ben (ch'io mi conosco alquanto)
> che di saver ver voi ho men d'un moco,
> né per via saggia come voi non voco,
> così parete saggio in ciascun canto. […] [Dante da Maiano]

(Whoever you may be, my friend, it seems that you are arrayed in such learning as commands respect […]. Know that my knowledge (for I do know myself a little) is less than a pea compared with yours; nor do I row my boat on a wise course as you do, so wise do you show yourself in every way. […])[9]

In Michele Barbi's edition, and also in Contini's, it is Dante Alighieri who does not know the identity of his 'friend', whereas Kenelm Foster and Patrick Boyde reverse the attributions of some of the questions and replies so that it is Dante da Maiano who finds himself corresponding with an unknown sonneteer of a probing, if serious, cast of mind.[10] In this latter, and perhaps more convincing, distribution of the poems, Dante Alighieri, probably still in his teens, is advertising himself anonymously so as to claim membership of a circle of love poets and mutual 'friends', and this matches his circulation of a sonnet, asking others to interpret a dream of his own. 'A ciascun'alma presa e gentil core' is addressed to all lovers,[11] the servants of their lord, Love, and asks for the explanation of

---

9 Foster and Boyde, I, 4–9.   **10** See Foster and Boyde, II, 6–9 where the problem of attribution is discussed with reference to earlier editors of Dante's *Rime*.   **11** Foster and Boyde, I, 12–13.

his dream of his lady's eating of his burning heart and of Love's departure in tears. According to his later account in the *Vita nuova*, Dante composed this poem at the age of about eighteen and sent it to many famous 'trovatori' of the time, the 'fedeli d'Amore', that is, the devotees or, in the feudal sense, vassals of Love (*Vita nuova*, III. 9–10). To this request, however, and perhaps unfairly, given Dante Alighieri's serious reply to the other Dante's own erotic dream, Dante da Maiano sent some coarsely medical advice to his 'amico', who is now no longer 'saggio' but 'di poco canoscente':

> Di ciò che stato sei dimandatore,
> guardando, ti rispondo brevemente,
> amico meo di poco canoscente, [...]
> che lavi la tua coglia largamente,
> a ciò che stinga e passi lo vapore
> lo qual ti fa favoleggiar loquendo; [...].
> Così riscritto el meo parer ti rendo;
> né cangio mai d'esta sentenza mea,
> fin che tua acqua al medico no stendo.

(Having considered, my rather ignorant friend, the matter you ask me about, I answer briefly [...] give your testicles a good wash, so that the vapours that make you talk nonsense be extinguished and dispersed; [...]. Such is my opinion, duly returned; nor will I ever alter my judgement without first showing your water to a doctor.)[12]

This anti-idealising response is an example of poetic correspondence between friends (or maybe ex-friends here) experimenting in the 'comic' style.

Of the other two known replies to Dante's sonnet, one came perhaps from Cino da Pistoia. The other, 'Vedeste, al mio parere, onne valore', from Guido Cavalcanti,[13] introduced Dante to his most important experience of friendship in the years before his exile. Cavalcanti must have sent his reply anonymously, for in the *Vita nuova* Dante records that when he found out who its sender was, it was 'quasi lo principio de l'amistà tra lui e me' so that Cavalcanti became 'quelli cui io chiamo primo de li miei amici', the first not so much perhaps in time as in their closeness as poets (*Vita nuova*, III. 14). Dante himself fell under the influence of his friend's love poetry, dominated by anguish, the imagery of conflict and battle, and the suffering of the 'spiritelli' (*Vita nuova*, XIII–XVII), until he turned to his new and nobler theme, based on Guinizzelli's doctrine

---

12 Foster and Boyde, I, 16–17. **13** Foster and Boyde, I, 14–15.

of Love, of praising Beatrice (*Vita nuova,* XVIII–XIX). Even though Cavalcanti's philosophy of Love, as expounded in 'Donna me prega', was very different from Dante's, the two continued to share certain beliefs in relation to their common craft: that a poet should be able to explain the true meaning of his verse beneath the covering of its figures and rhetorical colouring, unlike the foolish rhymers, known to both of them, who are incapable of doing so (*Vita nuova,* XXV. 10); and both agreed that Dante should write not in Latin but only in the 'volgare', a decision that shows Cavalcanti to have been in communication with Dante on the composition of the *Vita nuova,* which was, in effect, written principally for him, 'questo mio primo amico a cui ciò scrivo' (*Vita nuova,* XXX. 3).

Two sonnets in particular – three, if one includes the poem to Dante from Guido asking for news about Lapo Gianni's relationship with his lady, Monna Lagia – record the friendship between Dante and Guido in the context of love and their respective ladies. In 'Guido, i' vorrei che tu e Lapo ed io', Dante expressed his wish that a magician might whisk away the three poets and their ladies (including Guido's Monna Vanna) in a boat where they could form a small, closed circle devoted solely to their own company and to the uninterrupted discussion of Love.

> Guido, i' vorrei che tu e Lapo ed io
> fossimo presi per incantamento
> e messi in un vasel, ch'ad ogni vento
> per mare andasse al voler vostro e mio,
> sì che fortuna od altro tempo rio
> non ci potesse dare impedimento,
> anzi, vivendo sempre in un talento,
> di stare insieme crescesse 'l disio.
> E monna Vanna e monna Lagia poi
> con quella ch'è sul numer de le trenta
> con noi ponesse il buono incantatore:
> e quivi ragionar sempre d'amore,
> e ciascuna di lor fosse contenta,
> sì come i' credo che saremmo noi.

(Guido, I wish that you and Lapo and I could be taken by magic and placed in a boat that, whatever the wind, was carried over the sea wherever you and I chose to go, unhindered by tempest or foul weather – our desire to be together in fact always increasing, living as we would in unceasing harmony. And with this, that the good wizard should give us for company lady Vanna and lady Lagia and her who stands on number thirty, there to talk always of love; and that each of them should be happy, as I'm sure we would be.)[14]

What this poem expresses is a closed circle, indeed an élite, of friends and their ladies, and the friendship that for Aristotle and Cicero was the bond of the city-state is here the union of the 'signoria d'Amore', the common interests of the 'fedeli d'Amore', Love's vassals in the service of their lord, discussing and writing poems about Love. In reply, however, Guido dissociated himself from this delightful fantasy, stating that he is no longer worthy of such love, which is now but a memory, and that his relationship with his lady has changed, for he has been smitten by a new and anguished love. Perhaps dating from around the same time, Dante's sonnet, 'Io mi senti' svegliar dentro a lo core', records an occasion when Monna Vanna appeared, followed by Monna Bice. When he came to include this in the *Vita nuova*, Dante explained that Vanna, or Giovanna, 'fue già molto donna di questo primo amico' and that it was precisely with this event in mind that Love had inspired Guido, 'lo imponitore del nome', to give her the poetic code-name, the *senhal*, of Primavera. When he wrote the poem, he adds, he believed that his friend was still in love with this 'Primavera' (*Vita nuova*, XXIV. 4, 6). It is clear that Dante was not always up-to-date with the objects of his friend's love.

Dante mentions other friends too in the *Vita nuova*, presenting them unnamed but always because of their close connection with his poetry of Beatrice. As a result of the effects of Love upon his 'natural spirits', 'molti amici' are grieved by his weakened physical condition and appearance (*Vita nuova*, IV. I). It is an 'amica persona' who, 'credendosi fare a me grande piacere', takes Dante to see the ladies, including Beatrice, and Dante himself, 'credendomi fare piacere di questo amico', agrees to serve them; however, by unwittingly bringing his friend close to death by causing the crisis of the 'gabbo', this 'ingannato amico di buona fede' has to lead Dante away from the scene, and Dante, leaving him, goes home (*Vita nuova*, XIV. I–3, 7–9). A crucial role in Dante's development as a poet is played by the friend who, having heard 'Donne ch'avete intelletto d'amore' as it circulated, asked him what Love is, so inspiring him 'pensando che l'amico era da servire', to compose 'Amor e 'l cor gentil sono una cosa', his first statement of the Guinizzellian doctrine of Love and 'gentilezza' that underlies the new poetry of the praise of Beatrice later defined as the 'dolce stil novo' (*Vita nuova*, XX. I–2; *Purgatorio*, XXIV. 9–57). In Dante's delirious, apocalyptic vision he sees a friend who tells him that Beatrice is dead

14 Foster and Boyde, I, 30–I.

(*Vita nuova*, XXIII. 6). After her actual death, the friend who, 'secondo li gradi
de l'amistade, è amico di me immediatamente dopo lo primo' and who is the
closest possible relative by blood of Beatrice, asks him to write a poem for a
dead lady, whom Dante takes to be really Beatrice; Dante, however, is dissat-
isfied with the resulting sonnet and, before sending it as a gift to his friend, he
composes two stanzas of a *canzone*, one expressing the grief of 'questo mio caro
e distretto a lei', the other his own: 'E così appare che in questa canzone si
lamentano due persone, l'una de le quali si lamenta come frate, l'altra come
servo' (*Vita nuova*, XXXII. 1–3; XXXIII. 1–4). From this allusion to him as her
'frate', this second best friend of Dante's is commonly identified as Beatrice's
brother, Manetto Portinari.

Whilst these references give brief and tantalizing glimpses into Dante's social
friendships with other men in Florence in the years before his exile, the most
important motive for friendship remained the exclusive relationship that bound
together the practitioners of the poetry of Love. Ladies entered this circle by
joining this élite and, in particular, by achieving an understanding of the more
difficult concepts in the doctrine of love and 'gentilezza' – 'Donne, ch'avete
intelletto d'amore', the first *canzone* of the *Vita nuova* (XIX. 1) which Dante
addressed 'non ad ogni donna, ma solamente a coloro che sono gentili'.[15]
Beatrice in the *Vita nuova* does not have 'amiche' but 'compagne', the com-
panion-ladies who reflect and emphasize her dominance in the joining together
of love and virtuous 'gentilezza'. The one exception is her 'friendship' ('amistade') for her father when she grieves for his death (*Vita nuova*, XXII. 2), the
love between a virtuous father and a virtuous son (or in this case daughter) that
finds a place in the Aristotelian and Ciceronian doctrine of friendship in the
family and among kinsmen.

As Dante's poems did begin to circulate, he came to be regarded as an
authority in matters of Love. An unknown friend, humbly presenting himself
as Dante's inferior ('un tuo amico di debile affare'), sent him a sonnet which
opens with a fulsome hyperbole on Dante's unique intellectual gifts: 'Dante
Alleghier, d'ogni senno pregiato / che in corpo d'om si potesse trovare' (Dante
Alighieri, esteemed as having all the wisdom that may be found in a man).[16]
Describing how he had cited Dante to a beautiful young lady who had, however, cruelly rejected him, the friend wants Dante to help him by taking revenge
on her. Dante's reply, though sympathetic and optimistic that she might change

---

15 Dante in *De vulgari eloquentia* (II. viii. 8) cites this poem as exemplary in his discussion of
the *canzone*, and he recalls it in *Purgatorio*, XXIV. 49–63 as a poem that initiates a new way ('le
nove rime') of writing lyric poetry. On Dante's specific inclusion of women in his readership see also *Convivio*, I. ix. 5.   **16** Foster and Boyde, I, 154–7.

her mind, suggests merely that if he could be told her identity he might be able
to help by sending her a letter. And as the *Vita nuova* began to circulate, the
Sienese comic-realistic poet Cecco Angiolieri sent Dante a sonnet asking him
to resolve an apparent contradiction in its final poem, 'Oltre la spera'; it begins:
'Dante Allaghier, Cecco, 'l tu' servo e amico, / si raccomanda a te com'a
segnore [...]' (Dante Alighieri, your servant and friend Cecco commends himself to you as his lord [...]).[17]

Meanwhile, however, the friendship between Dante and Cavalcanti had
taken a negative turn. In its way, Cavalcanti's sonnet to Dante, 'I' vegno 'l
giorno a te 'nfinite volte', is the poem of one friend to another. Whilst emphasizing that Dante is always in Cavalcanti's thoughts, though not his presence, it
accuses him throughout of 'viltà', of betraying his high intellectual and moral
qualities, descending to frequent the company of 'annoiosa gente' whom he
once avoided, and of writing poems of which his friend no longer approves.
The poem was sent both as a rebuke and as a cure:

> I' vegno 'l giorno a te 'nfinite volte
> e trovoti pensar troppo vilmente:
> molto mi dòl della gentil tua mente
> e d'assai tue vertù che ti son tolte.
> Solevanti spiacer persone molte;
> tuttor fuggivi l'annoiosa gente;
> di me parlavi sì coralemente,
> che tutte le tue rime avie ricolte.
>
> Or non ardisco, per la vil tua vita,
> far mostramento che tu' dir mi piaccia,
> né 'n guisa vegno a te, che tu mi veggi.
> Se 'l presente sonetto spesso leggi,
> lo spirito noioso che ti caccia
> si partirà da l'anima invilita.

[To you I come a thousand times a day, and I find you thinking things
that are too base. I grieve greatly for your noble mind and your many
virtues that have been taken from you. Once you used to dislike many
people, and you always shunned the company of the tedious. You spoke
of me always so warmly that I collected all your rhymes. Now because

---

17 Foster and Boyde, I, 98–9. On correspondence in Angiolieri's poetry see Fabian Alfie,
Comedy and Culture: Cecco Angiolieri's Poetry and Late Medieval Society (Leeds: Northern
Universities Press, 2001), chapter v.

of your base life, I dare not reveal that your poetry pleases me, nor do I come into your presence. If you read this sonnet frequently, the tormenting spirit that pursues you will leave your debased soul.][18]

The occasion of this poem is unknown. It may have been directed against Dante's overwhelming demeaning grief at the death of Beatrice in 1290, or his later betrayal of Beatrice's memory by his attraction to the *donna gentile*, judged by Dante himself to have been a 'vile' or ignoble affair (*Vita nuova*, XXXVII. 1; XXXVIII. 2, 4; XXXIX. 2). In other ways too, the paths of the two friends diverged, both because of their differing philosophies of Love, and in their contrasting attitudes towards the conflict between the Cerchi and Donati factions that would later become the Whites and the Blacks. Whatever the cause, the poem is an example of a friend's (or ex-friend's) duty to reprimand his friend when he falls short of his moral and intellectual ideals – here the abandoning of that 'gentilezza' or moral nobility that accompanies true Love in favour of its opposite, 'viltà'.[19]

When Dante came to write *Inferno* X, he presented the parting of their ways as due to Guido's refusal or inability to accept guidance from a higher wisdom. In the middle of his dialogue with Guido's father-in-law, the Ghibelline leader Farinata degli Uberti, Dante is interrupted by Cavalcante dei Cavalcanti, Guido's father, who attributes Dante's journey through the afterlife to his 'altezza d'ingegno' and asks why his own son – also gifted with a 'lofty' mind – is not with him. Beneath the much debated words in Dante's reply, 'forse cui Guido vostro ebbe a disdegno', lies the poet's memory of the fact that in the spring of 1300 Guido's mortal and immortal destiny was in the balance, as he had only some five more months to live (*Inferno*, X. 58–63). Nowhere in *De vulgari eloquentia* does Dante refer to his principal fellow-Florentine poet as his friend, and in the *Purgatorio* he acknowledges his fame as a poet only as an exemplary lesson on its transience: just as one Guido, Cavalcanti, has superseded another, Guinizzelli (or, according to some critics, Guittone d'Arezzo), so Cavalcanti's claim to 'la gloria de la lingua' will 'forse' – but in the context inevitably – be eclipsed by another (*Purgatorio*, XI. 97–9).

The *Vita nuova* and some of the *Rime* show that, before his exile, Dante belonged to a group of friends joined together above all by their interest in poetry and the debate on the nature of Love. In the *Comedy*, he also expresses special affection for the singer, Casella, who proceeds to sing one of Dante's

---

18 Contini, II, ii, pp. 548–549. There were two translations in the author's notes; the editor has conflated them for greater accuracy. **19** Compare Virgil's accusation to Dante whose *viltà* is impeding his journey: *Inferno*, II, 45: 'L'anima tua è da viltate offesa', and again at 122 'Perché tanta viltà nel cor allette?'

own *canzoni* on love ('Amor che ne la mente mi ragiona'; *Purgatorio*, II), and in the Heaven of Venus, for the Angevin prince, Carlo Martello, who cites another ('Voi che 'ntendendo il terzo ciel movete'; *Paradiso*, VIII). Exile, however, broke this circle of literary and political friendships and community of interests within the civic context. Years later, acknowledging the work of a Florentine friend to negotiate his *repatriatio*, Dante wrote: 'et inde tanto me districtius obligastis, quanto rarius exules invenire amicos contingit' ('and so you have bound me so much the more closely to you in that it so rarely happens that exiles find friends').[20] One poet, however, Cino da Pistoia, who shared Dante's fate of exile, remained his friend in those later years.

In the *De vulgari eloquentia*, Dante identifies himself as Cino's 'friend' (X. 2), and his Epistle to Cino opens with affection: 'Exulanti Pistoriensi Florentinus exul immeritus per tempora diuturna salutem et perpetuæ caritatis ardorem' ('To the Pistoian exile from the unjustly exiled Florentine, wellbeing and the ardour of perpetual love for many a long time'); he goes on to give his answer to a philosophical question concerning Love which Cino has asked in order to give Dante a chance to increase the fame of his name. The letter ends with words of consolation for Dante's 'dearest brother' ('frater carissime'), virtuous advice to a friend in adversity, to bear the sharp arrows of Nemesis and to read Seneca's *Fortuitorum remedia*.[21] Apart from Cino's *canzone* written to console him on the death of Beatrice, and so probably composed around 1290 or a few years later, most of Cino's *canzoniere* and his correspondence with his fellow exile, Dante, seem to belong to the earlier years of the Trecento. In their poems they discussed love, in general and in particular.

In a sonnet written on behalf of Moroello Malaspina in reply to one of Cino's, Dante accused Cino of having a 'volgibile cor' in relation to Love;[22] later, Dante wrote Cino a sonnet of mild rebuke, as a true friend should, advising him to return to the principles of true, virtuous Love expressed in their earlier 'sweet' poems:

> Chi s'innamora sì come voi fate,
> or qua or là, e sé lega e dissolve,
> mostra ch'Amor leggermente il saetti.

---

20 *Dantis Alagherii Epistolae*, ed. by Paget Toynbee, 2nd edn, rev. by C.G. Hardie (Oxford: Clarendon Press, 1966), IX. 1, p. 153. **21** The Latin text is in Toynbee, *Epistolae*, III. address and 5, pp. 22, 25. The reference to Seneca is incorrect as the text recommended by Dante was written in the sixth century and attributed to Seneca because of his homonymous treatise then lost. **22** The opening line is 'Degno fa voi trovare ogni tesoro', see Foster and Boyde, I, 200–3.

> Però, se leggier cor così vi volve,
> priego che con vertù il correggiate,
> sì che s'accordi i fatti a' dolci detti.

(One who falls in love as you do, now here, now there, and both binds and looses himself, shows that Love wounds him but lightly. So, if a fickle heart thus whirls you around, I beg you to correct it with virtue, so that your deeds accord with your sweet words.)[23]

Cino defended himself by blaming his cruel exile for his separation from his lady:

> Poi ch'i' fu', Dante, dal mio natal sito
> fatto per greve essilio pellegrino
> e lontanato dal piacer più fino
> che mai formasse il Piacer infinito […].

(Dante, ever since harsh exile made me a wanderer from my birthplace and put a distance between me and the most exquisite beauty that ever the infinite Beauty fashioned […]).[24]

This is the reason why he seeks, in other women, the beauty which resembles hers. Here too, therefore, is an example of a poem of moral reproof within the secular and literary context of the correct approach to Love and to writing love poetry in the true sweet style.

There is one further aspect of friendship in Dante's Florence that goes beyond moral rebuke into the realms of violent abuse. In the famous *tenzone* with Forese Donati (died 1296), Dante accused his friend of abandoning his wife and leaving her cold and shivering in her bed at night; Forese replied by insulting the memory of Dante's father, and the two 'friends' continued with increasingly 'comic' and abusive language to accuse each other of thieving, guzzling, sponging off others, cowardice, and so on.[25] Whilst some critics insist that these poems are fakes, composed about a century later, and full of disguised obscenities, there seems little doubt, from the episode in *Purgatorio*, that some time in the 1290s Dante and Forese shared a life of some dissipation – after all, when he meets his friend in Purgatory (*Purgatorio*, XXIII–XXIV), it is among the gluttons and he makes Forese acknowledge his deep love for his widow, Nella. Similar charges, moreover, were made against Dante by the Sienese 'comic'

23 Foster and Boyde, I, 202–3. 24 Foster and Boyde, I, 204–5. 25 Foster and Boyde, I, 148–54.

poet Cecco Angiolieri, presumably in answer to a lost poem in which Dante rebuked his friend for bragging and sponging. Cecco turns the accusations back on Dante himself – he is just as bad, and neither of them has the right to castigate the other:

> Dante Alleghier, s'i' so' buon begolardo
> tu me ne tien' ben la lancia a le reni;
> s'i' desno con altrui, e tu vi ceni;
> s'io mordo 'l grasso, e tu vi sughi el lardo;
> s'io cimo 'l panno, e tu vi freghi el cardo;
> s'io so' discorso, e tu poco t'afreni;
> s'io gentileggio, e tu misèr t'aveni;
> s'io so' fatto romano, e tu lombardo.
>
>   Sí che, laudato Idio, rimproverare
> poco può l'uno a l'altro di noi due:
> sventura o poco senno ce 'l fa fare.
> E se di tal materia vo' dir piùe,
> Dante, risponde, ch'i' t'avrò a stancare,
> ch'i' son lo pugnerone, e tu se' 'l bue.[26]

(Dante Alighieri, if I'm a great braggart, so you're right behind me in the charge; if I'm dining with someone, you're supping there too; if I'm chewing the fat, you're sucking up the lard. If I'm working the wool, you're there, buffing up the carding comb; if I go over the top, you don't hold me back much; if I give myself the airs of a gentleman, you too like to be called 'Sir'; if I've been made a Roman, you're a Lombard. Thus – praise God – neither of us two can rightly rebuke the other; it is misfortune or foolishness that makes us do so. And, Dante, if you want to write more on this subject, answer me, for I'll wear you out, since I'm the goad and you're the ox.)

As said from the outset, Dante was to move on, in the *Convivio*, to apply Aristotle's and Cicero's doctrine of friendship to his own love for his native language and to his love for Lady Philosophy, as well as to that natural love which makes all men friends. Apart from numerous other references to friends in the *Comedy*, he puts into Virgil's mouth an expression of friendship, based on 'benvoglienza', for Statius even though the two Roman poets have never met (*Purgatorio*, XXII. 10–21). But it seems to me that these lesser known poems of

26 See Contini, II, i, p. 386.

Dante and others mentioned in this paper illustrate a more intimate – if secular and profane – sense of friendship between individuals in a particular social and moral context as fellow-servants or vassals ('fedeli') of Love, as an exclusive circle of friends and, above all, in their common profession that results from this – as fellow poets.

'Boccaccio could be better served': Harry McWilliam and translation criticism

Cormac Ó Cuilleanáin

G.H. McWilliam published incisive scholarly contributions on a variety of topics including Dante, Boccaccio, Verga, Pirandello, Ugo Betti, Italian literature in Ireland, and Shakespeare's Italy.[1] The present essay will touch on some issues surrrounding his contribution as a literary translator, particularly his fine Boccaccio version. An underlying question is this: how do translators and translations relate to each other over time, and how does the reception of translations reflect the interaction of writers and readers, including critics and scholars, across cultures and historical periods?

Translation is a marginal practice for some literary academics, but in McWilliam's case it allowed him to make creative use not only of his considerable writing skills but also of his erudition and his detailed knowledge of texts, writers and cultural backgrounds. He worked on the modern Italian playwright Ugo Betti, whose reputation (quite flourishing in the 1960s) he promoted by advocacy, scholarship and translation. His translation of *Three Plays on Justice* appeared in San Francisco in 1964, followed in 1965 by a Manchester University Press edition of *Two Plays* in the original Italian, with introduction, notes and vocabulary. Later, he worked on more enduring authors: his 1972 Penguin Classics version of Boccaccio's *Decameron*, revised in 1995, was followed by his 1999 Penguin Classics version of short stories by Verga.

He had in fact come to the earlier Boccaccio project by way of Verga. After his predecessor at Trinity College Dublin, Gwynfor Griffith, had recommended him to Penguin Classics as a translator, he had been approached by an editor at Penguin suggesting that he should translate one of Verga's two great novels: 'When I pointed out that Verga had been inconsiderate enough to survive until

---

1 His achievements and career, from postwar student in Leeds to foundation Professor of Italian in Leicester, have been chronicled elsewhere: for what he accomplished before retirement see the Biography and Bibliography provided in *Writers and Performers in Italian Drama from the Time of Dante to Pirandello: Essays in Honour of G.H. McWilliam* ed. by Julie R. Dashwood and Jane E. Everson (Lewiston: Edwin Mellen Press, 1992), pp. v–xii. See also the obituary for McWilliam in *Italian Studies*, 46 (2001), 1–3 (p. 2).

1922, and that therefore his work was still in copyright, I was sent a list of other possible candidates for inclusion in the series, one of whom happened to be Boccaccio [...].'² This episode is recalled in McWilliam's reflective essay 'On Translating the "Decameron"'. The essay opens with a stark verdict – 'The *Decameron* is untranslatable' – a view to which he still subscribed a quarter century later.³ Happily, the alleged impossibility did not in the least deter him. Quite the opposite: 'I was fascinated, and possibly a little hypnotized, by the sheer complexity and magnitude of the various problems that such an assignment entailed, and was sufficiently vain to suppose that I could devise solutions to some of them [...].' Years later, Gwynfor Griffith plausibly suggested that 'the very difficulties presented by such an author proved too much of a temptation, and McWilliam accepted the challenge. He did well.'⁴

Vanity, to which McWilliam cheerfully confesses in the passage quoted above, is a useful weapon in the translator's armoury. When approaching the translation task itself, an equally useful sense of humility creeps in:

> The untranslatability of the *Decameron* arises from its unique combination of various sophisticated stylistic features which are blended into a rich and intricate pattern that is both coherent in all its particulars and wholly inimitable. Boccaccio's prose [...] resembles a complicated and magnificently-wrought tapestry, consisting of a thousand different threads, of varying colour and texture, which have been interwoven in a uniquely personal fashion to produce an overall effect of breathtaking splendour and harmony.⁵

Wholly inimitable, perhaps, but one senses the translator flapping his own wings of rhetoric in that fine polysyllabic confession of inadequacy. We may also sense, in the style of that passage, a certain feeling of affinity and familiarity between translator and author, which if carried through the work should yield results

---

2 G.H. McWilliam, 'On Translating the "Decameron"', in *Essays in Honour of John Humphreys Whitfield, presented to him on his Retirement from the Serena Chair of Italian at the University of Birmingham*, ed. by H.C. Davis and others (London: St George's Press, 1975), pp. 71–83 (p. 71). In his obituary for McWilliam in *The Independent on Sunday*, 11 January 2001, Gwynfor Griffith remembers recommending McWilliam to Robert Baldick, a colleague of his at Oxford who was editor of Penguin Classics. 3 McWilliam, 'On Translating', p. 71. In the Introduction to his 1995 edition of the *Decameron* he wrote: 'it is inconceivable that a truly satisfactory English translation of this great European prose masterpiece will ever be produced': Giovanni Boccaccio, *The Decameron*, translated with an introduction and notes by G.H. McWilliam (London: Penguin Books, 1995), p. cxliv. 4 Griffith, 'Professor G.H. McWilliam'. 5 McWilliam, 'On Translating', p. 72.

beyond the purely technical. One would not wish to prescribe author-translator fraternization in all cases – there are promiscuous translators who can feel a strong affinity for more or less any text for the time it takes to translate it, and there are translators, including self-translators, whose work is fuelled by visceral antipathy – but in the case of Harry McWilliam and Boccaccio, the translation work was certainly sustained by strong aesthetic identification and deep scholarship that was worn lightly and woven almost seamlessly into the English text.[6]

The *Decameron* was going to be difficult to do in English, then, because of its daunting stylistic range, but no more so for McWilliam than for certain others he could name. And that is a strong ethical motive for taking on the task: 'Unless one is fortified by the belief that one can improve upon the efforts of one's predecessors, there can be no possible justification for translating any work that has already been translated, except in those cases where the only earlier versions, whilst still possessing considerable stylistic merit, are essentially of their own period.'[7] As we shall see, he later came to modify that somewhat stern and exclusve view, but the fortifying belief that he could do better was clearly an important consideration on first looking into the *Decameron* project. His most pertinent motive for translating Boccaccio was that

> the English versions already available seemed, for one reason or another, to fall short not only of perfection but even of an acceptable standard of competence or readability, or both. The truth of the old tag *Traduttore, traditore* seemed to me to be nowhere more persuasively illustrated than in the nine English versions of the *Decameron* we already possessed, and I was convinced that Boccaccio could be better served.[8]

Here we are approaching the central theme of the present essay. McWilliam's relative confidence in his own powers was accompanied by an acerbic awareness of the shortcomings of his fellow-translators, which he is prepared to expound in some detail. His 1972 Penguin *Decameron* is prefaced by a long, witty, sometimes sarcastic review of the fate of Boccaccio in English, mangled

6 Giuliano Dego, who translated Byron's *Don Juan*, wrote that 'perché il miracolo della traduzione in rima possa accadere, oltre a una conoscenza approfondita delle due lingue è necessaria una profonda affinità spirituale tra autore e interprete' (Byron, *Don Juan*: Canto Primo, traduzione in ottava rima di Giuliano Dego (Milan: Rizzoli, 1992), p. 42). This might be translated as follows: 'in order for the miracle of rhymed verse translation to happen, it takes not only a deep knowledge of the two languages involved, but also a profound spiritual affinity between author and interpreter'. I owe the reference to Corinna Salvadori Lonergan. **7** McWilliam, 'On Translating', pp. 71–2. **8** McWilliam, 'On Translating', p. 71.

by centuries of prudish or incompetent translators. He traces the disappearance
and substitution of certain of the more racy tales in the book, and notes the
faults as well as the virtues of his predecessors. As a translation critic, he can be
unkind. This is what he has to say, for example, about the 1930 version by the
distinguished poet, novelist, critic, essayist, biographer, translator and friend of
Pound, Richard Aldington:

> Finally we come to the Aldington translation, which has more faults than
> the servant of Friar Cipolla, and which it would be kinder to pass over
> in silence, except that for a large number of contemporary English read-
> ers it alone has served as their means of judging Boccaccio's worth.
> Aldington's version of the *Decameron* is littered with schoolboy errors,
> on the lines of 'I had better arms round your neck than you thought' (II.
> vi), where Boccaccio had written *'io t'ho avuti miglior bracchi alla coda che
> tu non credevi'* – a simple case of confusing *braccio* ('arm') with *bracco*
> ('hound'). Aldington has an uncanny knack of mistaking first-person end-
> ings for third-person endings, and seems blissfully unaware of the subtle
> distinction between subjunctives and indicatives, so that, for instance,
> *'quasi tutti dovessero dal toccamento di questo corpo divenir sani'* (II. i) becomes
> 'almost all of whom became well when they touched Arrigo's body'. But
> not only does Aldington frequently distort and sometimes wholly reverse
> Boccaccio's meaning, he also transmutes Boccaccio's rhythmical, majes-
> tic prose into a language that is jolting and totally commonplace. Where
> the texture of Boccaccio's prose is rich and complex, that of Aldington's
> version is plain and threadbare, so that anyone reading it might be for-
> given for thinking that Boccaccio was a kind of sub-standard fourteenth-
> century Somerset Maugham.[9]

Trenchant? Caustic? Yes, and eloquent too. The strongly negative tone of
some translation criticism makes it fun to quote. A major part of my argument
in the present essay is that critics should sometimes (not always) adopt a less
negative, more nuanced style of evaluation, a more flexible approach and a more

---

9 Boccaccio, *The Decameron*, translated with an Introduction by G.H. McWilliam (London:
Penguin Books, 1972), 'Translator's Introduction', p. 31. It might be pointed out in
Aldington's defence that the two detailed errors cited, though undeniable and symptomatic
of serious deficiencies in the translator's grasp of Italian (he doesn't know his *coda* from his
collo), are not hugely misleading in the overall context of their stories. The *bracchi alla coda*
mistake occurs (to be pedantic about it) not in 'II. vi' but in III. 6. 38, and Catella's speech to
Ricciardo, though unrelentingly doggy in its imagery, does occur in a context where 'arms
round your neck' is by no means an absurd assumption.

humble tone; yet it must be conceded straight away that the sweeping dismissal can have a charm all its own. In fact, McWilliam was not particularly cruel and patronizing by the standards of the genre. Here is Donald Carne-Ross, having pointed out some failings, and some alleged failings, in William Weaver's version of Calvino's *Cosmicomiche*:

> Mr Weaver's translation is the kind of routine job that most publishers, things being what they are, find themselves forced to accept. The purpose of this review is to argue that work of this sort is below the acceptable level. If no other translator could be found (admittedly they are hard to find in Italian), the publisher should have rented him an out-of-work poet for a couple of weeks who could have toned up his diction and improved his cadences and taught him a few dance steps.[10]

It is not the crude insult to Weaver and to the poetic profession, but the languid concessives ('things being what they are …', 'admittedly they are hard to find …') that give this judgment its delightfully supercilious flavour. Others go for a more vigorous frontal assault; here is William Arrowsmith prescribing good modern Italian works for adequate translation: 'Pavese was a great writer and he deserves immediate and complete translation. Several of the *racconti* have recently appeared (I do not mean by this the atrocious version of *La luna e i falò* published some years ago) and doubtless more will follow.' Or again: 'Brancati was a writer of narrow range but great intensity and vision, and he deserves, and will repay, skilful translation. *Il bell' Antonio* (which appeared recently in a butchered version) should be re-done.'[11] And the amusement of reading old critical denunciations is sometimes further heightened by the fact that their perpetrators – to take an example from music, the fearsome nineteenth-century critic Edouard Hanslick – can on occasion give eloquent expression to their comic inability to grasp what is going on.

Negative criticism sometimes fails to capture all the positive achievements of translators, and thus risks constructing an arbitrarily distorted and therefore invalid picture of the field. To return to McWilliam on Aldington: in my view, though far from perfect and nothing like as good as McWilliam, Aldington is not in fact all that bad. His style is literate and usually well balanced; the result-

---

10 D.S. Carne-Ross, *Writing between the Lines*: Italo Calvino's *Cosmicomics,* English translation by William Weaver, French translation by Jean Thibaudeau, *Delos*, 3 (1969), 198–207 (p. 207). 11 William Arrowsmith, 'Twentieth Century Fiction', in *The Craft and Context of Translation*, ed. by William Arrowsmith and Roger Shattuck (Austin: University of Texas Press, 1961), pp. 197–9 (p. 198).

ing *Decameron* is at least readable by a normal citizen, which is more than can be said for the previous version by J.M. Rigg (1903). Thus, in its day, Aldington represented a kind of advance. (In saying this, I realize that I have myself caught a mild dose of critical rabies and started being unkind to Rigg, whose own virtues were by no means negligible in his day.)

McWilliam is not the most unfair of translation critics; later we shall see him offer a genial though not unqualified welcome to his recent competitors. We also consider some more extreme critical hatchet jobs, the most amusing being those perpetrated (not on McWilliam) by Burton Raffel and Donald Carne-Ross.[12] Writers of such *stroncature*, when tempted to be trenchant, should perhaps bear in mind the protest of Irma Brandeis against the 'venomous' habit of 'pointing out many faults and skipping all virtues'.[13]

McWilliam's ease in writing salty and supple prose was certainly one of the reasons why his own 1972 *Decameron* turned out so well, a fact recognized by a number of readers. Consequently, the next part of the present essay will include some kind and positive comments. His version quickly became established as a leader in the field, even as the field became more crowded with the appearance of other new versions: in 1977 Norton published a selection of twenty-one *novelle* translated by Peter E. Bondanella and Mark Musa; this was followed in 1982 by the complete Bondanella and Musa *Decameron*; also in 1982 Charles S. Singleton's revision of the Victorian translation by John Payne was issued in three handsomely produced volumes by the University of California Press; and in 1993 Oxford produced Guido Waldman's version in its World's Classics series.[14] The co-translator of one of the later 'competitor' versions, Peter Bondanella, recognized the significance of the 1972 Penguin Classics version: 'Professor G.H. McWilliam produced a new translation of *The Decameron* whose superiority to currently available English translations, as well as its fortunate placement in the Penguin series, earned it popular and scholarly admiration.'[15] Another American scholar, Christopher Kleinhenz, undertook a fair-minded

---

12 See below, notes 19 to 24. **13** See below, notes 25 and 26. **14** Peter E. Bondanella and Mark Musa, *The Decameron: A New Translation: 21 Novelle, Contemporary Reactions, Modern Criticism*: A Norton Critical Edition (New York: W.W. Norton, 1977); Giovanni Boccaccio, *Decameron*, trans. by Mark Musa and Peter Bondanella, with an introduction by Thomas G. Bergin (New York: New American Library, 1982); Giovanni Boccaccio, *Decameron*: the John Payne translation, revised and annotated by Charles S. Singleton (Berkeley: University of California Press, 1982); Giovanni Boccaccio, *The Decameron*, trans. by Guido Waldman, ed. with an introduction and notes by Jonathan Usher (Oxford and New York: Oxford UP, 1993). **15** Peter Bondanella, 'Translating *The Decameron*', in *The Flight of Ulysses: Studies in Memory of Emmanuel Hatzantonis*, ed. by Augustus A. Mastri (Chapel Hill: Annali d'Italianistica, 1997), pp. 111–24 (p. 112).

assessment of the Payne/Singleton, Musa/Bondanella, and McWilliam versions, comparing a selection of parallel passages, identifying a number of nicely-taken points in each translation, but concluding that of the three,

> Payne/Singleton is the least successful and the least accessible for the modern reader, so encumbered is it with a difficult, enigmatic, and often tedious language. Both McWilliam and Musa/Bondanella furnish texts that are remarkably close to Boccaccio's original in meaning, tone, and nuance; moreover, they provide most enjoyable reading, and that is, after all, one of the principal reasons why Boccaccio wrote the *Decameron*.[16]

There were further endorsements, express and implied. McWilliam has been used as an authoritative English text for serious academic analyses of Boccaccio by scholars such as Guido Almansi (1975) and Pier Massimo Forni (1996).[17] In *The Oxford Guide to Literature in English Translation*, Virginia Cox notes 'the translator's stylistic virtuosity, apparent, for example, in his fine translation of the glorious gibberish of Fra Cipolla's sermon (VI. 10)', while the translation was warmly endorsed, both for its text and for its introductory matter, by Nancy M. Reale in the Fitzroy Dearborn *Encyclopedia of Literary Translation into English*:

> Wonderfully readable for a late 20th-century audience, and quite accurate, is the McWilliam translation [...] an introduction by the translator [...] contains an excellent summary of the English translation history of the *Decameron* [...] there is also an excellent account of the history of expurgation of licentious portions of the original. McWilliam's prose is sensitive to Boccaccio's tonal shifts and to variations in pacing as well as register of language.[18]

---

16 Christopher Kleinhenz, 'The Art of Translation: Boccaccio's *Decameron*', *Yearbook of Comparative and General Literature*, 36 (1987), 104–11 (p. 111). McWilliam was justifiably pleased with this assessment of his work, and quotes it in the preface to his 1995 Penguin *Decameron* (p. xxiii), erroneously citing it as having been published 'some years ago [...] in *Italica*'. **17** Guido Almansi, *The Writer as Liar: Narrative Technique in the 'Decameron'* (London: Routledge and Kegan Paul, 1975); Pier Massimo Forni, *Adventures in Speech: Rhetoric and Narration in Boccaccio's Decameron* (Philadelphia: University of Pennsylvania Press, 1996). Almansi, in his Introduction (p. vii), takes the opportunity 'to express [his] regard for the quality of the translation'. **18** *The Oxford Guide to Literature in English Translation*, ed. by Peter France (Oxford: Oxford UP, 2000), pp. 473–4; *Encyclopedia of Literary Translation into English*, ed. by Olive Classe (London: Fitzroy Dearborn, 2000), I, pp. 164–7 (p. 165). It should be borne in mind that 'quite', in American usage, reinforces rather than attenuates the adjective that follows it.

Another critic who noticed McWilliam's ability to move across the range of styles was Thomas G. Bergin, who pays him a wry *sotto voce* compliment. Referring to Boccaccio's original Italian, he writes: 'The combination of styles adds an element of aesthetic enjoyment to the reading of the work, even if the reader is barely conscious of it; so many-faceted is the language of the master that a contemporary translator has flatly stated that Boccaccio is untranslatable.' When we turn to the endnotes, we find the contemporary translator identified as McWilliam, and Bergin simply adds: 'His own translation (Penguin Classics, 1972) does little to support his statement.'[19]

Apart from such endorsements, McWilliam's most remarkable achievement may have been to escape unscathed – indeed unnoticed – from a 1994 onslaught on the evils of Penguin Classics by Burton Raffel. In *The Art of Translating Prose*, Professor Raffel has a raucous crow to pluck with the ubiquitous Penguin Classics series, which he sees as being based on a 'destructive' editorial policy:

> Penguin, one of our time's most consistent publishers of mediocre trans-
> lations (almost universally tepid rather than terrible, most usually boring
> rather than offensive) unfortunately puts out the largest volume of
> English-language translations. In handling poetry, indeed, Penguin prefers
> to print prose renderings, thus ensuring that aesthetic and stylistic mean-
> ings are not so much distorted as suppressed. In handling prose, Penguin's
> editors apparently aim at comfortable sameness of style – no sentences
> too long or too short; as little variety as possible in sentence structure
> and rhythm; and bland word-choices (monosyllables preferred). Balzac
> = Stendhal = Flaubert = Tolstoy = Whoever […].[20]

Penguin's policy of homogenizing mediocrity is applied, in Raffel's account, with impressive thoroughness. To Flaubert: 'Russell manages, as the Penguin translations so frequently do, to transmit neither the syntactic movement nor the lexicon'. To Balzac: 'This plodding, largely tone-deaf prose belongs, alas, to the translation published by Penguin'. To Rabelais: 'Lexically, Cohen seems determined to deflate, to flatten, whenever and wherever he conveniently can. (This is I suspect not a conscious and certainly not a malicious intent, but sim-ply a constitutional one; earlier in his career, significantly, Cohen not only trans-lated books for but helped the founding editor, E. V. Rieu, edit and shape the nature of the Penguin Classics series)'.[21] Raffel is himself an extraordinarily ver-

19 Thomas G. Bergin, *Boccaccio* (New York: The Viking Press, 1981), pp. 328, 362. **20** Burton Raffel, *The Art of Translating Prose* (University Park, PA: Pennsyvania State UP, 1994), pp. 126, 47–8. **21** Raffel, *The Art*, pp. 46, 79–80, 107.

satile translator; by a quirk of corporate ownership, the Penguin Group is among the publishers of his work.

Given his blanket condemnation of Penguin Classics, one might expect at least a few swipes at McWilliam when Raffel comes to the *Decameron* in his catalogue of 'Famous and Infamous Translations' (Chapter 3). After all, McWilliam's is a very British version, and Raffel is allergic to 'suitable British slang' and what he called '*TLS* condescension'.[22] Instead, unaccountably, he devotes his considerable energies to pummelling other Boccaccio translators. Having duffed up Richard Aldington's 1930 version – 'the reader of this translation can have no possible idea of Boccaccio's style, Boccaccio's literary approach, and, inevitably [...] Boccaccio's full meaning' – he drubs the 1982 American version by McWilliam's 'competitors' Musa and Bondanella – 'at times clumsy, even unidiomatic [...] Musa and Bondanella do not seem fully to understand English punctuation [...] they have chosen to quite closely ape the actual syntax of the Italian, a procedure that cannot produce good results in English or indeed in any other language' – before working over Singleton's 1982 revision of John Payne's translation – 'can language that was archaic in 1886 speak usefully yet another century and more down the road? Indeed, Singleton seems so unsure of what sort of diction his time requires that, astonishingly, not all the flailing archaisms here stem from Payne. [...] There are indeed many roads to failure [...].'[23]

So why no McWilliam? One is tempted to assume either that Raffel approved of it, or else that he had not seen it in the two decades since its publication. Had he been familiar with McWilliam's 1972 Introduction, he would surely have found himself in sympathy with its trenchant comments on previous Boccaccio translations in English, especially McWilliam's equation of Aldington's Boccaccio with Somerset Maugham, already noted. I say this because Raffel elsewhere quotes with amusement the 'wicked' assertion by a British reviewer that 'the founder of the Penguin Classics series, E.V. Rieu, in his versions of Homer had discovered that Homer was in reality Anthony Trollope'.[24]

One may note *en passant* that Burton Raffel was not the first American-based academic who had felt obliged to heap scorn on Penguin. In 1968 – well before the publication of McWilliam's *Decameron* – the distinguished British-born translation critic D.S. Carne-Ross had introduced a 'report' on 'Two Decades of Penguin Classics' in the Texan journal *Arion*, which he had helped to found. His verdict was expressed in the most insulting terms: 'As Miss Radice and Mr

22 Raffel, *The Art*, p. 57; *The New York Review of Books*, 18:2 (10 February 1972), Letters.
23 Raffel, *The Art*, pp. 59, 62, 65–6. **24** Raffel, *The Art*, p. 48.

Baldick survey the work done by Penguin Classics in this field over the last two decades, they must be aware that a good deal of it is at best mediocre, some very bad indeed. Assuming this critical awareness, do they – the interesting question is – propose to do anything about it?' His own prescription was somewhat high-handed:

> The proper course for a series of this sort would be to set up two flexible but well-defined categories. In the first category come the masterpieces, that is creative translations by writers of strong original gift. In the second come the service translations, competent versions by men with some scholarship and a decent prose style. With these categories in mind, the editor could draw a rough balance-sheet, the available talent on one side, the work to be done on the other'.[25]

One wonders whether McWilliam would have counted as a gifted writer or merely a man with some scholarship. Carne-Ross's lordly dismissals were not confined to Penguin Classics; Irma Brandeis decried the 'dogged consistency of his fault-finding' in his 'venomous' review of Allen Mandelbaum's translation of Dante's *Paradiso*, 'venomous in the approach gentle followed by the pounce deadly; venomous in pointing out many faults and skipping all virtues in the huge work'.[26]

McWilliam's *Decameron* was reprinted in expensive formats for series such as the Franklin Mint's Heirloom Library of the World's Greatest Books. At the other end of the market, a selection of his Boccaccian *novelle* figured among the inexpensive chapbooks issued by Penguin to celebrate the firm's sixtieth anniversary.[27] A recent Modern Language Association survey found that American college instructors rated McWilliam as one of their two favourite English versions of the *Decameron*, together with the American version by Musa and Bondanella.[28]

Together with the plaudits came the inevitable quotient of adverse comments, some more justified than others. No translation of the size and scope of the *Decameron* is without its faults. Quite apart from possible errors of detail, there are broad questions on which legitimate disagreements can arise: for exam-

---

25 See *The Translator's Art: Essays in honour of Betty Radice*, ed. by William Radice and Barbara Reynolds (London: Penguin Books, 1987), p. 23.   **26** See the letter from Brandeis in *The New York Review of Books*, 14 February 1985, available at <www.nybooks.com/articles/5562> [accessed 26 August 2005] (par. 1 of 8). His reply to her protest is no less spirited.   **27** Giovanni Boccaccio, *Ten Tales from the Decameron*, trans. by G. H. McWilliam (London: Penguin, 1995).   **28** James H. McGregor, 'Materials', in *Approaches to Teaching Boccaccio's 'Decameron'*, ed. by James H. McGregor (New York: The Modern Language Association of America, 2000), pp. 1–11 (p. 3).

ple, the issue of tone and register, on which translators tend to be vulnerable, whether they pitch their prose too high or too low. We shall see charges of stylistic inappropriateness being levelled by McWilliam, and at McWilliam.

Virginia Cox, in *The Oxford Guide to Literature in English Translation*, having cited J.M. Rigg's 'failure to do justice to the lower stylistic registers of the original, and particularly to Boccaccio's brilliant evocations of the rhythms of colloquial speech', continues:

> Subsequent translators' attempts to remedy this lack have not been uniformly positive: not only do colloquialisms age notoriously badly (Richard Aldington's 'Donna Windy-noddle'), but it might also be noted that certain modern renderings – particularly Aldington's and Guido Waldman's but also, to a lesser extent, G. H. McWilliam's – show a tendency to extend their use of a demotic register beyond the circumscribed use made of it by Boccaccio, with a resulting dilution of the stylistic variety of the original.[29]

Tone and register are widely accepted as being important, but readers tend to disagree on how well different translators have accounted for these features. Christopher C. Stevens, reviewing Waldman's 1993 version, specifically praised him for his skills in this regard: 'This new translation of *The Decameron* is especially valuable for the manner in which it accurately imitates the divergent tones and structures of Boccaccio's prose'.[30] McWilliam, while generally welcoming the new book, took a slightly different stance when he reviewed his Oxford 'rival' shortly before the reissue of his own 1995 revised edition. He commends Waldman's 'excellent command of modern colloquial English, which takes him with apparent ease through the narratives that pose most problems for the translator, though sometimes his evident delight in punning takes him a shade too far in his attempts to match the tone of Boccaccio's text'. The most striking example of this over-enthusiam is Friar Cipolla's nonsensical sermon (*Decameron*, VI. 10). McWilliam cites his own 1972 rendering of Cipolla's mythical wanderings through Funland, Laughland and Liarland (Truffia, Buffia, Menzogna), which hinted at 'a possible extension of the Friar's globe-trotting to include the Baltic region and the Celtic fringe' – but censures Waldman for his rather glorious version of the same passage, which now involves an imaginary trip to France: 'I crossed the straits and came to a town in utter Rouen, so on I went

29 *The Oxford Guide to Literature in English Translation*, ed. by Peter France (Oxford: Oxford UP), 2000, p. 473. **30** *Italian Studies*, 49 (1994), 166–7. Stevens also praises the translation's many felicitous touches, and the quality of Jonathan Usher's fine introduction.

as I had nothing Toulouse, though I had to go fast to escape from the Lyons.'
'The extract here quoted' – McWilliam generously points out – 'should not be
taken as typifying Waldman's overall approach to his task, which is in general
one of scrupulous regard for the meaning of the original. Where his translation
falters, like so many others, is in its occasional failure to match the style and tone
of the more formal registers of Boccaccio's prose [...].'[31]

A slightly longer extract from Waldman's text would have shown just how
the translator, matching Cipolla's nonsense-speak in a burst of Asterixian creativity, plays delightfully on British distortions of Continental placenames in a
dizzying spiral of phonic and rhythmic effects that lead him – with a certain
degree of hypnotic plausibility – not only to France but back to Italy:

> Be it known to you, ladies and gentlemen, that, when I was still but a
> lad, I was sent by my superior to the lands of the rising sun, and I was
> expressly charged with a quest: to seek out the fiefs of Saint Porker's
> Hospice, and never mind that they were picked up for a song, they're
> still bringing money to others and not to us. Off I set, therefore, and I
> set off from Venetia and passed through Magnesia, and on I rode through
> Nemesia and past Freesia and came out at Lutetia, and after that – it was
> a thirsty journey – I landed on the Isle of Sardines. But why do I dwell
> on all these lands where I conducted my quest? I crossed the straits and
> came to a town in utter Rouen, so on I went as I had nothing Toulouse,
> though I had to go fast to escape from the Lyons. When I arrived in a
> town called Boloney I found plenty of our friars and other religious liv-
> ing there.[32]

Peter E. Bondanella has a particularly well-phrased observation on the translation problems involved in such passages: 'It is nearly impossible to discover literal English equivalents for Italian nonsense words; the translator is left to rely
on his ingenuity in such instances, since nonsense words must be reinvented,
not merely translated.'[33] In our age of discontinuity, Waldman's 'reinventions'
could be seen as a justifiable take on what the *Decameron*, and specifically
Cipolla's speech, might have meant to its target audience. A more recent version felt encouraged by McWilliam and Waldman to venture even further afield.
Readers of Cipolla's adventures in that version may recognize, among other
things, a community of 'sisters' from San Francisco, a former Greek dictator
and his Iraqi counterpart, a questionable quarter of Paris, a stiff drink from

---

31 McWilliam's review is in *Translation and Literature*, 4 part 1 (1995), 115–18. **32** Boccaccio,
Decameron, trans. by Waldman, p. 408. **33** Bondanella, 'Translating *The Decameron*', p. 116.

Mexico, some former Soviet republics, detritus from the Internet boom of the 1990s, and a well-known American motor racing event. The effect is designed to be as confusing as the original Cipolla, who succeeded in convincing the simple burghers of Certaldo that he had collected the relics of a Roman saint by travelling to Palestine. It is to be hoped that no reader, or reviewer, will find these inventions in any way anachronistic or inappropriate.[34]

If McWilliam was capable of being somewhat stern (though never dour) in judging other translators, his own work was not immune from hostile criticism. The usual question of register surfaced in a long and detailed review of the 1972 Penguin Classics edition, in which Anna Laura Lepschy undertook a minute comparison of detailed renderings from the *Decameron* in order to see whether McWilliam could really be said to have improved on J.M. Rigg's 1903 version. She agrees with McWilliam's judgement that Rigg had done well in the formal passages but was 'not nearly so confident in his handling of the straightforward dialogue and colloquial speech to be found in the majority of Boccaccio's stories'.[35] In considering this new translation, she writes, 'it is necessary to see whether in fact McWilliam reaches Rigg's standards of accuracy and fidelity to the text whilst improving on the rendering of Boccaccio's various stylistic registers'.[36] She pays particular attention to four Decameronian stories, two written in an elevated style and two in a more demotic register. Having found dozens of spots where McWilliam is arguably less accurate than Rigg, she remarks:

> His text is certainly easier to read than Rigg's. But I have reservations, for Rigg's version is more accurate, and McWilliam in his attempts to be contemporary is sometimes jarring and anachronistic. His results are usually more satisfactory in the lower registers than in the higher, but he often introduces sudden contrasts between modern and dated, colloquial and literary, where the original does not require it.[37]

These contrasting views on different translators' degree of success in handling tone and register prompt several observations. Firstly, stylistic effects seem to be perceived in a highly subjective manner. Secondly, as already noted, translation criticism is sometimes written in punitive and prescriptive tones as though the translator had sat and failed an elementary language test devised by the

---

34 Giovanni Boccaccio, *Decameron*: A new English version by Cormac Ó Cuilleanáin, based on John Payne's 1886 translation (Ware: Wordsworth Editions, 2004), pp. lxxiv–lxxv, 456. **35** Anna Laura Lepschy, review of Giovanni Boccaccio, *The Decameron*, translated with an introduction by G.H. McWilliam (London: Penguin Books, 1972), in *Studi sul Boccaccio*, 8 (1974), 329–35 (p. 329). **36** Lepschy, review, p. 329. **37** Lepschy, review, p. 335.

reviewer. (Irritable reactions may sometimes be linked to a reviewer's love of the original text, its sounds and its rhythms, a love not mediated by translation.) Thirdly, it is naïve to think that ideas of 'high' and 'low' are any less subject to change than other cultural categories, and translation across language and time clearly involves translation across cultures and the transposition and re-orchestration of cultural categories. Modern English has its own ideas of the plain-spoken sublime; we might nowadays tend to smile at Dante's admiration, in *De vulgari eloquentia*, II.VII.6, for the hendecasyllabic word *sovramagnificentissima-mente*; it is equally possible that Dante might have missed the point of the 'red hills of Georgia' in Martin Luther King's address at the Lincoln Memorial, Washington DC, on 28 August 1963, when among other almost unbearably sublime cadences, he said: 'I have a dream that one day on the red hills of Georgia, the sons of former slaves and the sons of former slave owners will be able to sit down together at the table of brotherhood'.[38] If we feel allergic today to certain more traditional forms of 'high' speech, if Joyce and jazz and audio recordings have altered our ear for demotic prose, how far is the translator entitled, or obliged, to adapt to the new situation? Traditionally, modern language scholars tended to prescribe a strict standard of adherence to the original, and this includes, theoretically speaking, Harry McWilliam himself, when he questions Waldman's practice of cutting Boccaccio's rubrics so as to avoid giving away too much too soon. In a prefatory note, Waldman had explained that readers of the present day 'usually take it amiss if a publisher or reviewer gives away the tale's ending before they have started reading it'. McWilliam sounds sceptical: 'Whether one accepts such an explanation depends on one's view of the translator's remit. Should translators translate what writers actually wrote, or what they think they should have written?'[39]

Precisely the latter view is held by numerous literary translators, one of the more notorious assertions of their beliefs being Robert Lowell's claim in the preface to *Imitations* that 'I have tried to write live English and to do what my authors might have done if they were writing their poems now and in America.'[40] The translators of Goethe's *Italian Journey*, W.H. Auden and Elizabeth Mayer, were even more cavalier about bringing Goethe up to scratch. Introducing their translation, they explain that 'the translator's most difficult problem is not what his author says but his tone of voice. How is a man who thought and wrote in German to think and write in English and yet remain a

---

38 Martin Luther King, Jr.: 'I Have a Dream' <http://www.americanrhetoric.com/speeches/Ihaveadream.htm> [accessed 28 August 2005] (par 18 of 42).   **39** McWilliam, review in *Translation and Literature*, p. 116.   **40** Robert Lowell, *Imitations* (London: Faber and Faber, 1962), p. xi.

unique personality called Goethe?' They then admit that they have done some stylistic editing, cutting some repetitive passages and allusions to things that would have needed lengthy footnotes. One whole section is excised because it is 'verbose rubbish'. And they quote Goethe himself to answer 'those who regard such tinkering as sacrilege'. As they translate him, Goethe claims that 'if the translator has really understood his author, he will be able to evoke in his own mind not only what the author has done, but also what he wanted and ought to have done. That at least is the line I have always taken in translation, though I make no claim that it is justifiable.'[41]

Without entering into theoretical debates about the meanings of equivalence, or the choice between domesticating and foreignizing translation, we can at least note that writers and translators sometimes prove more flexible in practice than their theoretical pronouncements might suggest. Fortunately, McWilliam's idea of translating 'what writers actually wrote', when applied to his own translation practice, allowed considerable elbow-room for sensible adaptation at the level of clause, sentence and paragraph, so that his versions of Boccaccio ring true in English, even at the cost of distancing themselves slightly from the shape of the original Italian. That does not mean that Boccaccio has been repackaged as an Englishman, or that the natural flow of 'his' English prevents us from experiencing his foreignness. The case is more subtle and paradoxical than that. The 'native' illusion, the idea that it is somehow natural for the world to express itself in English, without detracting from its foreignness, is perhaps best conveyed by something that the critic James Wood said about McWilliam's later Verga translations:

> In English, they read superbly well. They are cleansing; a lot of wordy grime has been removed [...]. There is a vernacular ease of address, and yet hardly a moment at which the English version seems too local – i.e. English. The effect is oddly as if they had been translated twice, once into English, and then into a regional English which does not exist. The work retains its universality, and one suspects that these translations will last a long time.[42]

This is a fairly safe prophecy, although no translator can hope to reign unchallenged. McWilliam's Verga is of course hugely better than the efforts of D.H.

---

41 Johann Wolfgang Goethe, *Italian Journey, 1786–1788*, trans. by W.H. Auden and Elizabeth Mayer (London: Penguin, 1992), 'Introduction', pp. 17–19. 42 James Wood, 'Like a Mullet in Love', *London Review of Books*, 10 August 2000: a review of *Cavalleria Rusticana and Other Stories* by Giovanni Verga, trans. by G.H. McWilliam (London: Penguin, 1999).

Lawrence, but it is arguable that some of Verga's *novelle* in the recent version by J.G. Nichols – for instance, 'Nasty Foxfur' – may pack an even stronger punch than his.[43] The point to be borne in mind is that the vernacular can, paradoxically, release a work from the bonds of the local. When Edward Sapir asserts that 'with Heine, one is under the illusion that the universe speaks German',[44] that illusory Germanness does not prevent the universe from retaining its universality. The projection of a reader's consciousness into strange or familiar things, by means of strange or familiar language, is not a simple phenomenon. Whether with Verga or Boccaccio, the translator's language choices can help the work retain its universality. And it is precisely the flow of McWilliam's natural-sounding but de-localized English that justifies many of his departures from detailed matching of the vocabulary and syntax of Boccaccio's Italian original, identified in Lepschy's review.

Although it contains fifty-three numbered corrections and queries, as well as a quiverful of unnumbered objections, the Lepschy review is officially a favourable one, as a five-page litany of complaints is rounded off by an approving paragraph: 'It must be remembered that I have only listed objections and queries: I do not quote what I agree with, and this covers almost the whole translation. Keeping in mind, moreover, the difficulty of translating a text as long, as varied and as complex as the *Decameron*, I think that McWilliam has been successful in his enterprise'.[45] This being the case, how damaging are the points of detail on which she has taken him to task?

In the rubric of the tale of Masetto (III. 1) Lepschy asserts: '1. "*All the nuns vie with one another* to take him off to bed with them" is incorrect for "tutte concorrono a giacersi con lui", which is given the right meaning by Rigg: "with one accord make haste to lie with him"'.[46]

I cannot concur. Even in 1903, 'lie with him' may have come across as a coy bowdlerization, and although Rigg deftly deploys two verbs to render the etymological possibilities of 'concorrono', I do not find McWilliam's 'vie with' to be a particularly misleading image for the increasingly competitive demands that the nuns and the abbess make on Masetto's slender resources – even if it also reflects more modern Italian overtones of *concorrenza*, I find it suggestive of eager movement towards a goal which is by one accord found desirable.

Lepschy continues: '2. "As though some enormous and *diabolical* evil had been perpetrated against nature" introduces an extraneous element into "contra natura un grandissimo e scelerato male"; Rigg gives: "heinous and unnatural crime"'.

43 Giovanni Verga, *Life in the Country* (London: Hesperus Press, 2003), pp. 50–67. **44** Edward Sapir, *Language* (New York: Harcourt Brace, 1921), pp. 240–1. **45** Lepschy, review, p. 335. **46** Lepschy, review, p. 333.

Again, I wonder whether an English reader would spot the *diavolo* hidden in diabolical, rather than subconsciously hearing an entirely appropriate echo of 'bollocks'. 'Scelerato' is anyway a markedly hellish word (*Inferno*, XX. 28–30), and how extraneous are devils to a sin of impiety that involves Masetto 'lying with' ten nuns and thereby crowning a cuckold Christ with horns (*Decameron*, III. 1. 43)? The Rigg version, on the other hand, seems formulaic, with Boccaccio's heavy words and hint of sexual deviancy being condensed into what sounds like a bland courtroom cliché. Or at least so it sounds to me; perhaps I am becoming infected with the 'punitive and prescriptive' style of translation criticism to which I alluded earlier.

In the tale of Ghismonda (IV. 1), Lepschy objects that '"she decided to see whether she could find herself a secret lover who was *worthy of her affections*" strays unnecessarily from "si pensò di volere avere, se esser potesse, occultamente un valoroso amante". Rigg is more accurate, but archaic: "she cast about how she might come by a gallant to be her secret lover"'.[47]

Again, I fail to see how McWilliam is less accurate than Rigg. 'A gallant', even before the 'Two Gallants' of Joyce's *Dubliners*, did not have the entirely appropriate moral connotations of McWilliam's 'worthy'; rather, it summons up the image of a dashing military chap with a twinkle in his eye. 'Cast about' and 'come by' make Ghismonda sound a touch more raffish and less deliberate than Boccaccio painted her.[48]

There are of course some sound criticisms in Anna Laura Lepschy's closely attentive evaluation, and no doubt he should have taken them on board, as Jonathan Usher suggested in an unenthusiastic review of the revised 1995 edition.[49] But not all of her hits were palpable, and anyway, finding errors is not enough.

---

47 Lepschy, review, p. 331. **48** Compare the late Victorian street ballad 'The Gallant Hussar' which begins: 'A damsel possessed of great beauty, / She stood by her own father's gate, / The gallant hussars were on duty, / To view them this maiden did wait; / Their horses were capering and prancing, / Their accoutrements shone like a star, / From the plains they were nearer advancing, / She espied her young gallant Hussar'. Broadside printings of this ballad are catalogued in libraries including the National Library of Scotland (see <http://www.nls.uk/broadsides/index.html>) and the Bodleian (see <http://www.bodley.ox.ac.uk/ballads/ballads.htm>). The 1972 edition of Chambers *Twentieth Century Dictionary*, under 'gallant', includes the adjectival meaning 'attentive (esp. formally or obsequiously) to ladies', and, as a noun, 'a gay, dashing person: a man (*arch.*; woman *obs.*) of fashion: a lover'. In short, Ghismonda is looking for Captain Wentworth; Rigg has saddled her with Mr Wickham. **49** Usher writes: 'Those interested in a detailed analysis of the original, and who wish to make an assessment of the response of the translator in the second edition are advised to consult the review by A. L. Lepschy in *Studi sul Boccaccio*, 8 (1974), 329–35, but the translations remain unaltered, even where Lepschy rightly challenges their accuracy (e.g. note 1 on the rubric of Masetto da Lamporecchio: the meaning of "concorrono")'. See

The devil is in the detail, but the detail is not the book. Coherence and other translation constraints require that the translation of detail be done with an eye to various contexts: details may be displaced, and seemingly extraneous elements may be introduced to compensate for effects that get lost in translation. Thus, when Lepschy objects that 'an endless torrent of tears and sobbing' is 'an unnecessarily exaggerated version of "*tra' sospiri e tra le lagrime*"' (I. In. 3), one might defend McWilliam's expansion on the grounds that it is needed to weight the end of an ingeniously rebalanced English sentence that attempts an aesthetic equivalent of the extremely complex rhythms of the Italian original. When she finds no reason for translating '*una montagna aspra ed erta*' (I. In. 4) as 'a steep and rugged hill', one may find the choice fully justified not only by the euphony of the phrase and the balance of the sentence (the monosyllable 'hill' matches the monosyllable 'plain' at the end of the following clause), but also by the normal English collocation of hill with walkers (Boccaccio's *camminanti*, a key word in the passage), whereas mountains, for some reason, seem to be associated with climbers. Picking off individual points, without taking what Keith Harvey calls a 'text-holistic' approach, is in the end an undertaking of questionable merit. One cannot expect equivalent effects to be produced by identical means; interlingual translation involves constant adjustment and compensation to allow for differences in the linguistic terrain, and, as Harvey points out, 'compensation for a lost source text effect can be dispersed or displaced to a different part of the target text'; identifying the occurrences of compensation becomes more complicated when 'the displaced nature of compensation combines with the use of different linguistic devices in the source and target texts in order to approximate a similar effect'.[50]

What of the introduction of entirely new images, not found in the original? With reference to Boccaccio's little horror-story of the two pigs who died after chewing the discarded clothing of a plague victim (*Decameron*, I. In. 18), Lepschy objects that 'they both dropped dead to the ground, spreadeagled upon the rags that had brought about their undoing' introduces a new element into '*amenduni sopra gli mal tirati stracci morti caddero in terra*'.[51] Presumably the striking and anatomically improbable 'spreadeagled' is the unwanted element. To what in the original could it possibly correspond? What is it doing here?

There is more than one answer. Within the rhythm of the sentence, 'spread-eagled' neatly separates two too-similar phrases, 'to the ground' and 'upon the rags',

Italian Studies, 53 (1998), 180–1 (p. 181). For a more positive assessment of the 1995 revision, see Cormac Ó Cuilleanáin, review in *Modern Language Review*, 96 no. 2 (2001), pp. 531–2. **50** Keith Harvey, 'Compensation', *Routledge Encyclopedia of Translation Studies*, ed. by Mona Baker assisted by Kirsten Malmkjær (London: Routledge, 1998), pp. 37–40 (p. 40). **51** Lepschy, review, p. 330.

its bright stressed syllable contrasting with their darker vowel sounds and with those of the gloomy-sounding phrase that follows: 'that had brought about their undo-ing'. As an image, its very inappropriateness matches the obscene inappropriateness of Boccaccio's importation of a Dantean echo ('*mal tirati stracci*' from '*mal protesi nervi*') to the 'sin-excited nerves' of a former bishop of Florence, possibly homo-sexual, whose death in Vicenza (*Inferno*, XV. 114) parallels that of the pigs.[52] There was something gratuitous, something quite uncalled-for, in Boccaccio's Dantean echo, so perhaps we can allow something gratuitous in McWilliam's translation. Were one to apply the cultural compensation principle of 'replacing, say, a snatch of Dante with a snatch of Milton', as suggested by Ian Higgins and his co-authors when discussing 'categories of compensation' in *Thinking Italian Translation*, then perhaps McWilliam could have knocked his pigs headlong with hideous ruin. As it stands, 'spreadeagled' is a gratuitously creative response to a gratuitously creative phrase in Boccaccio, and an entirely legitimate exercise in reducing 'an unaccept-able translation loss through the calculated introduction of a less unacceptable one'.[53]

Should it be necessary to argue this obvious point in quite so much detail? A literary translator is bound to respond creatively to creative aspects of the original. In the 1958 collection *On Translation*, the American scholar and trans-lator Dudley Fitts argued that 'the translation of a poem should be a poem, viable as a poem, and, as a poem, weighable'. To understand a foreign poem, we need 'another poem [...], a comparable experience'.[54] Another essay by Jackson Mathews opened with the following assertion: 'One thing seems clear: to translate a poem whole is to compose another poem. A whole translation will be faithful to the matter, and it will 'approximate the form', of the original; and it will have a life of its own, which is the voice of the translator'. Mathews goes on to explain that 'in the "approximation of form" [...] the motive is invention, not imitation. The translator has to invent formal effects in his own language that give a sense of those produced by the original in its own.'[55] Fitts and Mathews are writing about poetry, but what they have to say, if valid, can be extended at least partially to prose. If we allow terms such as 'experience', 'life', 'voice' and 'invention' into the discussion of poetic translation, can we not allow at least some creative licence to a translator of prose, which has its

---

52 The 'sin-excited nerves' come from Longfellow's translation. The Dantean echo is noted in Giovanni Boccaccio, *Decameron*, ed. by Vittore Branca (Turin: Einaudi, 1992), I, p. 18, n. 7. **53** Sándor Hervey, Ian Higgins, Stella Cragie and Patrizia Gambarotta, *Thinking Italian Translation: A Course in Translation Method: Italian to English* (London: Routledge, 2000), pp. 38, 40. **54** Dudley Fitts, 'The Poetic Nuance', in *On Translation*, ed. by Reuben Brower (Cambridge MA: Harvard UP, 1959), pp. 32–47 (pp. 34–5). **55** Jackson Mathews, 'Third Thoughts on Translating Poetry', in *On Translation*, op. cit., pp. 67–77 (p. 67).

own complex formal demands, particularly if the translator generally stays as close to the original as McWilliam does with Boccaccio?

One problem with translation criticism is that, involving as it does both process and product, an adequate explication of even the simplest translation decision can take an inordinate amount of space. Having done that, I shall now hasten towards my end.

Harry McWilliam did not overhaul his text in the light of the Lepschy critique. Introducing the second edition of 1995, he states unapologetically that while the reprints since 1972 had involved 'occasional emendations of a distinctly minor complexion', the translation, which in his 'not altogether impartial judgement' still read 'surprisingly well', required only 'marginal adjustment'.[56] The major innovation for 1995 was the addition of a very useful and scholarly Introduction and bibliography, 121 pages in length, together with 68 pages of notes explaining local references, pointing out sources and parallels, defending translation choices, and offering incisive personal comments. (One wonders whether the style of the original translation might have been less explanatory in places, had he started out with the option of annotation in mind. Notes can free translators from the sometimes dangerous habit of clarifying.)

There are a few translation changes from the first edition. Some have to do with the flow of English phrasing; others are concerned with substantive meaning. Peter Bondanella's 1997 essay on 'Translating *The Decameron*' points out that McWilliam, in 1972, had given a mistaken interpretation of the words 'quelle del cane' in the ingredients for the disgusting sweet administered to Calandrino by Bruno and Buffalmacco as part of a comic trial by ordeal (VIII. 6. 1):

> any translator sensitive to Boccaccio's humour and unafraid to render slightly off-color passages accurately might be tempted to translate this opening passage as McWilliam has done: 'They give him two sweets, one after another, consisting of dog-stools seasoned with aloes, so that it appears that he has stolen the pig himself'. And yet, an extremely erudite argument by Manlio Pastore Stocchi makes it clear that 'quelle del cane' refers not to dog-excrement (a substance that was, indeed, employed by the period's apothecaries) but, instead, a cheaper version of the ginger used in the other cookies.[57]

In defence of McWilliam, one might note that the Pastore Stocchi article cited by Bondanella appeared in *Studi sul Boccaccio* volume 7 (1973), which was

---

56 Boccaccio, *Decameron*, trans. by McWilliam, 1995 edition, 'Preface to the Second Edition', p. xxiii.   57 Bondanella, 'Translating *The Decameron*', p. 123.

rather late for the first Penguin *Decameron* (1972), and moreover that the new interpretation had already been incorporated in the revised edition, albeit with a distinctly non-confessional note: '*dog ginger* Dog ginger is water pepper, a marsh weed having an acrid juice. B. wrote 'quelle del cane' ('those of the dog'), which until recently was misinterpreted by most of his English translators as 'dog stools' or 'dog turds'.[58]

More questionable is McWilliam's incorporation of a marginal comment from a medieval reader as if it were part of the text. The trickster Bruno is listing the mythical queens that Mastro Simone will see if he goes on the rampage with a group of revellers. These queens include '*la schinchimurra del Presto Giovanni; or vedete oggimai voi!*' (VIII. 9. 24), and in the margin of an early manuscript Francesco Mannelli adds: '*che ha per me' 'l culo le corna*'. As Bondanella points out, McWilliam's 1972 version adds Mannelli's remark as though it were Boccaccio's commentary: 'You would see every queen in the world there, not even excluding the Skinkymurra of Prester John, who has horns sticking out of her anus: now there's a spectacle for you!' Bondanella rightly protests that the spectacle is 'not one the author ever intended his reader to see!' – and one has to admit that the fault is not much improved by a silent correction in the 1995 edition, no doubt informed by scrupulous erudition: 'You would see every queen in the world there, not even excluding the Skinkymurra of Prester John, who has horns sticking out of his anus: now there's a pretty sight!'[59]

There are occasional infelicities, then, but the virtues of the translation are far more numerous and significant. The strength of McWilliam's *Decameron* is its fluency and the balance it strikes between exactness and naturalness. Without mechanically imitating Boccaccio's sentence structure, he has created a viable modern-day counterpart: readable, approachable, flavoured but also a little elevated above common speech. It can be argued that he captures the middle range of Boccaccio's style better than the extremes of solemnity or colloquial speech. One important achievement is that of maintaining a credible and consistent voice for the author.

For comparative purposes, it might be useful to quote a passage from the *Decameron* in Italian and in several English translations, not in order to show that McWilliam is the champion and the other translators are traitors, but rather to suggest that there are valid achievements to be found in many versions, and that

---

58 Boccaccio, *Decameron*, trans. by McWilliam, 1995 edition, p. 853. Clearly, there are limits to his personal humility.   **59** Bondanella, p. 123; Boccaccio, *Decameron*, ed. Branca, II, p. 989; Boccaccio, *Decameron*, trans. by McWilliam, 1972 edition, p. 653; Boccaccio, *Decameron*, trans. by McWilliam, 1995 edition, p. 619. These horns might have gone straight to the notes had the 1972 version been annotated from the start.

the broad range of available versions represents a cultural strengthening of the original work. The space spent on criticizing critics, however, does not allow further lengthy comparisons, so I will quote just two authors, Boccaccio and McWilliam,[60] as they present the story of an errant monk, a beautiful girl, and a far from impervious abbot (I. 4. 15):

> La giovane, vedendo venire l'abate, tutta smarrì, e temendo di vergogna cominciò a piagnere. Messer l'abate, postole l'occhio addosso e veggendola bella e fresca, ancora che vecchio fosse, sentì subitamente non meno cocenti gli stimoli della carne che sentiti avesse il suo giovane monaco, e fra se' stesso cominciò a dire: – Deh, perché non prendo io del piacere quando io ne posso avere, con ciò sia còsa che il dispiacere e la noia, sempre che io ne vorrò, sieno apparecchiati? Costei è una bella giovane, ed è qui che niuna persona del mondo il sa; se io la posso recare a fare i piacer miei, io non so perché io nol mi faccia.

> When she saw the Abbot coming in, the girl was terrified out of her wits, and began to weep for shame. Master Abbot, having looked her up and down, saw that she was a nice, comely wench, and despite his years he was promptly filled with fleshly cravings, no less intense than those his young monk had experienced. And he began to say to himself 'Well, well! Why not enjoy myself a little, when I have the opportunity? After all, I can have my fill of sorrow and afflictions whenever I like. This is a fine-looking wench, and not a living soul knows that she is here. If I can persuade her to play my game, I see no reason why I shouldn't do it.'

One could spend some amusing pages comparing this version to those by Aldington, Waldman, Rigg, Musa and Bondanella, Payne and others. Instead, I will simply draw attention to the appropriate use of sexist language, and the easy rhythm of the abbot's self-seducing thoughts. For me, the chief beauty of the McWilliam passage resides in the phrase 'If I can persuade her to play my game' for 'se io la posso recare a fare i piacer miei'. It has euphony, concision and concreteness to match the original, and it gives the abbot an entirely appropriate voice from British film comedy of the Nineteen-Fifties: this is an abbot from Ealing Studios, who could be played by Terry-Thomas or Alastair Sim. This slightly old-fashioned, avuncular tone, striking a brilliantly judged compromise between Boccaccio's contemporaneity with his own time and his temporal distance from

---

60 Boccaccio, *Decameron*, ed. Branca, I, pp. 86–7; Boccaccio, *Decameron*, trans. by McWilliam, 1995 edition, p. 47.

ours, allows the translator to render without undue strain the author's characteristic combination of indecent topics and decorous sentence structure.

How, then, do different translations relate to each other? How does translation work? We can start out from the simple concept of 'competition'. Initially,
as we saw, McWilliam was happy to compete with lesser translators on grounds
of quality. His sternly exclusive veto – 'Unless [...] one can improve upon the
efforts of one's predecessors, there can be no possible justification for translating [...]' – failed to appreciate the legitimate desire of different publishers to
produce their own versions of classic works, or the fact that a range of different translations, even if they sometimes vary in quality, collectively contribute
something new to our understanding of their source text. Later, in his 1995
review for *Translation and Literature* of Guido Waldman's version, McWilliam
was happy to acknowledge that competition can be good for everyone, including the author. He noted that his own translation of the *Decameron* had been
regularly reprinted, its popularity persisting despite 'stiff competition in recent
years' from the 1982 Bondanella and Musa version. Indeed, he noted,

> sales of the Penguin Classics version have actually increased steadily on
> the far side of the Atlantic over recent years, which suggests that a pol-
> icy of letting a hundred flowers blossom is grounded in common sense.
> The appearance of yet another complete translation into English of
> Boccaccio's master-work cannot be other than warmly welcomed by its
> competitors for the attention of the *Decameron*'s potential readership,
> whose numbers seem to increase exponentially with each new version
> that becomes available.[61]

The existence of 'competing' interpretations can even be good for scholars, as
witnessed by Marilyn Migiel's intelligent questioning of ambiguous meanings
in Boccaccio's original Italian, by reviewing particular points in the versions of
several translations, including McWilliam.[62] If, in the world of ideas, 'all great
texts contain their potential translation between the lines',[63] if 'it is the task of
the translator to release in his own language that pure language which is under

---

61 McWilliam, review of Waldman translation, *Translation and Literature*, p. 115. **62** Marilyn
Migiel, *A Rhetoric of the* Decameron (Toronto: University of Toronto Press, 2004), pp. 91–3,
105–6, 141–2, 199. **63** Walter Benjamin, 'The Task of the Translator', in *Illuminations*, ed.
with an introduction by Hannah Arendt, trans. by Harry Zohn (London: Jonathan Cape,
1970), pp. 69–82 (p. 82). Or, in the translation of James Hynd and E. M. Valk, 'For in some
degree, all great writings, but the Scriptures in the highest degree, contain between the lines
their virtual translation'. See *Delos: A Journal on & of Translation*, 2 (1968), 76–99 (p. 97).

the spell of another'[64] – or if, to put it another way, 'the task of the translator is this: in his own language to redeem universal language from exile in the alien, to free it by translation from the work that enthralls it'[65] – then perhaps we can see all adaptors and translators, and even all critics both sweet-tempered and sour-tongued, as working together to liberate Boccaccio's pure original ideas from the shackles of fourteenth-century Tuscan.

To end on an high note, let us simply admire how Harry McWilliam rewrote one of the *Decameron*'s most poetic recognition scenes, towards the end of its penultimate story:[66]

> Then the lady took hold of the cup, removed the lid, raised it to her lips to complete the ritual, and caught sight of the ring, which she inspected closely for a while without saying a word. Identifying the ring as the one she had given to Messer Torello at his departure, she picked it up and fixed her gaze upon the so-called stranger. And now that she could see who it was, she overturned the table at which she was sitting, as though she had gone berserk, and cried out:
>
> 'This is my lord; this truly is Messer Torello!'

64 Benjamin, 'The Task of the Translator', trans. by Harry Zohn, p. 80. 65 Benjamin, 'The Task of the Translator', trans. by Hynd and Valk, p. 94. 66 Boccaccio, *Decameron*, trans. by McWilliam, 1995 edition, p. 782.

Humanism in Ireland in the sixteenth century: the evidence of Trinity College Dublin MS 160

John Scattergood

I

Of the four great early Tudor manuscript collections of the new humanist poetry of Sir Thomas Wyatt, the earl of Surrey and their followers, TCD MS 160 is in many ways the most unusual.[1] As it is the book consists of two volumes, but only part II (fols 57–186) belongs to the Tudor period: the earlier part contains various late medieval moral and political items including a copy of Peter Idley's *Instructions to His Son*. But part II constitutes a separate entity, with its own definable set of interests, its own originally systematic programme of organization, its own partial contents lists, its own depleted system of foliation.[2]

TCD MS 160 is unique among Tudor collections in having an alphabetical arrangement of contents. It is clear from two *tabulae* – for the letters A and D – how the collection was conceived in terms of its original organization. The A tabula is as follows:

Tabula A

alone musyng	fo
absence alas	flo
absence abcentyng	flo
alas fortune	flo

---

1 The other three are London, British Library MS Egerton 2711, which is in Wyatt's handwriting, the Arundel Harrington MS, and the Devonshire MS (British Library MS Additional 17492). For an authoritative study of the Arundel Harrington MS see *The Arundel Harrington Manuscript of Tudor Poetry*, ed. by Ruth Hughey (Columbus, Ohio: Ohio State UP, 1960). For useful studies of the manuscripts in general see H. A. Mason, *Editing Wyatt* (Cambridge: Cambridge Quarterly Publications, 1972) and Richard Harrier, *The Canon of Thomas Wyatt's Poetry* (Cambridge, MA: Harvard UP, 1975). 2 The best published account of TCD MS 160 appears in *Sir Thomas Wyatt and His Circle*, ed. by Kenneth Muir (Liverpool: Liverpool UP, 1961). The most thorough investigation, however, appears in the unpublished MLitt thesis of Susan O'Keeffe, 'TCD MS 160: A Tudor Miscellany' (1986). I am much indebted to Ms O'Keeffe's work.

A my harte	flo	
alas dere harte	flo	
at last withdrawe youre crueltie	flo	
at moste myschyffe	flo	v ...
Alas dere harte	flo	ix
Alas all sorofull	flo	x
Away all care and payne	flo	xi
Alack alack what shall I doo	flo	xii
Alas that same swete face	flo	xiii
Alas my dere	flo	xiiii
alle ye that know	flo	xv
accusid though I be	flo	xvi
Agaynst the rock	flo	xvii
A. face that shuld	flo	
A.s from theys hylles	f ...	
A.		
A.		
A.		
A.		
A.		
A.		
A.		
A.		

The originator of the manuscript, Hand A, who alone of the contributors writes in a trained professional manner and who is identified by Helen Baron as John Mantell (?1516–41),[3] had access to a number of poems he wished to preserve and copied them into an already bound paper volume using an alphabetical system of organization: each poem was to begin on the recto of the folio and was to continue on to the verso if necessary. If the text was short enough to be completed on the recto the verso was left blank. Hand A also left a number of folios blank after he had entered all the poems that he had beginning with a particular letter, but appropriated them for more poems beginning with that letter by entering a capital letter at the top of the recto of a series of blank folios. Hand A, the first compiler of the manuscript, set the pattern for its future develop-

3 See Helen Baron, 'The "Blage Manuscript": The Original Compiler Identified', in *English Manuscript Studies, 1100–1700*, 1 (1989), ed. by Peter Beal and Jeremy Griffiths, 85–119. John Mantell was a friend of Wyatt. The scanty details of his life are usefully collected together by Helen Baron. However, not everyone accepts her attribution.

ment: he envisaged its completion being part of a dynamic process in which it would gradually be filled up with the addition of more poems. And this, in fact, is what happened. Hand A entered items only as far as fol. 109, part of the I section, and thereafter control of the book passed to others. Hand B, for example, contributed two poems to the A section, and noted their first lines in Tabula A, and added poems to other sections too. But Hand A's original conception of a handwritten humanist poetic anthology gradually gets dissipated: poems are entered on blank versos; work in progress begins to appear, with crossings-out and repeated drafts, whereas before all the poems had been fair copies; items begin to be entered under the wrong letter, sometimes squeezed into margins; items begin to get lost as pages disappear; prose starts to be included. The book becomes a generalized, but still largely humanist, miscellany.

The collection was put together over a number of years, but the evidence for dating it, or the successive stages of it, is sparse, fragmentary, and of different sorts – notes of actual dates, dates associated with the lives of people known to have contributed to it, and dateable allusions in the items themselves. So dating is difficult but not impossible, and it is also possible, in most cases, to establish in what order the ten people who contributed to the manuscript wrote their particular items – this by reference to the positions of their work in the alphabetical sections, for the earlier the hand the earlier the folios appropriated in the various sequences. The earliest contributor, Hand A, certainly intended to date his work: he entered a date at the top of fol. 57r., 'in ye yere of. ...' but the indicative part of the date has crumbled away through the fragility of the paper. The only useful item among his entries is a title entered in Tabula D, 'dryvyn by desire to set affection ...' which must have been composed before about 1538 when it was included in the Douce fragment of *The Court of Venus*.[4] In relation to Hand B the best evidence is provided by Wyatt's 'Who so lyst to hunt ...' (fol. 185r) which is to be dated around or after 1526 when Henry VIII first became interested in Anne Boleyn. The next major contributor, Hand C, copied 'In mornyng wyse ...' (fol. 114r. and v.) and 'Who lyst his welth ...' (fol. 183r.), both of which deal with the execution of Anne Boleyn and her supposed lovers, and so must have been composed in 1536 or after. At some stage the book passed into the possession of Sir George Blage, whose hand, Hand D, appears throughout, and who copied some of his own poems into it.[5] There

---

4 See E.K. Chambers, *Sir Thomas Wyatt and Some Collected Studies* (London: Sidgwick and Jackson, 1933), pp. 207–28 for an account of the fragments of *The Court of Venus*. For a text of the poem see p. 228. For a full edition see *The Court of Venus*, ed. by R.A. Fraser (Durham, NC: Duke UP, 1955). 5 For details about the life and career of Sir George Blage see *The History of Parliament: The House of Commons, 1509–1558*, ed. by S.T. Bindoff, 3 vols (London:

are several dates from this period of the manuscript's history: a financial note recording the payment of money to Elizabeth White, once a nun in the Dominican Convent at Dartford, dated 26 November 1545 (fol. 61r.); a poem written by Blage when he was awaiting execution for heresy in 1546 (fols. 101r.–103r.), from which he was saved by the intervention of Henry VIII; and two elegies on Katherine Parr, Henry VIII's sixth and final wife, who survived him but died at Sudeley Castle in 1548 (fols. 124r.–v.; fol. 177r.). Blage died in 1551 and may have possessed the book until then, but he made no will so it is impossible to determine what happened to his possessions. Six other hands contributed to the manuscript after Blage, including that of Sir John Harington the elder (1520–82), who wrote out one of his own poems on fol. 179r.[6] The latest hand, Hand J is responsible for several prose items. In one text, a fragmentary draft of a letter, which begins on fol. 107v., comes a passage in which the writer pledges himself, among other things, '… to geve dewe dutyfull obedience to the kynge hys mynesters and lawes …'. But 'kynge hys' is crossed through and 'queene hyr' is substituted – an alteration which must have been made in 1553 or later when Mary came to the throne, or after 1558 when Elizabeth succeeded Philip and Mary. This hand is that of 'John M …', almost certainly John Monye whose name appears elsewhere.

The note about Elizabeth White is particularly interesting in that it provides an insight into the shifting allegiances which the religious and political controversies of the mid sixteenth century generated. Most of the known contributors to this manuscript – Wyatt, Surrey, Blage, Sir John Cheke – were certainly humanists and most were also sympathetic to reformist positions on religion. So why should Sir George Blage, a year before he was condemned and almost executed for heresy, be giving money to an ex-Dominican nun? And Elizabeth White was no ordinary Dominican nun. She was the half-sister of John Fisher, bishop of Rochester, executed by Henry VIII on 22 June 1535 for his refusal to sign the Act of Supremacy, which, among other things, made the king the head of all the church in England, the *anglicana ecclesia*. Two of the three works written by Fisher when he was in the Tower awaiting execution, *A Spiritual Consolation* … (STC 10899) and *The Wayes of Perfect Religion*, were dedicated to Elizabeth White. When the nunnery was dissolved in 1539 she was evidently among those nuns who decided to maintain a sense of community by staying together, or, at least, keeping in touch, for, when the nunnery was refounded in 1557, in an old friary in King's Langley, she was one of the seven nuns to return. Forced into exile again in 1559, her resolution never wavered. A com-

Secker and Warburg, 1982), vol. I, 440–2. **6** See Ruth Hughey, *John Harington of Stepney* (Columbus, Ohio: Ohio State UP, 1971), especially the facsimile opposite p. 53.

ment made about her as the nuns of Syon Abbey and Dartford travelled together to Termonde in the Netherlands is perhaps indicative. It was said by a Dominican prior that the 'sister of the martyred bishop of Rochester [was] of no less constancy, could she be but put to the test, than was her brother'.[7] Blage had a lot to do with Kent. His father had left him two houses in Dartford; he was chief steward and bailiff of the manor of Maidstone from 1544 until his death; he was a justice of the peace for Kent from 1547 until his death. In 1550 he was granted a dissolved chantry in Dartford and other property in Kent. Whether George Blage's payment of money to Elizabeth White was because he was assisting her in some way, or whether it was the settlement of a debt, it does indicate that personal relationships could transcend doctrinal differences.

II

One of the most significant features of the later entries in TCD MS 160 is the presence of translations from humanist works into English. On fols 141r. to 144v. and on 149r. appears what may be the earliest translation of any length from Machiavelli – the opening of his essay 'Delle congiure' [Of Conspiracies] from *Discorsi* III. vi., written between 1513 and 1519, and first published in Rome by Blado in 1531. It begins:

> I have not thought it fyt to leave Conspiracie unspoken of, beinge so full of parell bothe to princes and privat men, because it ys probable that moo princes have loste bothe lif and stat therby then by open warr ...

What remains occupies fols 141r to 144v, the end of the 'O' section of the book which was blank until appropriated by this copyist, Hand H. But fol. 145 had already been written on by Hand B who had copied Wyatt's 'Perdy I sayd hytt nott ...' on the recto and verso. The next available space was right at the end of the 'P' section on fol. 149r where the translation from Machiavelli is briefly continued, before the copyist stopped. In all, about a fifth of Machiavelli's rather long essay is represented.

A brief consideration of a specific passage will give some indication of the nature of the text. Here Machiavelli is seeking to distinguish between individual assassination attempts against princes and conspiracies. The Italian is as follows:

---

7 For Elizabeth White see Paul Lee, *Nunneries, Learning and Spirituality in Late Medieval England: The Dominican Priory at Dartford* (York: York Medieval Press, 2000), pp. 115–16, 126–7, 169–70.

I pericoli che si portano, come io dissi di sopra, nelle congiure sono grandi, portandosi per tutti i tempi: perché in tali casi si corre pericolo nel maneggiarli, nello esequirli, ed esequiti che sono. Quegli che congiurano o ei sono uno o ei sono piú. Uno non si può dire che sia congiura, ma è una ferma disposizione nata in uno uomo di ammazzare il principe. Questo solo de' tre pericoli che si corrono nelle congiure manca del primo; perché innanzi alla esecuzione non porta alcuno pericolo, non avendo altri il suo secreto, né portando pericolo che torni il disegno suo all'orecchio del principe. Questa deliberazione cosí fatta può cadere in qualunque uomo di qualunque sorte, grande, piccolo, nobile, ignobile, familiare e non familiare al principe, perché ad ognuno è lecito qualche volta parlarli, ed a chi è lecito parlare è lecito sfogare l'animo suo. Pausania, del quale altre volte si è parlato, ammazzò Filippo di Macedonia che andava al tempio con mille armati d'intorno, ed in mezzo intra il figliuolo ed il genero. Ma costui fu nobile e cognito al principe. Uno Spagnuolo povero ed abietto dette una coltellata in su el collo al re Ferrando, re di Spagna: non fu la ferita mortale, ma per questo si vide che colui ebbe animo e commodità a farlo. Uno dervis, sacerdote turchesco, trasse d'una scimitarra a Baisit, padre del presente Turco: non lo ferí, ma ebbe pure animo e commodità a volerlo fare.[8]

The version from TCD MS 160 fols. 143r–v runs thus:

The parelles that conspiracie dothe bringe with it, as I saide, are greate evin in all times, for ther is parell in executinge and ther ys, parell after the execusyon. Those that conspire, either it is one or they be moe wheare ther ys […] but rather a determynd mynde in a man to kill a kinge. And of the thre pareills that passe in conspiracie this onely skapes the fyrste excucion: ther ys no dowbt of danger so longe as he hathe not discoverid hym to the prince. And this humore may be fed in any man of anie condision, small or great, noble or basse, familiar or unaquainted with the prince, ffor it ys lawfull somtime for anie man to speake with hym and so do. Phusania, of whome I have before speke, killed Philip of macedon betwen his son and hys son in lawe going to the temple with a thosand armed men abowt hym, but in deed he was a noble man brother in law to the prince. There was a poore and an abiet parson, a

---

8 The text is taken from Niccolò Machiavelli, *Il Principe e Discorsi sopra la prima deca di Tito Livio*, ed. by Sergio Bertelli, with an Introduction by Giuliano Procacci, 2nd edition (Milano: Feltrinelli, 1968), pp. 392–3.

spaniarde, that gave ferndo, kynge of spayne, a great wond in the necke.
It was not deadlye as it chanced, but by this we may ssee he hade bothe
corag & convenient place to it. Ther was one other, a truke called Deruis,
a priest, that drew a cimiter at baysit, father to the Turke that now ys.
He hurte hym not, yet he [...] bothe a redie waye and a good will.[9]

Several things are clear from this. Firstly, it looks certain that this is a translation directly from the Italian: the sentence 'Those that conspire, either it is
one or they be moe' is somewhat unEnglish in its syntax, but it replicates perfectly the Italian 'Quegli che congiurano o ei sono uno o ei sono piú'. Secondly,
in other places the Italian is handled with freedom and confidence. Machiavelli
ends his second and third instances with similar expressions:

> ... ebbe animo e commodità a farlo ...
> ... ebbe pure animo e commodità a volerlo fare ...

The English translator renders these as:

> ... he hade bothe corag & convenient place to it ...
> ... yet he [...] bothe a redie waye and a good will ...

In the cause of elegant variation he clearly eschewed repeating himself and chose
to paraphrase rather than render literally: 'good will' takes in something of 'puro
animo' and the intentionality of 'volerlo'. And yet, thirdly, it seems from the
garbled nature of the text that the copyist was not the translator. The word
'hade' (for *ebbe*) is missed out in the last sentence. And earlier in the passage the
whole structure and economy of Machiavelli's argument are ruined: the three-
fold dangers of conspiracy 'pericolo nel manieggiarli, nello esequirli, ed esequiti
che sono' is rendered as two, a contrast instead of a list, 'parell in executinge
and, ther ys, parell after the executyon.' And yet a few lines later the text correctly deals in 'thre pareills'. The phrase 'nel maneggiarli', which means literally 'in the handling of them', that is, devising or plotting them, is not a difficult one, and is unlikely to have defeated this translator, and it seems certain
that the copyist inadvertently omitted the phrase. In the sentence 'wheare ther
ys [...] but rather a determynd mynde in a man to kill a kinge' he also omits
something which would have corresponded to the Italian 'Uno non si può dire
che sia congiura' [A plot by one man cannot be called a conspiracy]. So it follows that this was not the only manuscript text of the translation: the exemplar

---

9 The punctuation is mine. The translator evidently read *cognito* (=known) as *cognato* (=
brother-in-law).

was presumably better and may well have been more complete, since there would not be much point in translating only part of the essay which, like all the discourses, has an elegant and cumulative argument.

The reception of Machiavelli's work in sixteenth-century England is a complex issue, which has been much studied. The first English printed translation of the *Discourses* was that of Edward Dacres in 1636.[10] But at least four manuscript versions, incomplete but substantial, have been identified, which are usually said to date from somewhere between *c.*1580 and *c.*1610. Only one, however, can be precisely dated – that of John Levytt in 1599 which is preserved in London, British Library MS Additional 41162.[11] The *Discorsi* were also available in England after 1584 in John Wolfe's pirated Italian edition. But otherwise Englishmen appear to have acquired texts from Italy and read the book in Italian, or read it while in Italy. Richard Morison, one of Henry VIII's chief apologists, who had been among the humanists in Cardinal Reginald Pole's household in Padua, adverts frequently and with approval to the *Discorsi* in *A Remedye for Sedition* of 1536 (STC 18113.5) written in the aftermath of the Pilgrimage of Grace.[12] A little later, William Thomas, who spent the years between 1545 and 1549 in Italy, returned to England enthused by the sophistication of Italian culture: he produced an Italian grammar and dictionary in 1550, and in the previous year he published *The Historie of Italie* (STC 24018). In his section 'Of the edification and success of the citee of Florence' he opens with the following:

> Conferryng the discourse of divers authours together, toucheyng the Florentine histories, and findyng the effectes of theim all gathered in one by Nicholas Macchiavegli, a notable learned man, and secretarie of late daies to the common wealthe there: I determined to take hym for myne onely auctour in that behalfe.

In 1551 Edward VI made him Clerk of the Privy Council, and a little later he writes to the king offering political advice, specifically 'the notes of those discourses, that are now my principal study, which I have gathered out of divers authors', and he adds a list of eighty-five headings of political topics on which

---

10 For the importance of Edward Dacres in relation to the spread of knowledge of Machiavelli in England see Felix Raab, *The English Face of Machiavelli: A Changing Interpretation, 1500–1700* (London: Routledge and Kegan Paul, 1964), pp. 96–100.   **11** For this translation see Felix Raab, *The English Face of Machiavelli*, pp. 65–6.   **12** For Richard Morison see Felix Raab, *The English Face of Machiavelli*, pp. 34–40. For a more detailed account see W.G. Zeefeldt, 'Richard Morison, Official Apologist for Henry VIII', *PMLA*, 55 (1940), 406–25.

he claims to be able to instruct the king on the basis of his reading: 'divers authors' is a little disingenuous, for the topics turn out to be subjects treated by Machiavelli in the *Discorsi*. The king evidently invited him to develop some of his ideas, and four essays, each of which he calls a 'discourse', were evidently produced: from the summaries of them which remain they appear to be heavily Machiavellian, and use not only the *Discorsi* but *Il principe* as well.[13]

So far as is known neither Richard Morison nor William Thomas translated Machiavelli, though both knew his works well and each (and no doubt a good many others) would have been well capable of making a translation. So too could Lodowick Bryskett, or Lodovico Bruschetto (1546/7–1612), an Italian born in Hackney to Genoese parents, who, after he came down from Cambridge, was in the household of Sir Henry Sidney, and spent most of his life from 1574 to 1598 as a government official in Ireland. In 1606 he published *A Discourse of Civill Life* (STC 3959), a translation of the second part of Giambattista Giraldi Cinzio's *Hecatommithi* (1565), which he says he wrote in or near Dublin, and which some say may have been done originally as early as 1567 though it is likely to have been much later.[14] The name of the translator of the passage in TCD MS 160 is not known, though the name of the copyist, Hand H, is – though his identity is obscure: an entry in his hand on fol. 135r is followed by a name '... ietere Tayllyor', which is presumably 'Pietere'.

III

In addition to this, on fols 132r.–134v. comes an almost complete translation of Marguerite of Navarre's *Heptameron* I. 9., the end of which is fragmentary because of the loss of folios from the manuscript. This text may be the earliest translation into English of one of the stories from this famous collection, and as such is interesting. But what the text can reveal about the provenance of TCD MS 160 and about the spread of humanist culture is even more significant.

Marguerite worked on this collection until her death in 1549: it appears that she had intended to emulate the hundred stories of Boccaccio's *Decamerone*, but only completed some seventy. In the edition of A.J.V. de Lincy and Anatole de Montaiglon (4 vols; Paris, 1880) it is suggested that Nouvelle 9 may have been written in 1544, and it is possible that the translator of it may have had

---

13 For details of the life and career of William Thomas see Felix Raab, *The English Face of Machiavelli*, pp. 40–8. The quotation from *The Historie of Italie* is from p. 41. 14 For details of his life and for the dates of composition of his works see Lodowick Bryskett, *Literary Works*, ed. by J.H.P. Pafford (Farnborough, Hants.: Gregg, 1972), pp. x–xv.

access to a manuscript version.[15] But it is more likely that his source was one of the earliest printed editions. The earliest of these entitled *Histoires des amans fortunez* dates from 1558: it was edited by Pierre Boiastuau and was published in Paris by Gilles Robinot. It contains sixty-seven tales, not divided into days, with no linking introductions or discussions, and in a seemingly random order: Nouvelle 9, for example, appears seventeenth in the order.[16] In the following year 1559 Pierre Gruget brought out a much more authoritative version, published again in Paris by Jean Caveillier. This is entitled *L'Heptaméron*, is attributed to Marguerite, and advertises itself as containing the stories '... remis en sa vray ordre, confus auparavant en sa premiere impression'. Gruget's version contains seventy-two stories, in the standard order, with links – but Nouvelles 11, 44 and 46 are Gruget's own substitutions; he evidently omits three stories which are particularly derogatory to the friars.[17] Thereafter there are many editions. The earliest English translation dates from the last years of Elizabeth's reign: *The Queene of Navarres Tales. Containing Verie pleasant Discourses of fortunate lovers* was printed for V. S[immes] by John Oxenbridge in London in 1597 (STC 17323). It contains seventeen stories only: the first nine from Day One; 2, 4, 5, 6 from Day Two; 9 and 10 from Day Three, and two stories which do not appear in Marguerite's collection at all. From the title it looks as though this book is based on Boiastuau's edition, yet it clearly attributes the stories to Marguerite and adds stories, so there was clearly some independence of thought which went into it. There was no full translation into English until that of John Codrington in 1654.

In Gruget's edition Nouvelle I. 9. is headed 'Piteuse mort d'un gentil-homme amoureux poer avoir trop tard recu consolation de celle qu'il amoit'. It is a tragic story of a love which is idealized, chaste and self-denying and which leads to unhappiness and death. It opens as follows:

> Entre Daulphiné et Provence, y avoit ung gentilhomme beaucoup plus riche de vertu, beaulté et honnesteté que d'autres biens, lequel ayma tant

15 See *L'Heptaméron des nouvelles de la Reine de Navarre*, ed. by Le Roux de Lincy and Anatole de Montaiglon, 4 vols (Paris: Eudes, 1880), vol. 4, 233. For a list of manuscripts see I, 149–75. For more up to date but less detailed manuscript descriptions see *L'Heptaméron*, ed. by Michel François (Paris: Garnier, 1967), pp. xxi–xxvi, and *Marguerite de Navarre Heptaméron*, edition critique par Renja Salminen (Helsinki: Suomalainen Tiedeakatemia, 1991), pp. ix–xvii. **16** For a description see Le Roux de Lincy and Anatole de Montaiglon, vol. 1, 176–81. **17** For a description see Le Roux de Lincy and Anatole de Montaiglon, vol. 1, 181–3. I should like to record my gratitude to the late Professor Michel Simonin of the Centre d'Études Supérieures de la Renaissance, Université François Rabelais, Tours, who generously allowed me to use his first edition of Gruget and shared his considerable knowledge of Marguerite de Navarre with me.

une damoyselle, dont je ne diray le nom, pour l'amour de ses parens qui sont venuz de grandes et bonnes maisons; mais asseurez vous que la chose est tresveritable. Et, à cause qu'il n'estoit de maison de mesme elle, n'ousoit descouvrir son affection, car l'amour qu'il luy portoit estoit si grande et parfaicte qu'il eust mieulx aymé mourir que de desirer seullement chose qui eust esté à son deshonneur. Et, se voyant de si bas lieu au pris d'elle, n'avoit nul espoir de l'espouser. Parquoy son amour n'estoit fondée sur nulle fin, synon de l'aymer de tout son povoir le plus parfaictement qu'il luy seroit possible, ce qu'il fist sy longuement que à la fin elle en eut quelque congnoissance. Et, voyant l'honneste amytié qu'il luy portoit tant plaine de vertuz et bons propoz, se sentoit honnorée d'estre aymée d'un si vertueux personnaige, et luy faisoit tant de bonne chere que luy, qui n'avoit nulle pretente à myeulx, se contantoit tresfort.

Mais la malice, ennemye de tout repoz, ne peut souffrir ceste vye honneste et heureuse, car quelques ungs allerent dire à la mere de la fille qu'ilz s'esbahissoient que ce gentilhomme pouvoit tant faire en sa maison, et que lon soupsonnoit que la beaulté de la fille le y tenoit plus que autre chose, avecques laquelle on le voyoit souvent parler. La mere, qui ne doubtoit en nulle façon de l'honnesteté du gentilhomme, dont elle se tenoit aussy asseurée que de nul de ses enfans, fut fort marrye d'entendre que on le prenoit à mauvaise part. Tant que, à la fin, craignant le scandalle par la malice des hommes, le pria pour quelque temps de ne hanter pas sa maison comme il avoit acoustumé, chose qu'il trouva de dure digestion, saichant que les honnestes propoz qu'il tenoit à sa fille ne meritoient poinct tel eslongnement. Toutesfoiz, pour faire taire les mauvaises langues, se retira tant de temps que le bruit cessa; et, luy retourna comme il avoit acoustumé.[18]

But when he resumes his visits the gentleman hears talk that the girl is to be married to someone not much richer or of much greater status than he is, and, thus encouraged, he persuades his friends to speak on his behalf. But the other man is, nevertheless, somewhat richer and he remains the choice of the girl's family. The poor gentleman then despairs and dwindles away: he loses all desire to eat or drink; he can neither sleep nor rest. When he is confined to his bed and close to death he asks to see the girl, who visits him accompanied by her mother. When he explains to them that his imminent death is the result of his unrequited love for the girl they are overwhelmed by grief: the mother promises that he shall marry her daughter, and the daughter agrees. The gentleman,

18 I use the text in Renja Salminen's edition, pp. 41–2.

however, feels that they are only trying to raise his spirits and says that, in any case, the offer is too late to save his life. He asks as a final wish that the girl should be placed in his arms, and that he should be able to embrace and kiss her, and it is while she is in his arms that he dies. Long after his lifeless arms had loosened their grip on her the girl lay embracing him, and it was only with great difficulty that her mother and the servants could separate their united bodies. The gentleman was buried with due honour, but the greatest tribute to him, says the story, consisted in the tears and lamentations of the girl. While the gentleman was alive she had always concealed her love for him, but at his death she made it known to all. And though she was later married, she never knew true happiness in her heart. Though the listeners are all moved by the story, in the discussion which follows reactions to it are polarized: there are some (mainly women) who admire the selfless restraint of the love it exemplifies, and others (mainly men) who think it misguided and foolish, that fortune favours the brave and that women are to be actively pursued.[19]

The English translation in TCD MS 160 occupies fols 132r. to 134v., and ends fragmentarily at the gentleman's death, making no mention of his funeral, or the grief of the girl, or her subsequent marriage. And, of course, there is no discussion of the story. Some text has clearly been lost, but how much is impossible to say. In the old foliation, the pages it occupies are numbered ccxxii, ccxxiii, ccxxiiii, and the next folio (fol. 135 in the manuscript as it is at present) is numbered ccxxx – so five folios have been lost, enough for the end of the story, the discussion, and much more. The translation opens as follows:

> [fol. 132r.] Betwen Dolphyne and Provence, in France ther lyvid a gent[leman] much more riche in vertiu, bewtye and hones[tey] then endued with temperall goodis or possessions, who enterlye loved a gent[le]woman, whose name I leve untolde as well for the howse she ys desended of as for movynge hyr modestye. Thys gent[leman], not beynge of so great parentage as she, so that he dorst never discover hys synguler affection unto hyr, and the extreme and covarde love he allwayes bare unto hyr was so iust and perfect that he had leaver dey then do or move hyr or to sturre hyr to any thynge that sholde seme to ether hyrs or hys dissoner or susspect. And revolvynge yet hys dyvers wordlye wantis, and scarsite of frendes wherby he was the more unable to compas or obtayne al hys wish or gett hyr goodwyll in the end was past hope to atcheve hyr

19 For a good discussion of this tale see André Tournon, 'Rules of the Game', in *Critical Tales: New Studies of the Heptaméron and Early Modern Culture*, ed. by John D. Lyons and Mary McKinlay (Philadelphia: University of Pennsylvania Press, 1993), pp. 188–99.

as hys wyff. Amyddis which maze so muche the more hys love and entere affection semyd gronded almost to no effect, save onlye to love and honer hyer with al hys power in most perfect and humble wysse possible durynge hys lyff as he had done longe tyme before. Wherof I knowe not by what meanes the gent[le]woman had perseverance and intellygence, whoe consyderynge the honest proffessyd frendshyp borne unto hyr so fully intendyd of vertwe and to good purpose, demed hyr selfe verye happye in the end to be favored of one so well adorned with vertu and stored of good behavior, in the end entertaynd hym as well with hyr good chere, as lovers use also, as hyr lovely and frendly contenance, dertermynd allwayes to honor and content hym in the best maner she could possible, the more because she iudged hym a most fytt and semlye fere, [fol. 132v.] equal to hyr hart and fancy. But envye, the accuser and dispriser of every happi delyght or sportis, could not longe permyt thys honest lyf. So some envious person declared unto hyr modest mother the lover whom hyr doghter lovyd, pronouncynge they undrestood thys gent[leman] found great favor in hyr howse, and that nothynge alloured hym therto but the bewtye of hyr doghter, which he eastemed more then any tresure. Which report moved the mother to send presentlye for the sayd gent[leman] to be spoken wyth. The mother, that doubted by no meanes the iust dealynge and honestye of the gent[leman], and also held herself assured of the stayednes of hyr chyld, wherby she could discreatlye dissearne and waye anye attempt sundynge [of] dishonestye in any wyse. But in the ende, the mother, pausynge a whyl, consydered thys brute reysed by the malice of pernicious men, and hou yt myght breed a defame unto hyr, hyr house and chylde, besought the gent[leman] frelilye for a certayne tyme not to frequent hyr howse as he had been accustomed, a doome and comaundement which the gent[leman] found verye hard of digestyon and grevos to observ, wherof and wherwith luvers be judge, waynge hyt was doone uppon no other honest purpose then for to savgard of hyr chylds good fame, that by no meanes meryted suche appoynted severance but onlye to werye and trede undrefoote spekyn the evell tonges. And so when sertayne tyme ys spent and that former brut ys qwaylde, quod she, you maye retorne as you have been accustomed ...[20]

What is immediately apparent is that the translation presents a problem. If the translation is a literal one, it is based on a text which has not survived. If, on the

---

[20] The punctuation is mine.

other hand, it is based on a text such as Gruget's, or something similar to it, then the translation is a relatively free one – though not inaccurate. The second of these possibilities is the more likely, because the English text is extensively revised: there are current revisions as the text was being written; and there are later corrections in the same hand but using a darker ink. The revisions do not reveal any consistency of purpose. Sometimes the translator's second thoughts take the translation back closer to a more literal rendering of the French: for 'riche de', for example, he originally wrote 'riche and endued with' but went back to the simpler original and settled for 'riche in'; and similarly for 'aima fort' he originally wrote 'loved and favoured' but settled for 'loved' and inserted 'enterelye' suggested by the French 'fort', which he had not initially rendered. Usually, however, his instinct is to expand in the cause of greater explanatory adequacy: he inserts the defining phrase 'in France', for example, in his opening sentence, and for 'd'autres biens' he initially wrote 'goodis or possessions' and as a second thought added 'temporall'. Sometimes he simplifies the French and expands it at the same time: the sequence 'pour l'amour de ses parens, qui sont venuz de grandes et bonnes maisons' appears first as 'bothe for her parentis sake ther of as for hyr modesty', but he crosses out 'bothe for her parentis sake' and inserts the second part of the French 'as well for the howse she is descended of' – he could legitimately have kept all of this – and not only leaves in place the phrase about her modesty, which is not in the French, but adds 'movynge' to it. It is also of interest that he originally translated Marguerite's asseveration about the truth of her story 'mais asseurez vous que la chose est veritable' as 'and assure you the tragedye to be verye trewe', but crossed it out, perhaps realizing that he himself did not know whether the story was true or not.

The text as I have given it is what, so far as I can determine, are his final thoughts, so far as he went, but it is clear that it is in no way a definitive text. At the top of fol. 132v, for example, the word 'envye' has 'malice' written above it, but 'envye' is not cancelled, and a little later he contemplates 'honest intent' for the phrase 'honest lyf' but 'lyf' is not crossed out – so presumably he had not finally made up his mind which he preferred. This has all the appearance of being work in progress, a working translation, and it suggests that the translator had ready access to the manuscript over some period.

It is possible to give a name to the translator, though not to establish his identity. He signs himself at various places in the manuscript as John Tayllyour or Taillior. The translation of *Heptaméron* I. ix. is undoubtedly his, and a number of other items in his hand may be attributable to him – but not all, for on fol. 129v appears his copy of Wyatt's 'Nature that gave the bee so fayre a grace'. Most of his entries appear in secondary positions in the manuscript, that is, on

previously blank versos or on the blank spaces of rectos previously used for
something else. On fol. 70r, following an acrostic poem, which appears in *Tottel's
Miscellany* (STC 13860), on Lady Anne Stanhope, wife of Henry VIII's Master
of the Horse, appears a six-line moralistic stanza, not found elsewhere, in a neat
version of Taylor's hand:

> A sobre maide, asswrde of looke and mynde;
> a stayed yonge man, not wilful, wise and chast;
> a hwsband, trewe, vngelous and vnblynd,
> a qwieat wyf not geven to lwst and wast –
> be needfull thynges, more often soght then fonde,
> as chefest goodes in lyf that least abonde.

Most of the poems in his hand, however, are complaints of one sort or another,
or depressed reflections on the nature of things. The poem on fol. 96v beginning 'You iudge or you knowe and condempne or you trye ...', which consists of a single six-line stanza, is followed by 'Ta', presumably short for Taylor,
so he presumably is claiming it as his, though the first four and a half lines were
copied on fol. 95r in a different hand:

> You iudge or you knowe and condempne or you trye.
> it is but your fancye that moveth thus to blame.
> I se where he dothe lourke, hys fayth to iustefye,
> abydinge tyme to conquere worthie fame.
> yf you therfore shoulde hate hym or hys name
> a iuste reward of spites sport should rightly frame.
>
> Ta

A quatrain beginning 'where favores do boldly prese or bost ...' also appears on
for 96v, and is also signed 'Ta':

> Where favores do boldly presse or bost
> of giltles good, and deemes that ys not so;
> where will and rage doth dailye rule the rost
> needes must that state contynewe longe in woo.
>
> Ta

It looks as though there may have been another poem as well, because a catch-
word 'To condemne' is written at the right-hand bottom of this folio. Both
stanzas seem to be rather gnomic meditations on seeking fame in a courtly set-

ting. In the top margin of fol. 145r John Taylor has written a quatrain which
appears to be the beginning of a poem:

> these wofull wydous and the stressed maryners on seas
> And the unhappi servynge man that may hys lord not pleas
> The wronges wroght to fatherles and strangled chyldren eke
> the poyson sett and well eskapt who lyst to learne may seke.

But where one is to seek never appears. On fol. 174r appear two six-line stanzas in John Taylor's hand again reflecting deep disillusionment with something
unspecified, to which he appears to react with a rather trite stoicism:

> repentance, ranson of each offence,
> discowrse of gyle and fawlty fact.
> now learne to flee, sith the disspence
> vnto thy gayne is trwly sakte.
> of doble blame he ys, be swre,
> to burne hys fancy wyll aloure.
>
> happy hoope to harmefull hate,
> gyrte with the gayne of fructles toyle,
> into the pitt of poremens state,
> charged vnawares as yeldynge moyle;
> In yoye to froune, at harme to smoile;
> golde glitters not with so pale foyle.

He was evidently still working on this poem too, for there are many crossings-
out and revisions, especially in relation to the last two lines.

Surprisingly, perhaps, some of his entries in the manuscript are love poems.
The four stanzas of rhyme-royal followed by a quatrain beginning 'Where shall
my hevi syghes unfold ther payne ...' on fol. 111v. look as though they are
again John Taylor's version of a poem already in the manuscript, for on the
opposite recto of 112 appear four rhyme-royal stanzas beginning 'I knowe not
where my hevy syghys to hyd ...' which are very close in sentiment and word-
ing. These poems are complaints of a lover separated from his beloved: John
Taylor's version has a refrain varying the sentiment 'Sith bitter yt ys out of hyr
syght to be.' He actually intervenes in the text of 'I knowe not where my hevy
syghys to hyd ...', revising and emending it. But why he feels the need to devise
another version of it is difficult to know. His version is not an improvement.

It is not known to whom this love poem is addressed – if anybody. But that may not be the case with the ten-line stanza which appears in John Taylor's hand on fol. 127v:

> My lady ys suche one to whome our Lord hath lent
> even such assured hope as Judeth in hym had;
> that earnest care of poore he also to hyr sent;
> Lyke Hestre to deffend the danger to be drad;
> as Lydya she lowes and keps hyr Lords law
> With great delight of grace, and excersyse of yoy;
> with faythfull Pheabe eake she standeth aye in awe;
> Lyke Sara humble styll, and fre from each anoye.
> hir vertu shyneth so yt doth the best excelle.
> hyr honor ys so clere yt sondeth lyke a bell.

This is signed 'Tay', so it is evidently John Taylor's poem, but it appears to be based on ideas which appear at the end of a poem written earlier in the manuscript – George Blage's 'Let the hethen whyche trust not in the Lorde ...' on fols 124r and v. In the top left corner of the folio, in very faded ink, appears what seems to be the name of a woman 'mabell kylcare' or perhaps 'kyldare' (though the 'k' is very rubbed and indistinct) perhaps the name of the 'lady' to whom the poem is addressed, though Irish placenames (which both of these are) rarely double as surnames.[21] Kylcar is an Irish placename and surname (as is Kildare), so it may be that the object of his affection in this poem was Irish. The subject of the two short poems on fol. 153r is certainly to be associated with Ireland from the 1540s onward:

> E(ar)ly[22] the elect on the sabathe dothe praye,
> callynge to repencance all strayed in syne.
> in noz abarb I set my trust allwaye,
> and railliatt may not from fayth declyne.
> In barons fayre feeldes each headge ys featly bak[t]
> with swett of strange flowres that other soyles hath lakt
>   tayllyer.

---

21 Many thanks to Eiléan Ní Chuilleanáin for pointing this out to me. Professor Greg Walker, on the other hand, suggests to me that this may not be a name, but should perhaps read 'ma bell kyl care' (= my beautiful destroyer of grief). 22 This word is written with a capital E followed by a contraction mark.

Bragg not of goodes put gg unto ther flyght;
baye ys all green with vertwe right repleat;
ye out ys bett then aye a sore in sight.
son nome mon cwer per grace still doth heate.

These verses refer to Elizabeth Brabazon: her christian name appears in the first line of the first poem 'Ely ... sabathe', and her surname written backwards in the third line 'braba zon'; in the second poem 'Bra ... ba ... son' appears as an acrostic. The name 'tailliar' appears written backwards in the fourth line of the first poem. Elizabeth Brabazon, née Clifford, was the wife of Sir William Brabazon, who, in 1534, was appointed vice-treasurer and receiver general in Ireland, and who became one of the strong men of the English administration there – during which time he enriched himself and some of his allies considerably though not particularly honestly.[23] He was lord justice of Ireland in 1543, 1546, and 1549, and became a member of the privy council of Ireland in 1547. He died in Ireland on 9 July 1552 and was buried in St Catherine's church, Dublin. His wife, two sons and two or three daughters survived him.[24] It is possible that these poems were written to Elizabeth Brabazon while her husband was alive, but not very likely. It is much more plausible to assume that John Taylor became her admirer in her widowhood.

IV

Two tentative conclusions may be drawn from all this. The first concerns the translation of *Heptaméron* I. ix. Assuming that John Taylor read the story in Boiastuau's or Gruget's editions, why did he choose to translate this tale rather than another? It is at least possible that this story of a man hopelessly in love with a woman of higher social standing appealed to him because of his feelings for the, for him, unattainable Elizabeth Brabazon. It is also possible to assume that he wrote it into this manuscript because so many of its original contents are poems about disappointed love, and that he saw himself as not dissimilar to Wyatt and Surrey as a lover of an unattainable lady. He appears to have fashioned himself on his illustrious predecessors.

The second deduction which may be made concerns where this story was translated – and indeed where the manuscript was for the later years of its his-

23 On this see Ciaran Brady, *The Chief Governors: The Rise and Fall of Reform Government in Tudor Ireland, 1536–1588* (Cambridge: Cambridge UP, 1994), especially pp. 33–6. **24** On his varied and eventful career see *Dictionary of National Biography*, ed. by Leslie Stephen and Sidney Lee, 22 vols (London: Smith, Elder, 1908–1909), vol. 2, 1046–7.

tory. It seems highly likely that it was in Dublin or at least in the Dublin area.[25] What precisely happened to Elizabeth Clifford after her husband's death is not known, but it is clear that she stayed in Ireland. She remarried, first to Captain Christopher Blunt, and then to Captain Humphrey Warren, who died on 13 November 1561. Ten years later, in 1571 she married Edward Moore of Mellifont.[26] By this time she was extremely wealthy. Lord Justice Fitzwilliam, writing to Burghley on 26 November 1571, recommends Edward Moore for employment praising his probity and mentioning that he 'has married Lady Brabazon, whose living is on the border of Uriell, and may by his wife spend yearly £500 sterling.'[27] Moore was later knighted, and became sheriff of Louth and constable of Phillipstown castle. Elizabeth Clifford's eldest son Edward Brabazon, who succeeded his father when in his fourth year, was MP for Wicklow in 1585, became a benefactor of Trinity College Dublin in 1591, was knighted by the lord deputy in 1595, became a member of the council of Munster in 1615, and, like his father, was buried in St Catherine's church Dublin after his death in 1625. On 19 July 1616 he was created Lord Brabazon, baron of Ardee (Co. Louth), and his son, William, was created earl of Meath on 16 April 1627. The Brabazons had possessions in England – in Nether Whitacre (Warwicks.) and possibly in Staffordshire – but the main centre of their activities was Ireland where they became powerful and influential landowners.[28] Exactly how John Taylor related to the Brabazons is not clear, but it is likely that it was in Ireland, and that it was there where the earliest translation from the *Heptaméron* was made.

Another piece of evidence concerns Pietere Taylor – perhaps a relative of John – who copied a number of items into the manuscript, including the passage from Machiavelli's *Discorsi* in English. It seems likely that Pietere Taylor was also in Ireland because of a note in his hand on fol. 135r:

> Doing your mastershipp to understand that wher you willede me for to receve of master Thomas Myght twenti pound I cannot

This is written out, with slight variations, four times, and at the end of the fourth version is the signature, 'Pietere Tayllyor'. It looks as if he is practising a letter.

---

25 For the connection of MS 160 with the Dublin area, and for the identification of a number of the people mentioned in the manuscript, I am much indebted to Dr Jim Murray of Dublin City University. **26** See *The Complete Peerage*, ed. by George Edward Cokayne, revised by Vicary Gibbs and H.A. Doubleday (London: St Catherine's Press, 1916), vol. 4, 462. **27** See *Calendar of State Papers Ireland: Tudor Period, 1571–1575*, ed. by Mary O'Dowd (Dublin: Irish Manuscripts Commission, 2000), No. 159, p. 94. There are many records relating to Edward Moore in this volume. **28** See *The Complete Peerage*, vol. 2 (1912), 269–70.

Thomas Myght was the victualler to the English armies in Ireland, and so a likely enough person with whom one might be engaged in a financial transaction. The best idea of the scale of his activities can be deduced from the long and precise 'articles of order and agreements made between the queen and Thomas Mighte, gent[leman], surveyer of victuals within Ireland, concerning the victualling of the garrisons of soldiers and the maintenance of a staple of victuals and other possessions, 24th May 1568'.[29] This lays out in great detail what he is to provide, and what he is to receive in terms of money. But on 4 March 1570 appears a more interesting record. Myght writes to Cecil from Ireland that he cannot come to court because he is ill, that he is happy that Thomas Sackford, the lord deputy's cousin, should replace him, and requesting some consideration for the 24 years of 'painful travel' he has undertaken – all of which suggests that he was engaged in victualling activities from about 1556 onwards,[30] though he was officially appointed victualler with Henry Colley in 1563 and on his own in 1569.[31] So he could have had dealings with Pietere Taylor on a financial matter from that time onwards. On 2 November 1573 Walter, Earl of Essex writes complaining about Myght: he 'hath showed himself careless in uttering the provisions to victuallers and other that would pay him ready money, whereby I am forced to set a comptroller over him'.[32] And Myght's propensity for dealing in ready money might explain the nature of Pietere Taylor's plaintive note. He writes here as a servant to his 'mastershipp', and two texts in the latter part of the manuscript, in the hand of John Monye, deal with the duties of household servants: there is an account of the duties of the clerk of the kitchen beginning on fol. 162v.; and an account of 'The offyce of a Steward in the house of estate' beginning on fol. 163v. It may be that the later contributors to the manuscript were household officials, the professional administrators and bureaucrats of the emerging Anglo-Irish ruling class in and around Dublin in the latter part of the sixteenth century. Of those mentioned by name in the manuscript John More may have been a relative of Edward Moore who later married Elizabeth Brabazon. John Money was mayor of Dublin in 1550, and he and other members of his family were prominent in the municipal government of Dublin in this period. So too were members of the extensive Taylor family of Swords, to which John and Pietere Taylor possibly belonged. The connection of the Moneys with this manuscript is significant because they were one of the few families in Dublin who became Protestant in

29 See *Calendar of the Carew Manuscripts, 1515–1574*, ed. by J.S. Brewer and William Bullen (London: Public Record Office, 1867), pp. 379–83. **30** See *Calendar of State Papers: Ireland 1509–73* (London: Longmans, 1860) p. 427. **31** See *Calendar of State Papers of Ireland: Tudor Period 1571–1575*, p. 925. **32** See *Calendar of the Carew Manuscripts, 1515–1574*, p. 446.

the Tudor and Elizabethan periods, along with their relatives the Usshers, the Balls and the Chalenors.[33]

On the evidence of TCD MS 160, therefore, it appears that humanistic culture of a reformist and Protestant kind had taken root in Ireland around Dublin in the late 1550s: the Anglo-Irish had access to the poems of Wyatt and Surrey, Sir John Harrington, Sir John Cheke, Sir George Blage and others. But they were also making their own contributions – copying translations of Machiavelli, and making translations from Marguerite of Navarre. Dublin in the latter half of the sixteenth century was not isolated culturally, and not provincial except in a geographical sense, but was in touch with much that was modern in English and European literature.

---

[33] See Alan Ford, 'The Protestant Reformation in Ireland', in *Natives and Newcomers: Essays in the Making of Irish Colonial Society*, ed. by Ciaran Brady and Raymond Gillespie (Dublin: Irish Academic Press, 1986), pp. 50–74.

'Angelicafugata': from Ariosto to Lampedusa

Daragh O'Connell

Persse turned to address Angelica, but she had disappeared. 'Was there ever such a girl for disappearing?' he muttered to himself in vexation. 'It's as if she had a magic ring for making herself invisible.'

David Lodge, Small World

'That Angelica, Mr. Curate,' said Don Quixote, 'was a desolate damsel, a wild, flirting, wanton creature and somewhat capricious besides. She left the world as full of her impertinencies as the fame of her beauty. She despised a thousand princes, a thousand of the most valiant and discreet knights in the whole world, and took up with a beardless page [...].'

Cervantes, Don Quixote, II. i

[...] Angelica non so chi sia.

Giuseppe Tomasi di Lampedusa, Letter to Baron Enrico Merlo di
Tagliavia, 30 May 1957.

Of all the literary characters that have come down to us from the Renaissance, few can be said to hold the same resonance and influence as Ariosto's figure of Angelica. Impossibly beautiful, dangerous to behold, cunning and elusive, this pagan princess is notorious for driving so-called chivalrous knights mad with love for her – love that on closer inspection is more akin to unbridled lust. Ariosto's much-maligned Angelica has received a great deal of bad press throughout the centuries from poets and commentators alike, who squarely lay the blame at her door for seducing and distracting those poor defenceless knights.[1] To add insult to injury, she shunned all only to marry Medoro, a nobody ('d'oscura stirpe'),[2] well beneath her social standing. How dare she!

---

1 Recent studies which have reappraised critical approaches to Ariosto's Angelica and begun the rehabilitation of her character include: Mario Santoro, 'L'Angelica del *Furioso*: fuga dalla storia', in *Esperienze letterarie*, 3 (1978), pp. 3–28; Corinna Salvadori Lonergan, 'Angelica Redenta? Reflections on one more sinned against than sinning', in *Renaissance and Other Studies: Essays Presented to Peter M. Brown*, ed. by E.A. Millar (Glasgow: University of Glasgow, 1988), pp. 94–110; Deanna Shemek, 'That Elusive Object of Desire: Angelica in the *Orlando furioso*', *Annali d'Italianistica*, 7 (1989), pp. 116–41; Judith Bryce, 'Gender and Myth in the *Orlando furioso*', *Italian Studies*, XLVII (1992), pp. 41–50. 2 Ludovico Ariosto, *Orlando furioso*,

She weaves her way through Ariosto's poem, disappearing and suddenly reappearing, leaving only havoc in her wake. Always pursued, escaping and in flight, Angelica represents that elusive object of male desire, but once she has given herself to Medoro all male desire disappears in the poem, and quite abruptly so too does she from Ariosto's *Furioso*. But such is the force of her attraction, she does, from time to time, reappear in later literary texts and cast that spell of hers over male characters, who are unable or unwilling to look beyond their primary instincts. When the Ferrarese poet takes leave of Angelica in the *Furioso* he sings: 'Quanto, Signore, ad Angelica accada / dopo ch'uscì di man del pazzo tempo; / [...] forse altri canterà con miglior plettro / Io son a dir tante altre cose intento, / che di seguir più questa non mi cale' (XXX, 16–17). But follow her we must.

One case in point, and perhaps with 'peggior plettro', is that of Giuseppe Tomasi di Lampedusa's beautiful and seductive Angelica Sedàra in his only novel *Il Gattopardo*. Interestingly, Lampedusa makes many veiled allusions to her name-sake and counterpart in the *Furioso* and weaves many Ariostan motifs into his novel. This may at first seem strange given that Lampedusa's text is ostensibly an historical novel detailing and charting the decline of the old ruling class in Sicily in the period of the Risorgimento – very little here of chivalrous knights and damsels in distress. Moreover, Lampedusa had a stated dislike for Italian Renaissance literature, the *Orlando furioso* in particular, and criticised Ariosto for his ignorance in handling temporal shifts within the poem. He considered Ariosto to be the classic example of those 'cattivi scrittori, [...] senza interiorità'.[3] One wonders what this terrible literary snob would have made of all the criticisms levelled at his own novel had he lived to see its publication in 1958.

None of this augurs well for uncovering fertile ground for a comparison between the two Angelicas. Nevertheless, this ground does exist, although perhaps in 'chiave minore'. A recently published letter written by Lampedusa in 1957 outlines the parallels between the various characters of the novel and their real-life historical counterparts. On the figure of Angelica, however, he is decidedly enigmatic and elusive when he states: 'Angelica non so chi sia'.[4] She therefore has no fixed historical equivalent, yet within the novel Angelica assumes an

ed. by Lanfranco Caretti (Turin: Einaudi, 1966), XVIII. 165. All references to the *Furioso* are from this edition.   **3** Giuseppe Tomasi di Lampedusa, *Letteratura inglese* in *Opere* (Milan: Mondadori, 1995), p. 1229. In his *Letteratura francese* Lampedusa writes that 'uno dei non pochi difetti del *Furioso* è l'assoluta ignoranza di Ariosto del problema temporale: non si sa se l'azione si prolunghi per un pomeriggio o per venti anni; o per esser più precisi, si sa soltanto attraverso esplicite dichiarazioni che toccano l'intelletto ma non commuovono il sentimento'. Lampedusa, *Opere*, p. 1798.   **4** Cited from Gioacchino Lanza Tomasi, *I luoghi del Gattopardo* (Palermo: Sellerio, 2001), p. 63.

increasingly important role, rendering this statement somewhat disingenuous.

The aim of this study is to examine Angelica's role within the novel and detail how Lampedusa, despite his reservations and obvious prejudices in matters relating to Ariosto, knowingly or unknowingly borrowed from Ariosto and the Renaissance tradition in the construction of her character. Furthermore, on a textual and editorial level, Angelica is up to her old tricks again by disappearing and suddenly reappearing between two different editions of the novel at a decisive moment in the narrative. The second half of this study will focus on this discrepancy, a discrepancy quite in keeping with our image of an elusive Angelica.

An examination of any Angelica, though, should begin with her name and the use of that favoured practice of early Italian poets: the aptronym – according to which the poet's love object should have a name befitting her immeasurable qualities. The name Angelica, however, is no aptronym but an ironic play on the rich tradition of the *donna angelicata* in the poetry of the 'stilnovisti'. One need only look to the apex of that tradition, Dante's Beatrice, whose name denotes 'she who makes blessed', for an example of the true *donna angelicata*. Angelica, however, is quite a different matter. The pun in Angelica's name articulates a parodic intent, and though they treat the character differently, for both Boiardo, who invented her, and Ariosto Angelica is anything but 'angelicata'. We should perhaps heed Marfisa's words in the *Orlando innamorato*: 'E quella dama Angelica se appella / che ha ben contrario il nome a sua natura'. Although how faithful a witness we take Marfisa to be is perhaps tempered by her description of Angelica in the previous octave: '[…] meretrice iniqua e prava, / piena di frode e de incantazione […]' (*Orlando innamorato*, I. xx. 43–44).[5]

Nevertheless, in both poems the language of 'stilnovismo' is employed to great effect. We read descriptions of Angelica such as 'ad angelo del ciel rassomigliava' in the *Innamorato* (I. i. 42), or in the *Furioso* 'l'angelico sembiante' (I. 12; I. 53) and 'l'angelica faccia' (I. 81). However, in one of the few studies that does Angelica's character justice C.S. Lonergan points out that while Angelica 'turns out to be 'tanto gentile e tanto onesta' she does not come 'da cielo in terra a miracol mostrare'. She is no Beatrice and has no sanctifying role'.[6] Angelica is obviously, and very deliberately, a different incarnation to the *donna angelicata*. But if we look at their respective roles we may glimpse some parallels, though with opposite results. Beatrice is sent by a heavenly parent, the Virgin Mary, to Dante to lead him on the path of salvation. Conversely, Angelica is sent by her earthly father to lure the knights eastwards to their supposed destruction and the collapse of Christendom. Jumping forward in the

5 Matteo Maria Boiardo, *Orlando innamorato*, ed. by R. Bruscagli (Turin: Einaudi, 1995). 6 Lonergan, p. 96.

centuries to *Il Gattopardo*, we may well ask: is not Angelica Sedàra also sent by her father on a mission? Does not don Calogero Sedàra, proto-mafioso and *homo novus* of the fledgling Italy, send his daughter into the Salina household to seduce Tancredi and thereby increase his own power, prestige and wealth?

Lampedusa too, plays with nomenclature, but with quite unexpected results. In chapter III the protagonist Don Fabrizio, Prince of Salina, on hearing the story of Angelica's grandfather, who had been shot with 'dodici "lupare" nella schiena', is more shocked to discover the deceased man's nickname, Peppe 'Mmerda:

> Molte di queste cose erano già note a Don Fabrizio [...]; ma il soprannome del nonno di Angelica non lo conosceva; esso apriva una prospettiva storica profonda, svelava abissi [...]. Sentì veramente il terreno mancargli sotto i piedi; come avrebbe fatto Tancredi a mandar giù anche questo? e lui stesso? [...] Angelica era Angelica, un fiore di ragazza, una rosa cui il soprannome del nonno era servito solo da fertilizzante. (pp. 118–119)[7]

The passage offers an intriguing link to Rodomonte's ineffectual comic attack on women in the *Furioso*: 'che delle spine ancor nascon le rose / e d'una fetida erba nasce il giglio' (XXVII. 121). Beyond establishing Angelica's truly chthonic origins, the reference to the rose in the novel is deeply redolent of the poetry of the Cinquecento. Floral imagery abounds within *Il Gattopardo* in relation to Angelica. The Prince's first words to Angelica in the novel are: 'È una fortuna per noi, signorina Angelica, di avere accolto un fiore tanto bello nella nostra casa; e spero che avremo il piacere di rivedervelo spesso' (p. 82). Or later, when Angelica makes her first official visit to the palace as Tancredi's fiancée we read: 'Il Principe si attardò un attimo, forse più del necessario, a fiutare l'aroma di gardenia delle guance adolescenti' (p. 135).

In these and in similar such examples, Lampedusa fuses his narrative with Ariostan patternings. Here he is drawing from the flower-virginity *topos* running throughout the *Furioso*, and more specifically the rose. In this context such passages recall Orlando's misguided, anguished words in canto VIII:

> E il fior ch'in ciel potea pormi fra i dei,
> il fior ch'intatto io mi venìa serbando
> per non turbarti (ohimè) l'animo casto,

---

7 Unless otherwise stated all references to *Il Gattopardo* are taken from the *Opere* (Milan: Mondadori, 1995).

ohimè, per forza avranno colto e guasto.
Oh infelice! Oh misero! Che voglio
se non morir, se 'l mio bel fiore colto hanno? (VIII. 77–8)

More significantly, these passages recall Sacripante's infamous 'La verginella è simile alla rosa' speech (I. 42). In the *Furioso* the knights prize Angelica's virginity above all else, whereas in *Il Gattopardo* it is just one more vital ingredient to her dangerous and inviting beauty.

As with the Angelica of Ariosto's poem, this Angelica is desired by all who gaze on her. Where any Angelica is concerned gazing occupies a specific role in the narrative: it activates desire, but also diminishes the gazer's ability to reason correctly. In short, her character functions by characterizing others. Angelica's first appearance in world literature is a significant example. Her entrance into Charlemagne's great hall at the beginning of Boiardo's *Innamorato* aptly details the 'effect' her physical beauty has on her gazing admirers:

> ma nova cosa che ebbe ad apparire,
> fe' lui con gli altri insieme sbigotire.
> [...], e lor nel mezo una donzella,
> [...]
> Essa sembrava matutina stella
> e giglio d'orto e rosa de verzieri:
> in somma, a dir di lei la veritate,
> non fu veduta mai tanta beltate. (I. i. 20–1)

In Lampedusa's novel, Angelica's first entrance into the Palace of Donnafugata shares striking similarities with its Renaissance precursor, yet Lampedusa is quick to undermine his character from the very outset and will continue to do so throughout the narrative:

> La prima impressione fu di abbagliata sorpresa. I Salina rimasero col fiato in gola; Tancredi sentì addirittura come gli pulsassero le vene delle tempie. Sotto l'impeto della sua bellezza gli uomini rimasero incapaci di notare, analizzandoli, i non pochi difetti che questa bellezza aveva, molte dovevano essere le persone che di questo lavorio critico non furono capaci mai. Era alta e ben fatta, in base a generosi criteri; la carnagione sua doveva possedere il sapore della crema fresca alla quale rassomigliava, la bocca infantile quello delle fragole. Sotto la massa dei capelli color di notte avvolti in soavi ondulazioni, gli occhi verdi albeggiavano [...]. (p. 81)

Significantly, the only physical description of Angelica in the *Furioso* relates that she has 'vermiglie gote', 'auree chiome' and 'begli occhi neri' (XII. 33). By keeping physical description to a minimum, Ariosto succeeds in enhancing her beauty through suggestion and thus renders her more powerfully alluring. Conversely, Lampedusa builds on her physical beauty to undermine that same beauty, though the use of 'doveva' loses all objectivity and sinks the descriptive passage back to the level of desire, suggesting a very unreliable narrator. This 'adolescente voluttuosa' sparks off in Padre Pirrone 'una successione di Dalile, Giuditte ed Ester' (p. 82) which is an ironic touch given that they were all at some stage adulterous wives to important men, and one which prefigures Angelica's own adulterous marriage to Tancredi. Later in the novel Padre Pirrone also lets slip the verse '*Veni, sponsa de Libano*' (p. 137) from the *Canticum canticorum* at the sight of Angelica.[8] It may also, however, be a playful allusion to the same verse in Dante's *Purgatorio* (XXX. 11) where the subject is Beatrice, which further suggests Lampedusa's parodic handling of the *donna angelicata* figure through Angelica. Jeffrey Meyers comments that 'if Solomon's bride is the very essence of the earthly and carnal, Dante's Beatrice personifies the heavenly and the spiritual, and comments ironically on the rapture with which the Salinas receive Tancredi's goddess'.[9] Her promise of sexual gratification is made even more explicit by the animal epithets given to her. On listening to Tancredi's crude story about his incursion into a convent: 'Angelica, ancora appoggiata, rideva, mostrando tutti i suoi denti di lupatta. Lo scherzo le sembrava delizioso; quella possibilità di stupro la turbava, la bella gola palpitava' (p. 86). Later in the novel we read that Angelica 'da quella canaglia che era, gli aveva detto: "Sono la tua novizia"' (p. 156) in a ready conflation of story and desire.

This motif suggests the numerous instances in the *Furioso* in which Angelica was almost the victim of rape – she cleverly eludes Sacripante and most notably Ruggiero. Yet Lampedusa had his Angelica become a willing participant in the idea of it, though not its action. If anything, where the *Furioso* plays out the actions of its characters, whether it be a movement towards sexual possession or a near miss and subsequent escape from it, Lampedusa's characters literally 'play out' their actions in their minds at the level of unspoken desire. All actions are ludically interiorized and no real action takes place – Tancredi never takes his 'novizia', though she seems willing.

---

8 In the same chapter the Lombard Cavriaghi again quotes from the *Canticum canticorum* in reference to Angelica: 'Sa, principe, a sentire lui è la regina di Saba! Andiamo subito a riverire la *formosissima et nigerrima*. Muoviti, testone!' (p. 143).   9 J. Meyers, 'Symbol and Structure in *The Leopard*', in *Italian Quarterly*, 19, nos 34–5 (1965), p. 159.

But what of Angelica's character? How does the Sicilian author, in comparison with the Ferrarese poet, reveal the true Angelica – if she exists at all? At one point in the novel we read that 'gli occhi verdi albeggiavano, immoti come quelli delle statue e, com'essi, un po'crudeli' (p. 81). This is then rendered more explicit by the intervention of the narrator in the course of the novel:

> Se da questa abitudine di Angelica si volesse dedurre che essa amava Tancredi, ci si sbaglierebbe: essa possedeva troppo orgoglio e troppa ambizione per esser capace di quell'annullamento, provvisorio, della propria personalità senza il quale non c'è amore. [...] nel corso degli anni, divenne una delle più viperine Egerie di Montecitorio e della Consulta. (pp. 138–139)

In the *Furioso*, Angelica's deceitful or necessary use, depending on which way you view her, of Sacripante in canto I has some fine parallels:

> Con molta attenzion la bella donna
> al pianto, alle parole, al modo attende
> di colui ch'in amarla non assonna;
> né questo è il primo dì ch'ella l'intende:
> ma dura e fredda più d'una colonna,
> ad averne pietà non però scende,
> come colei c'ha tutto il mondo a sdegno,
> e non le par ch'alcun sia di lei degno.
> [...]
> ma alcuna finzione, alcuno inganno
> di tenerlo in speranza ordisce e trama;
> tanto ch'a quel bisogno se ne serva,
> poi torni all'uso suo dura e proterva. (I. 49–51)

Ariosto's cold 'colonna' and Lampedusa's cruel 'statua' are similes for a duplicitous Angelica, but whereas Ariosto's Angelica is forced into this position in order to escape impending harm, no such excuses can be made for her Sicilian equivalent. Ariosto's comments on Angelica are all from the viewpoint of disappointed males, he himself takes no position and entrusts his multifaceted narrative to his several personæ. The most frequently encountered, though deeply erroneous, epithet for Ariosto's Angelica, 'perfida', is one that is better levelled at Lampedusa's sly creation. With regard to female characters in Sicilian literature Gianvito Resta writes that 'la figura femminile emerge ad un livello per certi aspetti "demoniaco", continuamente riproposta dall'elemento oscuro, dionisiaco, delle valenze di cui si carica la sua presenza'. He further states that 'le due funzioni del personaggio femminile, causa di perdizione o *mater* salvifica, sono quelle che hanno operato in tutta la letteratura siciliana'.[10] Angelica Sedàra is definitely the former.

Lampedusa, in describing Angelica's character, gently hints at associations between her and the name of the town and palace of Donnafugata where chapters II, III and IV take place. Her entrance into the palace on the night of Tancredi's return is suggestive in this regard: '"Si può?" Era Angelica. Nella fretta e nell'emozione non aveva trovato di meglio per ripararsi dalla pioggia dirotta che mettersi uno "scappolare", uno di quegli immensi tabarri da contadino di ruvidissimo panno' (p. 147). It is evident that the Sicilian author is alluding to Angelica's humble origins which are in stark contrast to the exalted history and ancestral memory of the Salina palace. Yet, it is also here that a distant echo emerges from her precursor. Here again we may recall the scene in the *Furioso* when Angelica, having taken refuge from Ruggiero, reappears disguised in rustic dress:

> in certi drappi rozzi aviluppossi,
> dissimil troppo ai portamenti gai,
> che verdi, gialli, persi, azzurri e rossi
> ebbe, e di quante fogge furon mai.
> Non le può tor però tanto umil gonna,
> che bella non rassembri e nobil donna. (XI. 11)

In the *Gattopardo* reference there is also a hidden allusion, which significantly lends weight to the importance of Angelica's role within the narrative and suggests an association with her and the toponym Donnafugata. The name Donnafugata hints at many of the vital themes in the novel. Its components, woman-fled or woman-driven away, immediately suggest the ideas of 'fuga' and 'possesso', both joined and qualified by 'donna'. Sciascia wrote, referring to the small town of Donnaventura connected to the Tomasi feudal home of Palma, which in itself suggests the name Donnafugata, that 'l'onomastico ha nel *Gattopardo* un ruolo di segrete allusioni storiche o private, non è gratuito andare al di là di quel che letteralmente questo nome contiene – e cioè una donna in fuga – e scorgervi, magari inconscia, una simbolizzazione del possesso (la terra come donna) ormai perduto, della proprietà come in fuga e dissolta: dalla donna-ventura, e cioè avvenire e fortuna insieme, alla donna-fugata, e

---

10 Gianvito Resta, 'Prolusione', in *Letteratura siciliana al femminile: donne scrittrici e donne personaggio*, ed. by S. Zappulla Muscarà (Caltanisetta, Rome: Salvatore Sciascia, 1984), pp. 5–7.

cioè passato, sfortuna, sconfitta'.[11] The term 'scappolare' from the previous passage has two meanings in Italian: the first, an old religious cloak pertaining to the Benedictine order; the second indicates 'sfuggire', drawing attention to the idea of the 'fuga'. Lampedusa's choice of word is deliberate; its double meaning is highlighted by the use of inverted commas in the text. Tancredi even defines Angelica in his mind as 'la donnafugasca' (p. 159), which, though it may only denote her place of origin, more than suggests the association between her and the toponym.

Furthermore, the binomy Angelica/Donnafugata is made more explicit not only by reference to 'flight', but also through the tortuous courtship of Angelica and Tancredi, which entails a mimetic representation of the meaning of the name Donnafugata. This is set against the backdrop of the 'ciclone amoroso' of chapter IV. In the disused rooms of the palace, hidden from the living, Tancredi and Angelica embark on their *Voyage à Cithère*. Lampedusa variously describes this secret interior of the palace as a 'labirinto', 'Nuovo Mondo' and 'oceano di stanze'. Their journey into the 'nucleo segreto' of the palace represents an uncovering of the unconscious sublimated through history. It is a world of both religious and carnal excess, played out and filtered through their 'gioco a nascondere' – a game deeply redolent of the 'fuga'. It is also a game which intimates a relationship with the activities of flight, evasion, pursuit and possession, activities abundantly present in the *Furioso*. In the novel we read that 'l'indomani avrebbero ripreso il loro pazzesco gioco a nascondersi, a mostrarsi' (p. 158), suggesting repetition and replay. Could we not substitute this labyrinth with the 'selve spaventose e scure' or the 'lochi inabitati, ermi e selvaggi' of canto I. 33 in the *Furioso*? Lampedusa, knowingly and playfully, transports his dales, rocks and verdant forests into the hidden interior of the Donnafugata palace, condenses the numerous pursuits and escapes of Angelica to just over a few days, and transforms all the action into a game, with Angelica as a more than willing participant – a case of parodying the parody. How to possess Angelica is key to both works.

The nominal representative of the urge towards possession in the novel is Tancredi, whose marriage to Angelica reaps only material gain in that he never fully possesses her – much like Ariosto's knights. Their marriage is a fruitless one, she does not conform to the norms which are expected from her, she does not become 'madre' and she retains that quality which renders her 'altra', that is, desirable. Both Angelicas are fleeting objects of desire, they are *fugaci* and characterised through the gazes of their pursuers/admirers. Furthermore, both are subverters of male imposed categories informing their respective ages. But if Medoro, as the only one capable of genuine love, is Angelica's chosen one

11 Leonardo Sciascia, *Fatti diversi di storia letteraria e civile* (Palermo: Sellerio, 1989), pp. 102–3.

in the *Furioso*, who or what does Angelica desire in *Il Gattopardo*?[12] A possible answer may be Don Fabrizio Prince of Salina himself. As protagonist in the novel, Don Fabrizio represents the subject by which all objects of desire are viewed. The Prince is not immune to 'un'avventura galante di basso rango' (p. 31), and much of the conflict that exists within the Prince is based on the wavering impulses between carnal and celestial love. References to the Prince's attraction to Angelica are scattered throughout the novel. The Prince is jealous of his nephew Tancredi, even if he treats him with his usual paternal affection: 'gelosia carnale: Tancredi aveva assaporato quel gusto di fragole che a lui sarebbe rimasto sempre ignoto' (p. 124).

Before his death Lampedusa began an additional chapter to the novel. Of this unfinished chapter, he wrote six pages. Chronologically the chapter was to come after chapter VI; it was to recount the details of the Prince's passion for Angelica, a passion already well manifest in the preceding chapters. Archibald Colquhoun writes that this chapter 'would have been set in a place of assignation where Angelica was to meet her lover. Don Fabrizio hears of this and substitutes himself'. Two short poems and an anagram beginning 'Angelica mia' were also supposed to have existed.[13]

This additional chapter, or at least the idea of it, should come as no real surprise. Throughout the scenes in which Angelica is present the narrative voice almost seems to be that of Don Fabrizio himself. The line between narrator and protagonist is deliberately blurred, save for Lampedusa's more telling intrusions. Gioacchino Lanza Tomasi writes: 'L'erotismo del *Gattopardo* ha troppo sapore per essere soltanto finzione.'[14] He goes on to suggest the existence of some real-life Angelicas in Lampedusa's formative years. The underlying idea, however, is clear: Angelica is the focal point of desire for Tancredi, Don Fabrizio and the author himself. Andrea Vitello writes that Angelica 'non è una donna. Né, tan-

---

12 Despite his modest origins Medoro has 'buon cuor' (XVIII. 169) and 'di cor ama' (XIX. 1). For an excellent reading of Medoro's role in the *Furioso* see Richard Andrews, 'Cloridano, Medoro, Angelica: Patterns of Loyalty and Love in the *Orlando furioso*', in *The Cultural Heritage of the Italian Renaissance: Essays in Honour of T.G. Griffith*, ed. by C.E.J. Griffiths and R. Hastings (Lampeter: Edward Mellen Press, 1993), pp. 215–34. **13** Archibald Colquhoun, 'Lampedusa in Sicily: The Lair of *The Leopard*', *Atlantic Monthly*, 211 (Feb. 1963), p. 109. In 2002 Feltrinelli published what remains of this unfinished chapter for a new edition of the novel: G. Tomasi di Lampedusa, *Il Gattopardo: Nuova edizione riveduta* (Milan: Feltrinelli, 2002). In the 'Postfazione' G. Lanza Tomasi states that he remembered that Lampedusa had 'composto alcune poesie, ascritte a don Fabrizio, e che in queste si aveva la rivelazione del suo amore per Angelica' (p. 276). This new chapter had as its title 'Il Canzoniere di casa Salina'. Sadly, the reproduced fragment does not touch upon this episode. **14** Gioacchino Lanza Tomasi, '*Il Gattopardo*: Un romanzo quale soluzione della discrepanza tra realtà e desiderio', *Forum Italicum* 21, no. 1 (1987), p. 11.

tomeno, la donna. [...] invece, sa di impersonare la femmina-tipo, quella di sempre: fonte di seduzione, oggetto di desiderio e strumento di piacere.'[15] This stereotypical reading advocates an Angelica akin to Calvino's reading of Ariosto's Angelica as an 'irresistibile seduttrice'.[16] I would suggest that Lampedusa's Angelica is much more. Here we must leave Ariosto aside and examine the history of the novel's text to view how Lampedusa invests his Angelica with meanings that go beyond the merely parodic and demonstrate how even editors have fallen for Angelica's elusive charms.

The polemics which followed the publication of Lampedusa's *Il Gattopardo* in 1958 were succeeded ten years later by fresh controversy regarding the authenticity of the text in its published form. Giorgio Bassani's editorial work on the novel came under fire through the discovery of the 'definitive' autograph manuscript. Carlo Muscetta, the instigator of this new polemic, declared that the first published version was incorrect and demanded that the text conform to the manuscript.[17] He based this judgement on the supposition that the manuscript, which had been written after the typescript, was closer to the author's true intention than the synthesis arrived at by Bassani who, although relying heavily on the typescript, had combined the two. This was later confounded by Antonio Dipace's study *Questione delle varianti del 'Gattopardo'*, in which he argued that the typescript was superior and that the manuscript had not been transcribed from the typescript, but from an earlier draft.[18] Lampedusa's adopted son, Gioacchino Lanza Tomasi, conceded that variations existed, though he stressed that they were exaggerated by Muscetta.[19] However, publications successive to this discovery have amended the text with the hundreds of minor variations.[20]

One of the so-called 'minor' variations between the two texts which has escaped the attention of most critics, involving the absence and sudden appearance of Angelica at one point in the novel, is noteworthy in this regard. The significance of this point is that it helps establish an association between the character of Angelica and the figure of Death. Tom O'Neill was the only critic to draw attention to this variant and argue that there is an association between Angelica and Death.[21] This 'gioco a nascondere' is purely a textual one, but does, nevertheless, call into question the seriousness and interpretative considerations

15 Andrea Vitello, *Giuseppe Tomasi di Lampedusa* (Palermo: Sellerio, 1989), p. 388. 16 *Orlando furioso di Ludovico Ariosto raccontato da Italo Calvino* (Turin: Einaudi, 1970), p. 161. 17 Carlo Muscetta, 'Saggio di correzioni del *Gattopardo* completo', *Mimesis*, no. I, 1968. 18 Antonio Dipace, *Questione delle varianti del "Gattopardo"* (Rome: Argileto Editori, 1971). 19 David Gilmour, *The Last Leopard* (London: Collins Harvill, 1990), p. 191. 20 The 2002 Feltrinelli edition claims to be the definitive version. 21 Tom O'Neill, 'The Leopard's changing spots: which version should we read?' in *Renaissance and Other Studies*, pp. 280–97.

of those who went about re-constructing the novel in 1969. Lampedusa's surviving statements regarding *Il Gattopardo* highlight his aesthetic aims and draw attention to the way he would have us read the text: 'Tutto il libro è ironico, amaro e non privo di cattiveria. Bisogna leggerlo con grande attenzione perché ogni parola è pesata ed ogni episodio ha un senso nascosto. [...] tutto vi è soltanto accennato e simboleggiato; non vi è nulla di esplicito e potrebbe sembrare che non succeda niente. Invece succedono molte cose, tutte tristi.'[22]

With the support of this authorial reference to hidden allusions and symbolic undercurrents, it is worth re-examining the penultimate chapter of *Il Gattopardo*. In the first edition (*l'edizione bassaniana*), with the Prince on his death-bed in the Hotel Trinacria, Lampedusa writes:

> Doveva aver avuto un'altra sincope perché si accorse a un tratto di esser disteso sul letto. Qualcuno gli teneva il polso: dalla finestra il riflesso spietato del mare lo accecava; nella camera si udiva un sibilo; era il suo rantolo, ma non lo sapeva. Attorno vi era una piccola folla, un gruppo di persone estranee che lo guardavano fisso con un'espressione impaurita. Via via li riconobbe: Concetta, Francesco Paolo, Carolina, Tancredi, Fabrizietto. Chi gli teneva il polso era il dottor Cataliotti; credette di sorridere a questo per dargli il benvenuto, ma nessuno poté accorgersene: tutti, tranne Concetta, piangevano; anche Tancredi che diceva: "Zio, zione caro!"[23]

In the later edition of the novel (*l'edizione conforme al manoscritto del 1957*), however, we read the following:

> Doveva aver avuto un'altra sincope perché si accorse a un tratto di esser disteso sul letto: qualcuno gli teneva il polso: dalla finestra il riflesso spietato del mare lo accecava; nella camera si udiva un sibilo: era il suo rantolo ma non lo sapeva; attorno vi era una piccola folla, un gruppo di persone estranee che lo guardavano fisso con un'espressione impaurita: via via li riconobbe: Tancredi, Concetta, *Angelica*, Francesco-Paolo, Carolina, Fabrizietto; chi gli teneva il polso era il dottor Cataliotti; credette di sorridere a questo per dargli il benvenuto ma nessuno poté accorgersene: tutti, tranne Concetta, piangevano; anche Tancredi che diceva: "Zio, zione caro!"[24]

22 The passages are taken from letters Lampedusa wrote to his friend and wartime companion Guido Lajolo between March 1956 and January 1957. Cited from A. Vitello, pp. 229–30.
23 Giuseppe Tomasi di Lampedusa, *Il Gattopardo* (Milan: Feltrinelli, 1959), p. 297. 24 Lampedusa, *Opere*, p. 234 (my italics).

Angelica is clearly missing from the group in the first edition, yet mysteriously present in all editions after 1969. The difference in the two editions is due to the discrepancies between the typescript and the manuscript.[25] Angelica is not among the list of mourners in the typescript, but present in the manuscript. Angelica's presence, in a passage where all of the relatives were considered likely to be present during the Prince's last hours, was deemed to be more appropriate by those editing the 1969 version. Does this constitute an error on the part of the editors or was the first edition's 'absence' an interpretative decision by Bassani?

Antonio Dipace's study makes no mention whatsoever of the exclusion/inclusion of Angelica's name between the two versions, which seems strange given the fact that he publicly advocated the superiority of the type-script over the manuscript. Closer attention to this passage would certainly have lent greater weight to his thesis over Muscetta's. The adoption of the manu-script in 1969 resulted in only minor changes, mostly in punctuation and in certain nomenclature, but the final paragraphs were substantially modified. This is no minor variant in a supposedly imperfect text, since it implies that Angelica's role is more symbolic than has hitherto been thought. The question of whether her later 'appearance' at the death-bed in the revised text is of importance at a place in the novel where the main focus of interest is on the dying Prince, depends on whether we take her absence to be important to the aesthetic aims of the author. Her presence in this scene is of little importance if she is there solely to make up the numbers, but her absence from the list of mourners can be shown to imply a direct association between Angelica and the 'creatura bra-mata', Lampedusa's image of death.

Her presence among the group of mourners destroys any association, implicit or otherwise, between Angelica and Death. The richness of the *Eros* and *Thanatos* association is impoverished by her presence at this point in the text. Angelica may be said to represent an earthly Venus. Plato in the *Symposium* (180ff) posits the idea of two Aphrodites, each representing a different form of *Eros*. The celestial Venus represents love aroused by the contemplation of the eternal and divine; the earthly Venus represents love aroused by beauty found in the material world and is based on sexual and procreative principles. In *Il Gattopardo* Don Fabrizio's love for astronomy and for his faithful 'Venere' sug-gests the *Venus coelestis*, while the Prince's obvious attraction to Angelica, and his sexual transgressions with various mistresses, illustrate the conflicting figure of the *Venus vulgaris* in the Prince's life. It is Don Fabrizio's desire for Angelica which illustrates this point.

---

25 I am grateful to Gioacchino Lanza Tomasi for providing me with photocopies of both the typescript and the manuscript of this particular passage.

Most critics of *Il Gattopardo* have associated Death with the celestial 'Venere' so much longed for by Don Fabrizio. They have based this judgement on the explicit association made between Venus and 'la creatura bramata'. At the end of chapter VI the Prince, walking alone on the streets of Palermo, thinks: 'Venere stava lì, avvolta nel suo turbante dei vapori autunnali. Essa era sempre fedele. [...] Quando si sarebbe decisa a dargli un appuntamento meno effimero, lontano dai torsali e dal sangue, nella propria regione di perenne certezza?' (p. 222). By the end of chapter VII his wish is fulfilled: 'Giunta faccia a faccia con lui sollevò il velo e così, pudica ma pronta ad esser posseduta, gli apparve più bella di come mai l'avesse intravista negli spazi stellari' (p. 235).

Death then is personified as Venus, that perennial object of desire. But this should not preclude the possibility that the physical form of the lady is, in reality, that of Angelica. Both Venus and Angelica are objects of desire for the Prince, the one spiritual and the other carnal. The very sensual nature of the 'creatura bramata' suggests carnal desire, and the language of the chapter is filled with images of escape, elopement and possession through an illicit love affair: 'adesso il corteggiamento era finito: la bella aveva detto il suo sì, la fuga decisa, lo scompartimento nel treno, riservato' (p. 224).[26] Lampedusa's description of Death implicitly points to the figure of Angelica.

Moreover, chapter VII reveals more striking instances for an association between the two. The figure of Death is described as 'una giovane signora: snella'. This recalls an earlier descriptive passage in chapter IV in which the subject was Angelica: 'il corpo di lei appariva snellissimo'(p. 147). Further comparisons between the two are implied as in a passage at the ball scene in chapter VI when Lampedusa writes of Angelica: 'I suoi occhi ridevano di *malizia*' (p. 213).[27] Later in chapter VII he describes the straw hat the 'creatura bramata' is wearing as having a veil which 'non riusciva a nascondere la *maliosa* avvenenza del volto'. What is striking about this parallel is that in the *edizione bassaniana* we read the following: 'Fra il gruppetto ad un tratto si fece largo una giovane signora; snella, ... con un cappello di paglia ornato da un velo a pallottoline che non riusciva a nascondere una *maliziosa* avvenenza del volto' (p. 297).

Though the difference between the two adjectives is significant – 'maliosa'/ enchanting or bewitching and 'maliziosa'/malicious or mischievous – within the context of the novel preference of one over the other may be deemed to have little import. But it more than suggests that the revised edition neglected some of the more telling associations made by the author.[28] The comparison between

26 Significantly, Angelica is referred to as 'matutina stella' (Venus) in Boiardo's *Orlando innamorato* (I. i. 21). 27 All italics are mine. 28 It is interesting to note that the two words are placed together in an earlier passage detailing the deeds of *Eros*. This prefigures the fusion

the two is obviously intended and rendered more ironic by the fact that in chapter VI at the ball scene Angelica had just come to the Prince to invite him to dance with her. Her words: 'spero che non me la rifiuterà' are met with acceptance by her interlocutor. It is worth noting that moments before Tancredi had asked: 'Corteggi la morte?' This sensual invitation/acceptance anticipates a fuller re-enactment in chapter VII. Both passages also share a delicate movement of the hands which mirror each other. In the ball scene we read that 'La sua mano si posava sulla manica di Don Fabrizio' (pp. 213–14), while during the death-bed scene Lampedusa's figure of Death 'Insinuava una manina inguantata di camoscio fra un gomito e l'altro dei piangenti' (p. 235). In both instances the Prince desires and accepts the gratifying feminine invitations. The echoes between Angelica and the 'creatura bramata' are also evident in chapter VII itself. The scene at Palermo train station, in which all the relatives await the return of the dying Don Fabrizio, suggests such an echo. Lampedusa's description of the scene, in which the Prince's children are quickly passed over, is clearly focused on the figure of Angelica: 'Angelica con la seta del suo corpetto ben tesa dai seni maturi, fu allora che si fece udire il fragore della cascata' (p. 226).

The sight of Angelica on the platform causes the first of a series of blackouts for the Prince. With each successive blackout he moves ever closer to death. Again, Angelica is described by her clothes and in sexual terms. The final passage of the chapter has a direct correspondence with this one. Like Angelica, the figure of Death is described by her clothes and her femininity. The sight of this figure finally brings to an end the 'fragore' set off by Angelica: '[…] il fragore del mare si placò del tutto' (p. 235).

The personification of Death, then, in *Il Gattopardo* is a combination of many of the feminine elements at work in the novel. She represents the finale of the 'fuga', embodied in both Angelica and Donnafugata, which runs throughout the novel. Despite his studied distaste for Italian Renaissance literature, Lampedusa weaves many Ariostan motifs into his rich Sicilian tapestry. Yet, as Angelica grew in his imagination she began to accrue additional meanings and move away from her model. C.S. Lonergan trenchantly observes that Ariosto's Angelica has 'become a symbol of our pursuit of chimerical fancies, […] new versions of her have somehow falsified the original'.[29] Lampedusa's falsified copy is invested with many extraneous meanings, though she remains equally elusive. More significantly, she frequently nods in the direction of her forebear, even if she is unable to live up to her standards.

---

of *Eros* and *Thanatos*: 'E l'Eros era sempre con loro, malizioso e tenace, il gioco in cui trascinava era pieno di azzardi e di malia' p. 151.   **29** Lonergan, p. 94.

Motives of translation: reading Thomas More's translation of Pico della Mirandola's Life and Works

Eiléan Ní Chuilleanáin

Thomas More's *Lyfe of Iohan Picus Erle of Myrandula* [...] *with dyuers epistles & other warkis of the seyd Iohan Picus* is a translation of the humanist Gianfrancesco Pico's biography of his famous uncle. The *Life* is supplemented by a brief selection of its subject's writings, consisting of three letters, a Commentary on Psalm 15, and four English versifications of brief spiritual works. The small volume was printed, probably in 1510,[1] by John Rastell, and reissued about 1525 by Wynkyn de Worde; it is included also in the 1557 collection of More's English works. All three early editions include a dedicatory letter to a nun named Joyce Leigh, describing the book as a new year's gift, but there is no surviving manuscript. More's earliest published work in English, it was to appear last of all (in 1997, with the *English Poems* and the *Last Things*) in the Yale edition of More's *Complete Works*, though it is volume I – volume II had appeared in 1963, thirty-four years earlier. The size of the Yale enterprise matches the range and weight of Thomas More's work and influence; the comparative brevity and the belated appearance of this early work may be appropriate to its lesser and lighter place in the canon.

Yet though a minor work, the Pico translations have occupied, as we shall see, a significant position in the development of biographical speculation about More's own mental life. The choice to make Pico's life and work known in England seems significant; but what was it about Pico that made him an attractive subject? One response would be his appropriateness as an intellectual forerunner for the English humanist. The career of Pico should have had an intrinsic fascination for a young man beginning to make a name for wit and learning. By 1510, More's literary activity – his studies in Greek, his (now lost) lectures

---

1 *The Complete Works of St Thomas More* (henceforth *CW*), 15 vols (New Haven and London: Yale UP, 1965–1997), I, ed. by Anthony S. G. Edwards, Katherine Gardiner Rodgers and Clarence H. Miller, cxx–xxi. The first edition of the *Life of Pico* is undated, but Rastell's son William who printed the *English Works* gave the date of the book as about 1510.

on St Augustine, his translations from Lucian which associated him with Erasmus, and his English poems – had obtained a reputation for him as a highly promising young scholar.[2]

In this context, Pico's career was both exemplary and ominous. Born in 1463 to a noble Italian family, handsome and well educated, his early studies in Latin, Greek, Hebrew, and Arabic learning, at Bologna, Ferrara, Florence, Padua, and Paris led to the extraordinary challenge (in 1486 at the age of 23) to scholars from all the world, to debate 900 questions on 'dialectic, mathematics [...] natural phenomena and theology'[3] at Rome. The debate never took place; the printed questions were suppressed by Pope Innocent VIII, as thirteen out of the 900 were suspected of possible heresy, and Pico wrote an *Apologia* in which he protested that he had intended them to be understood in an ortho- dox sense.

His philosophical studies continued and seem to have taken a more religious turn as he grew older, but though officially pardoned by Alexander VI, he remained a figure of controversy. Before his death in 1494 he had apparently contemplated joining an order of mendicant friars, had given away much of his property and had come under the influence of the Dominican preacher Girolamo Savonarola. Savonarola's sermon after his death claimed supernatural information as to his state in the other world; he declared that Pico was being punished in purgatory for not having carried out his intention of entering the religious life. Pico's complete works were published at Bologna in 1496, com- piled by his nephew Gianfrancesco Pico whose *Life* was prefaced to the book; it is this that formed the main text of More's translation.

More's associates, John Colet, Thomas Linacre, and Cuthbert Tunstall, have been suggested as possible conduits for his first acquaintance with Pico's fame,[4] which continued to be widely known in England throughout the sixteenth cen- tury and into the seventeenth. Pico's early death was lamented by humanists and his name remained a synonym for promising youth into the seventeenth century. Izaak Walton repeats a statement by an unknown admirer of the young John Donne, who thought '*That this age had brought forth another* Picus Mirandula; *of whom Story says, That he was rather born, than made wise by study*'.[5]

2 See W. Nelson, 'Thomas More, Grammarian and Orator', in *Essential Articles for the study of Thomas More*, ed. by R.S. Sylvester and G.P. Marc'hadour (Hamden, Conn.: Archon Books, 1977), pp. 150–60.   3 *CW*, I, 299 (translation of the original Latin text).   4 *CW*, I, xli; Roberto Weiss, 'Pico e l'Inghilterra', in *L'opera e il pensiero di Giovanni Pico della Mirandola nella storia dell'Umanesimo*, ed. by Mario Salmi, 2 vols (Firenze: Istituto nazionale di studi sul rinascimento, 1965), I, 143–58.   5 Marc Laureys, 'The reception of Giovanni Pico in the Low Countries', in *Giovanni Pico della Mirandola. Convegno internazionale di studi nel cinque- centesimo anniversario della morte, 1494–1994*, ed. by G.C. Garfagnini (Firenze: Olschki, 1997),

To nineteenth and twentieth-century students of the Renaissance he was known above all as the author of the exciting manifesto of human potential, *De hominis dignitate*, as the student of Cabbala and the heir of Ficino; to Renaissance readers of his nephew's *Life* he is presented rather as ascetic exemplar of a definitive turning away from profane learning to sacred studies. It is in this light that More's translation appears, in spite of its small size, as a spiritually 'profitable'[6] enterprise for him and his readers, making available in English an (abbreviated but instructive) *Life* and a choice of the most edifying and accessible works, 'full of grete science vertew and wysedome: whos lyfe & warkys bene worthy & digne to be read, and often to be had in memory', in the words of its title-page.

My present object is less to look at this piece of translation in itself than to consider some implications of the emphasis on the 'profitable' in the context of translation. I want also to consider the reception and the use of the *Life* by More's biographers, and especially to look at the way the selection of Pico's life to translate has been read in terms of More's own inner life. And I want to end by considering the ideas on translation, recent ones as well as those belonging to the Counter-reformation, which emerge from these readings.

The Yale editors, Anthony S. G. Edwards and Clarence H. Miller, point to the 1504 Strasbourg edition of Pico's *Works* as the one most likely to have been used by More.[7] The significance of this date – if it is correct then 1504 is the earliest date for the translation – is the opportunity it offers for speculation about the place of Pico's life in More's own development. A number of commentators have followed the tradition begun, well after More's death, by the latest of his sixteenth-century biographers, Thomas Stapleton. He connects this translation with More's decision to marry Joan or Jane Colt, an event which took place around January 1505. Stapleton suggests – I will be looking presently at his exact words – that More had originally planned a life of religious celibacy, but then, finding his sexual nature recalcitrant, had decided to marry and had selected the (unmarried) Pico as a model for his life as a layman. Furthermore, Stapleton suggested that guilt at this surrender to human sexuality dogged him throughout his life. A number of twentieth-century biographers of More have taken up the hint, several selecting a date of 1505 for the Pico translation, and one, Richard Marius, speaking of More's decision to marry as 'agonizing' and the translation as 'evi-

pp. 625–40; Weiss, p. 153; *The lives of Dr John Donne, Sir Henry Wotton, Mr Richard Hooker, Mr George Herbert written by Izaak Walton*, London, 1675. B6r–B6v. **6** The volume is described in the dedication to Joyce Leigh as 'more profitable then large', 'I suppose of ye quantite ther commeth none in your hande more profitable' (CW, I, pp. 50–1), thus valuable for their brevity as well as quality. **7** *CW*, I, 291.

dence of brooding'.[8] A closer look at the language of the biographers before Stapleton should, I suggest, make the drama surrounding More's marriage plans look less intense. The date of 1505 which associates the translation with the marriage is probably unsound; the Yale editors observe that there is 'no real evidence to place the *Life* substantially earlier than the date of original publication, c. 1510'.[9] Before his marriage, More had indeed, it seems, lived as a lay guest in the London Charterhouse, following the rhythm of the monastery, but if this was unusual it was far from unique: London religious houses, including Syon as well as the Charterhouse, had provision for such secular guests.[10]

The dedication to Joyce Leigh has also, in the eyes of some commentators, seemed relevant to More's decision to abandon his leanings towards the religious life. She was the sister of a friend of his, and she was a nun. Does this suggest that More was as it were detaching himself from the cloister by degrees, or that the barrier between a religious life and a life in the secular world did not seem as enormous to him as talk of 'agonizing' decisions might suggest? Another possibility is that the choice of a dedicatee might also connect with the enterprise of translation. While sometimes overstated, the connection of women with the production of vernacular translation has been profitably studied in recent years.[11] If Joyce Leigh was well educated, as is not unlikely, is the dedication a hint that the translation of pious works, as later undertaken by More's own children and grandchildren of both sexes, would be a suitable task for her? Books are often dedicated to people whom the author thinks capable of appreciating the issues they treat, and one issue invoked implicitly, in the choice of a text to translate, is the gap between Pico's polyglot world and the culture of the vernacular, a gap which translation sets out to bridge.

Women, even when they are patrons of scholars, like Margaret Beaufort, 'Lady Margaret', Henry VII's mother, may be often seen as the typical consumers rather than producers of literature in vernacular languages, but they could also be, as Lamb, Hannay, and others have shown, producers, in particular of translations. Thus, to take an example very close in time to the publication of More's version of the Pico *Life*, Bishop John Fisher, later More's fellow-martyr, praises Lady Margaret in his commemorative sermon in 1509, for her read-

8 See *CW*, I, xxxviii–ix; Richard Marius, *Thomas More* (New York: Knopf, 1985), pp. 35, 37. 9 *CW*, I, xxxix. 10 See James McConica, 'The Patrimony of Thomas More', in *History and Imagination: Essays in Honour of H.R. Trevor-Roper* ed. by Hugh Lloyd-Jones et al. (London: Duckworth, 1981), 56–71 (pp. 59–62). See also Barbara Harvey, *Living and Dying in England, 1100–1540: The Monastic Experience* (Oxford: Clarendon Press, 1993). 11 See e.g. Mary Ellen Lamb, 'The Cooke Sisters: Attitudes toward Learned Women in the Renaissance', in '*Silent but for the Word': Tudor Women as Patrons, Translators and Writers of Religious Works*, ed. by Margaret Hannay (Kent, Ohio: Kent State UP, 1985), pp. 107–25.

ing and translation of devout French works, mentioning her regret that she was not learned enough to translate from Latin.[12] Some recent scholars, struck by the erudition of Protestant women translators and patronesses, have drawn an unwarranted contrast between them and earlier Tudor women like Lady Margaret;[13] it is probably safer to conclude that under Catholic as well as Protestant dispensations women with literary capacity frequently expressed it by translating religious works, thus putting what learning they possessed at the service of readers of the vernacular. A nun with humanist connections might well undertake the task.

Even if the dedication does not quite give us the work's raison d'être it may help us to decide how we are meant to read it. The *Life of Pico* as we have it is not a private manuscript gift but a printed book, and the dedication is thus intended for others besides the dedicatee. We know from the elaborate epistles and prefatory material to *Utopia,* full of publicity about the author's international connections and ironic hints as to how the book might be read,[14] that More like Erasmus was a master of the strategic dedication. The epistle to Joyce Leigh, with its emphasis on 'profitability', prescribes an attentive reader willing to apply everything that is learned to some good use in her own life, to make Pico's life her own, and in so doing to manipulate the meaning of the text. This would continue a process already begun, as we shall see, by the biographer and the translator.

The original biographer, Gianfrancesco Pico, had his own imperatives.[15] Writing a *Vita* as preface to the *Opera omnia,* he must assert the value and uniqueness of his subject's writings and the prodigious learning that underlies them. It is also worth his while, long before the Tridentine *Index of Prohibited Books,* to stress their orthodoxy, since the volume contained the 900 questionable theses as well as Pico's *Apologia* and Pope Alexander VI's letter absolving him. As Pico's heir and close relative, he goes to much trouble to emphasize the nobility of the family, their descent from the Emperor Constantine, and their connections with the major Italian ruling families. More personally,

---

12 John Fisher, *Here after foloweth a momynge remembrau[n]ce had at the moneth mynde of the noble prynces Margarete countesse of Rychemonde* (London, 1509), A3r. **13** See for this view John N. King, 'Patronage and Piety: the Influence of Katherine Parr', in Hannay, p. 43, who writes that Parr broke 'with the tradition of Lady Margaret and Catherine of Aragon' who patronized 'works of monastic piety and scholastic learning for an elite aristocratic readership' by promoting 'devotional manuals and theological translations for the edification of a mixed audience of elite and ordinary readers'. The distinction seems to me a doubtful one. **14** See P.R. Allen, '*Utopia* and European Humanism: the Function of the Prefatory Letters and Verses', *Studies in the Renaissance,* 10 (1963), 91–107. **15** The whole of the Latin original, with a modern translation, is in *CW,* I, 294–340.

Gianfrancesco Pico's devotion to the memory of Savonarola, of whom he was much later to write a *Life* in which Alexander VI appears as the villain, may have led him to lay especial emphasis on the closeness of Savonarola to Giovanni Pico. And, as Thomas More's earliest biographer, William Roper, was later to do, he writes himself in as witness to many of Pico's private thoughts, to the tenor of his private life and his religious austerities.

More's translation is selective. It omits much of the family detail, much information on the philosophical works, and a number of statements and phrases emphasizing the privileged status of Gianfrancesco Pico as witness to his uncle's life.[16] The effect is to exclude some material which might seem less 'profitable' to the English reader, and to turn the biography even more into a conversion narrative with a turning-point. Pico having studied deeply for seven years puts forward his celebrated theses. The forbidding of the public disputation he covets leads to a total change in his life. More inserts section headings which emphasize this drama: *Of his mynde and vaingloriouse dispitions at Rome; Of the chaunge of his life* [...] *The burning of wanton bokis; Of his study and diligence in holy scripture*. The translator is not misrepresenting his source: Gianfrancesco Pico had indeed wished to present his uncle as a man engaged in a progress from worldly to heavenly concerns; More heightens this narrative by suppressing some matters less relevant to an English readership. Whether the original biographer misrepresented his subject is another question. In 1963 Paul Oskar Kristeller suggested that Gianfrancesco Pico had exaggerated his uncle's closeness to Savonarola, and quite recently Cesare Vasoli has reminded scholars that the two Picos had different agendas.[17]

The criterion of 'profitability' invoked in More's dedication affects the freedom of the translator. If the reader's spiritual profit is the prime aim, the translator may use his discretion to select, add, transpose — for example into verse — without much regard for fidelity providing the result is edifying. We can find this process at work in both More's version and his original, and in other writings of Gianfrancesco Pico as well. When More omits the fact that Pico was interested in the discrepancies between the standard Latin versions of the Bible and the original Hebrew and Greek — an issue which was to become acutely controversial a couple of years later, with More defending in Latin letters the enterprise of the 'grammarians' who criticized the Vulgate[18] — we may see him

---

16 See e.g. *CW*, I, 294, 298, 304–14, 320, 322 (passages on the greatness of the family, on Pico's learning, a long passage on his philosophical book, the *Heptaplus*, Gianfrancesco's assertion that he often saw the whip with which his uncle punished himself).   17 See P.O. Kristeller, 'Giovanni Pico della Mirandola and his sources', in Salmi, I, 35–142 (pp. 77, 79); C. Vasoli 'Conclusioni' in Garfagnini, 641–95 (p. 643).   18 *CW*, xv, ed. by Daniel Kinney,

as revising in order to produce a profitable epitome, rather than censoring the text. And it is perhaps on the principle of identifying and emphasizing the core of relevant moral instruction that he uses freedom in verse translations of Pico but sticks much closer to the original in his handling of the letters to his nephew exhorting him to virtue. The concern for the reader's welfare expressed in his letter to Joyce Leigh can be seen as guiding him in these choices; we may note that the same concern is invoked by Pico, by his nephew, by Savonarola, and indeed by Alexander VI. Pico 'begged friends and enemies alike, learned and unlearned, to read the Apology but to leave unread the pamphlet containing those unqualified conclusions [the 900 theses], since it included many things which he had brought up not so that they could be bruited about on every street-corner but so that they could be discussed in a private, small gathering of learned men'.[19] Pope Alexander's letter on the same subject mentions that some of the theses had seemed 'erroneous, scandalous and evil-sounding' and had been suppressed lest 'the minds of the faithful and especially of simple people who crowd to this kind of public disputation should be corrupted'.[20]

The concern for the unlearned reader of vernacular texts is continuous with the biographer's presentation of his subject as constantly tending towards simple edification. In Gianfrancesco Pico's other exemplary biography, his *Life* of Savonarola, the great Dominican preacher 'laid aside sharp and subtle questions and gave himself entirely to Christian simplicity, studying those books which aroused devotion and filled him with the things of God'.[21] Elsewhere he distinguishes between the elevated style which is 'pro doctibus' and Savonarola's which was 'pro rudibus'.[22] Gianfrancesco's godson, the anonymous translator of the Savonarola *Life* into the Tuscan vernacular, in turn elected to omit from his version 'those subtle things which belong more to disputation than to the story' and 'the doctrinal passages, the erudite examples, the quotations [and details of the charges against Savonarola at his trial] because these are subtle matters belonging to the learned, qualified theologians and canon lawyers, so we decided to omit them, both because they are hard to render from Latin into the

1–311; see also E. Ní Chuilleanáin, 'The Debate between Thomas More and William Tyndale, 1528–33: Ideas on Literature and Religion', in *The Journal of Ecclesiastical History*, 39.3 (July 1988), 382–411. **19** *CW*, I, 303. **20** 'aliquas erroneas: scandalosas: & male sonantes [...] ne fidelium mentes & praesertim simplicium qui ad huiusmodi publices disputationes confluere solent corrumperentur.' G. Pico della Mirandola, *Opera omnia* (Venice, 1557), h4r. **21** 'ambitiosa quaestionum subtilitate seposita, christianae simplicitati se penitus dedit, eos libros sibi familiares deligens quorum lectione ad pietatem identidem provocaretur et divinarum rerum ...' G.F. Pico, *Vita Hieronymi Savonarolae*, ed. by Elisabetta Schisto (Firenze: Olschki, 1999), p. 116. **22** See F. Tateo, 'I due Pico e la Retorica', in Garfagnini, 451–64 (p. 452).

vernacular and because the Father [Savonarola] no longer needs to be defended, especially among upright people, simple and holy, since he defends himself with his frequent and great miracles'.[23] Repeated revisions, re-emphasizing the essential message, are of a piece with the self-censorship of the scrupulous geniuses who are commemorated in these texts. Biographers and translators see themselves as cooperatively serving the reader by reiterating the central truths of the subject's life.

The concern for the simple reader is conditioned by the omnipresent, often unspoken, fear of 'scandal', which in Christian theology means not undesirable publicity, but the sin of leading astray, even to their damnation, by words or actions possibly in themselves innocent, 'one of these little ones', in the words of St Luke's gospel.[24] This was a subject on which confessors regularly interrogated penitents, and the conscientious really did agonize.[25] It is prominent in the Christian thought of the Savonarolan milieu and the period as a whole, and can be emphasized, as we have seen, particularly in relation to vernacular translation, which is addressed to the unlearned. Having chosen to translate a work, the translator has the responsibility of choosing what to emphasize or embellish for the benefit of the reader, and what to omit. Philosophy, indeed all learning, is unprofitable compared to what stirs the heart to devotion.

For Gianfrancesco as biographer of Savonarola and Pico this includes miracles; about these More is rather more sceptical, as we shall see. Miracles and supernatural revelations play a prominent part in the denouement of Gianfrancesco's *Life of Giovanni Pico della Mirandola*. The subject's withdrawal from the world, though it involved burning his love-poems, giving away property and refusing the offer of a cardinalate, as well as his private penances, and was validated by a period in which his saintly wisdom was exhibited – all this was not, according to his nephew, enough. Giovanni Pico had told Gianfrancesco once, walking in an orchard in Ferrara, that when he had finished writing certain books he planned to give away the last of his possessions

---

23 'quelle cose sottili et più da disputare che all'historia pertinenti ho lasciato [...] le parti doctrinale, gli esempi eruditi, le citazioni colte [...] perché sono cose sottili e da huomini dotti e instrutti in teologia e nelle legge canoniche, ci è paruto meglio lasciare, si perché male si possono in lingua toscana acconciare che latine non paiano, sì perché non ha più il padre di difesa bisogno, maximo presso alle persone rette, santamente semplici, difendendosi egli stesso con i frequenti e gran miracoli'. Giovan Francesco Pico della Mirandola, *Vita di Hieronimo Savonarola (volgarizzato anonimo)*, a cura di Raffaele Castagnola (Florence: Galluzzo, 1998), p. 57. 24 Luke, XVII, 1–2. 25 See e.g. Aquinas, *Summa Theologiae*, IIa–IIae; St François de Sales, *Advice to Confessors*, trans. fr. J. Baraniewicz (Hyatsville, Maryland: Institute of Salesian Studies, 1969); Lindsay Bryan, 'Scandle is Heaued Sunne', in *Florilegium*, 14 (1995–6), 71–86.

to the poor, and walk forth barefoot to preach Jesus Christ in towns and villages. The implication is that he thought of joining a Franciscan group; later, Gianfrancesco reports, he changed his mind and resolved to join the Dominicans – Savonarola's own order. (More's translation adds 'by the especiall commaundement of god';[26] no doubt simple readers needed to be warned against shopping around between different varieties of the religious life.) In the biography this resolution is followed by the sudden illness which caused his death. His nephew tells of his deathbed vision of the Virgin, of the spiritual comforts offered by the Dominicans, from hearsay, since he did not get to Florence in time to see him alive. He was however present at Savonarola's sermon which made public Pico's secret calling to enter the religious life, blamed him as ungrateful and 'distracted by the senses' in failing to follow that calling and announced that he was suffering in purgatory because of his failure.[27]

It is surely this passage, which resonates strongly if perhaps misleadingly with More's later defences of the doctrine of Purgatory and of celibate priesthood, which has appealed to the biographers who have seen his decision to marry as a wrenching move away from a treasured vocation. We may notice that More's rendering of Savonarola's account of Pico's motives seems to allow for weakness rather than lust predominating,[28] and that he omits the Latin passage immediately following the account of the sermon, which defends visions in general and those of Savonarola in particular, and repeats only one, the briefer one, of two confirmatory visions of Pico's state after his death. The original biographer was concerned to assert Savonarola's status as a true prophet, a matter which More, who in 1513, writing his *History of King Richard III*, was to show some scepticism about visions and prophecies, who in 1529 in the anti-Lutheran *Dialogue concerning Heresies* joked about miracles,[29] and who in the early 1530s may have believed in the visions and revelations of the Nun of Kent, probably regarded as less 'profitable' than the moral example of Pico's life.

---

26 *CW*, I, 330, 70. See S.E. Lehmberg, 'Sir Thomas More's Life of Pico della Mirandola', *Studies in the Renaissance*, 3 (1956), 61–74 (p. 62). **27** *CW*, I, 334. **28** The Yale editor translates 'ab sensibus euocatus' and 'delecatae [...] temperaturae' as 'called away by sensuality' and 'a voluptuous temperament' (p. 335) whereas More (p. 73) has 'called bak by the tendrenes of hys flesh' and 'delicate complexion'. Is More avoiding scandal here too, or is Professor Miller going for a 'strong' and possibly scandalous reading? **29** In *Richard III* the Archbishop of York defends the privilege of sanctuary, 'proving' that St Peter himself consecrated Westminster by the fact that 'they have yet in the abbey St Peter's cope to show' (*History of King Richard III, and Selections from the English and Latin Poems of St Thomas More*, ed. by R.S. Sylvester (Yale: Yale UP, 1976), p. 28; in the *Dialogue* More himself tells a miracle story of which the point is that it contains nothing miraculous (*CW*, VI., ed. by Thomas M.C. Lawler, Germain Marc'hadour, Richard C. Marius, 1, 79).

I am arguing here that More, who undoubtedly, on the evidence of many of his works,[30] valued the idea of a sacred priesthood while recognizing the inadequacy of many priests, is not necessarily in the *Life of Pico* writing from a position which polarized the lay and clerical conditions. But by the end of the sixteenth century the biographical tradition surrounding More had reached the point where a polarization was assumed, and thus a choice between ways of life which, as with the central figure's choice in the Pico biography, had quasi-tragic implications. The earlier biographers do not have quite the same emphasis. More's son-in-law William Roper's account, the earliest, of his father-in-law's courtship of his first wife, suggests a gradual process by which the virtuous and learned young man finds himself ready for a suitable marriage in circumstances we may think of as typical for his time and class, which was also Roper's own:

> After which time he gave himself to devotion and prayer in the Charterhouse of London, religiously living there without vow about four years, until he resorted to the house of one Mr Colt, a gentleman of Essex that had oft invited him thither, having three daughters whose honest conversation and virtuous education provoked him there especially to set his affection.

More was attracted to the second of the girls, we are told, but then, considering that the eldest ought to be married first, 'framed his liking' to her – for Roper it is the choice between the Misses Colt that gives the interest to the story.[31]

Roper's biography, full not only of his own insights as a member of More's household, but we must assume also of knowledge gained from his wife, More's beloved daughter Margaret, was originally composed to assist the 'official' biographer Nicholas Harpsfield, whose *Life* perhaps was planned as a companion piece to the 1557 *English Works*.[32] In the event, the death of Queen Mary meant that neither of the two Catholic lives of More could be published in England. But Harpsfield's book, written in her lifetime, is full of that sense of the triumphs of God's providence which had led the popes to order Te Deums to be sung at the

---

30 For example *Utopia*, which expresses gratitude to, and admiration for, Cardinal Morton, and contempt for monks and friars who regard only the interest of their own order, and presents a fictional Utopian priesthood which is limited in numbers, virtuous (though emphatically not celibate), and enjoys a privileged position in Utopian society (*CW*, iv, ed. by Edwards Surtz, J.H. Hexter, 226–9). Much but not all of More's criticism of clergy is found in his Latin works, e.g. *De tristitia Christi* (see *CW*, xiv, ed. by Clarence H. Miller, 351–7, 391, and 740–1). 31 W. Roper, *The Life of Sir Thomas More*, in *Two Early Tudor Lives*, ed. by R.S. Sylvester and D.P. Harding (New Haven, London: Yale UP, 1962), pp. 198–9. 32 M.A. Anderegg, 'The Tradition of Early More Biography', in *Essential Articles*, 3–25 (p. 6).

death of Edward VI, and it is in this light that he sees the story of More's marriage. We may observe that he is aware of the marriage as a problem for some readers – we will see why presently – but it is one he robustly dismisses:

> Nowe, if any man will say that, seing the contemplative life farre exceedeth the active, according as Christe him selfe confesseth: *Optimam partem elegit Maria, quae non aufertur ab ea,* that he meruaileth why Master More did not folow, embrace and pursue the saide inclination, To this I answere, that no man is precisely bound so to doo; I aunswere farther, that were it so that he had such propension and inclination, God himselfe seemeth to haue chosen and appointed this man to another kinde of life, to serue him therein more acceptably to his diuine honour, and more profitably for the wealth of the Realme and his owne soule also.
>
> In conclusion therefore he fell to mariage, in and vnder the which he did not only live free from dishonouring the same with any vnlawfull and filthie company, leaving his owne wife (as many, especially such as be of great wealth and authoritie, the more pitie, often doo) but liued himselfe, his wife, his children and familie, after such a godly and vertuous sort as his house might rather be a mirrour and spectacle, not onely to the residue of the laitie, but euen to many of the Clergie also.[33]

More's marriage is for Harpsfield a licit moral choice of a way of life in which moral struggle has not been left behind, and where moral excellence can be, and is, achieved. It has however another dimension, the providential. More as a learned man is destined to vindicate the church's claim to the loyalty of the learned as well as the simple, the laity as well as clergy:

> So God prouided that euen in this Realme also should be those that should first of all people in the world confirme and seale the vnitie of the said Churche with their innocent bloud. Among whom of all laye men (for afterwarde manye other as well of the Clergie as the laitie, especially one excellent learned man, Master Germaine Gardiner, Secretary to my Lord Gardiner, Bishopp of Winchester, and should haue beene also for his grauitie, wisedome and learning Secretary to the King himselfe after the Lord Writhesley, dyed for the sayde vnitie) the very first was our woorthy Sir Thomas More. Which notable part to playe, and to be therein his messenger for the laitie, it seemeth that God did pur-

33 N. Harpsfield, *The Life and Death of Sir Thomas Moore, Knight,* ed. by E.V. Hitchcock (Oxford: EETS, 1963), p. 8.

posely choose and reserue him, though for the time he were propense
and inclined to some lyking towarde a solitarye and religious life.[34]

Harpsfield's providential theorizing, his cool account of More's interest in a
monastic life as 'propension' and 'inclination' and his assertion that the choice of
marriage is a legitimate one, might have been hard to defend in any other Catholic
religious dispensation than Queen Mary's. One of the last of the old-fashioned
Christian humanists, her cousin Cardinal Reginald Pole, was Mary's chief ecclesiastical adviser, and he was regarded as suspect by the new Counter-reformation
regime in Rome. His imminent recall to Rome for investigation was precluded
by his death in 1558, coinciding with that of Mary herself. On the Continent the
Protestant attack on celibate priesthood and monasticism was being resisted by a
reinforcement of traditional clerical defensiveness. By 1548 Ignatius Loyola was
including his rules on 'The Mind of the Church' in the *Spiritual Exercises:*

> 352. The following rules are to be observed in order that we may
> hold the opinions we should hold in the Church militant.
> 353. We should put away completely our own opinion and keep our
> minds ready and eager to give our entire obedience to our holy Mother
> the hierarchical Church [...].
> 356. We should speak with particular approval of religious orders,
> and the states of virginity and celibacy, not rating matrimony as high as
> any of these.[35]

In 1563 the Council of Trent at its twenty-fourth session defined as Canon
X, 'If any one saith, that the marriage state is to be placed above the state of
virginity, or of celibacy, and that it is not better and more blessed to remain in
virginity, or in celibacy, than to be united in matrimony; let him be anathema.'[36]
It is perhaps easier in the light of these statements to see how, for Thomas
Stapleton, writing in 1588 in exile in Louvain, More's decision to marry is seen
as something to be excused, as well as attributable to the sexual 'motions' which
as a young man he despaired of overcoming:

> But when it seemed to him that it was not possible with these austeri-
> ties to vanquish those motions of the flesh which are usual in the height

---

34 Harpsfield, pp. 212–13.   35 *The Spiritual Exercises of Saint Ignatius,* translated by Thomas
Corbishley (Wheathamstead, Hertfordshire: Anthony Clarke, 1973), 2nd edition, p. 120.   36
*The Canons and Decrees of the Sacred and Oecumenical Council of Trent, Celebrated under the
Sovereign Pontiffs, Paul III, Julius III, and Pius IV,* translated by J. Waterworth (London: Burns
Oates; New York: Catholic Publication Society Company, 1888), p. 195.

and heat of youth, he decided to take a wife. He would later speak of this with great sadness and mourning, saying that it was much easier to conquer the flesh in celibacy than in marriage. [...] So he decided to place before his eyes some outstanding man from the ranks of the laity, after whose example he could pattern his life. Then out of all those that he could remember, whose names were famous at that time for learning and piety, both at home and abroad, he happened on Giovanni Pico count of Mirandola, whose exalted reputation for excellent and varied learning resounded throughout Europe, and who was no less known for his piety and virtue. He translated his Life from Latin to English, as well as his letters and twelve precepts on leading a good life, not just for others' benefit but to familiarize himself with all of them.[37]

Stapleton drew for his account of More on the surviving members of the More household who were part of the exiled Catholic community. They told him stories which reveal that the hagiography of the subject was well developed, including miracle tales of considerable charm. They may also, I suggest, have told him what he needed to hear, supplying the biographer of More, as Gianfrancesco Pico had supplied More himself, with a drama of choice and regret which conformed to the demands of hagiographical narrative. Alternatively, Stapleton may have found the 'sadness and mourning' of the later More, over his choice of a life in 'the world', in Roper's account of More's self-comparison with the martyred Carthusians.[38]

---

37 T. Stapleton (Stapletonus), *Vita Thomae Mori*, in *Opera omnia,* 4 vols (Lutet. Paris., 1620) IV, p. 992. [translation mine] 'Sed quum exercitiis praedictis adhibitis, motus carnis qui in iuuentutis flore & ardore accidere solent, euincere non posse sibi videretur, vxorem ducere instituit. Solebat haec ille postea narrare non sine magna animi tristitia & moerore; dicebatque multo esse facilius legem carnis in coelibatu vincere quām in matrimonio. [...] Statuit igitur aliquem sibi praeclarum virum ex ordine Laicorum ante oculos ponere, ad cuius exemplum vitam suam conformaret. Omnibus itaque qui tunc vel domi vel foris pietatis & eruditionis nomine florebant, ad memoriam reuocatis, occurrit illi Ioannes Picus Mirandula comes, de cuius sanè multiplici & excellenti eruditione per totam tunc Europam fama celeberrima peruolitabat, qui etiam pietate et morum integritate non minus erat celebris. Huius vitam Thomas Morus Latine conscriptam, Epistolas quoque eius, & duodecim bene viuendi praecepta in linguam Anglicam vertit: non tam vt aliis ea communicaret (quamquam & id quoque) quam vt sibi ipsi magis familiaria illa omnia redderet.' **38** Roper (p. 242) recounts how More 'said unto my wife, then standing there beside him, 'Lo, dost thou not see (Meg) that these blessed fathers be now as cheerful going to their deaths, as bridegrooms to their marriages? Wherefore thereby mayest thou see (mine own good daughter) what a difference there is between such as have in effect spent all their days in a strait, hard and penitential life religiously, and such as have in the world, like worldly wretches, as thy poor father has done, consumed all the time in pleasure and ease licentiously. For God, considering their long-

As has been pointed out by others,[39] the Pico *Life,* though it includes an unfulfilled religious vocation, does not really match More's decision to marry and take on the responsibilities of a family. I suggest that we need to detach the *Life of Pico* from the later preoccupations of More, the embattled, often depressed, defender of the hierarchical church, and return it to the period around 1510. We may note that Harpsfield, the earliest biographer to pay attention to More's writings, classes it with 'the foresaide life of king Richarde, and some other fewe prophane thinges'.[40] He dissociates it, that is to say, from the religious and controversial writings of his subject's later career and ascribes to it no particular religious significance.

If Harpsfield, writing less than twenty-five years after More's death, when information from the immediate More family was still available, sees no connection between the *Life of Pico* and any spiritual crisis, can we see a significance in it as a secular work? While Gianfrancesco Pico treats Pico's call to the religious life with the utmost seriousness, he relates with obvious approval the refusal by his uncle to accept ecclesiastical dignities, and declaration that he did not intend to take Holy Orders as would have been necessary if he had accepted them. His refusal is coupled with a similar rejection of secular rewards for service to kings, in More's words 'y^t he might ye more quietly giue him self to studie & ye seruice of god'.[41] The long description of his unworldly temperament which precedes the account of his final illness brings in the possibility of marriage (using More's words again):

> Weddyng / & worldly besynes / [the original has 'Militiam saeculi & conjugale vinculum'] he fledd almost a like: notwithstonding whan he was axed onys in sport whither of those two burdeyns semed lighter and which he wolde chese if he shuld of necessite be dryuen to that one & at his election: which he stiked thereat a while but at ye last he shoke his hede and a litle smylyng he answered y^t he had leuer take him to mariage / as y^t thing in which was less seruitude & not so moche ieopardie. Liberte a boue all thing he loued to which both his owne naturall affection & ye study of philosophy enclined him [...].[42]

continued life in most sore and grievous penance, will not longer suffer them to remain here in this vale of misery and iniquity, but speedily hence take them to the fruition of his everlasting deity: whereas thy silly father (Meg) that, like a most wicked caitiff, hath past forth the whole course of his miserable life most pitifully, God, thinking him not worthy so soon to come to that eternal felicity, leaveth him here yet, still in the world further to be plunged and turmoiled with misery'. Could this be a source for the 'customary' ('solebat') sadness? **39** See *CW*, I, xxxix.   **40** Harpsfield, p. 107.   **41** *CW*, I, 66.   **42** *CW*, I, 69, cf 329.

The concern with 'liberty' recurs in More's earlier career[43] and is an important theme of *Utopia,* where More's dedicatory letter includes an account of the responsibilities of parenthood and marriage and its consequences: 'relinquo mihi, hoc est literis, nihil' (I leave to myself, that is to literature, no time).[44] In the body of that work Raphael Hythlodaeus, a Pician figure – unsettled in abode, devoted to philosophy – has disposed of all his property and declares his unwillingness to accept servitude to kings. If we want to relate the *Life* of Pico to More's own preoccupations, the importance of liberty rather than the call of the cloister seems a likely focus.

However, another link between the Pico biography and those of More's works written up to 1518, which largely predate the Lutheran challenge and his own not quite contemporary acceptance of service to Henry VIII, is the concern they show with literary and linguistic scholarship. The letters in defence of humanist 'grammatical' and 'poetical' studies, especially of Erasmus's Bible scholarship and translation, explore the full implications of the relationship between the new learning and moral and religious life.[45] The list of his other works is full of evidence of More's awareness of translation as a various and pregnant activity. The Lucian versions (Greek to Latin) of 1505–6 certainly do coincide in time with his first marriage; he wrote the history of Richard III in two languages, Latin and English, in 1513; for *Utopia* in 1515–16 he invented an imaginary language & produced 'translations' from Utopian into Latin;[46] he was again translating poems from the Greek anthology into Latin for the *Poems* of 1518. This literary activity, this play with languages and fictions, is the 'poetry' with which his Protestant opponents were later to reproach him. Its totality shows how lively was More's awareness of the multiple trajectories between texts which occur when translation, including self-translation, happens.

In conclusion: a reading of More's version of the *Life* of Pico della Mirandola shows us a translation formed by a concern for the welfare of the vernacular reader. More uses his dedication to influence the attitude of that reader who may be, but need not be, an educated Englishwoman, capable perhaps of engaging in translation herself. It is a story of the revision and selection of his own works by a writer, and an analogous remaking and revision of that writer's life by himself. It also shows how that life was understood, its supposedly secret drives and callings manipulated by intimate confidants, a confessor and a nephew. More's own strategies of choice and secrecy have puzzled many commentators and have led to probably erroneous judgements on the place of this work of translation in his life.

---

43 See Lehmberg, pp. 66–7 on Erasmus's statement to Ulrich von Hutten that More disliked the idea of taking public office. **44** *CW*, IV, 38. **45** See note 18 above. **46** *CW*, IV, 18–20.

In considering the biographical tradition we may observe that readers of such figures as More (and Pico), fascinating as human beings as well as writers, will, whether justified or not, make connections between the life and work, will insist willy-nilly on being edified or scandalized. Readers of translations too are less than docile, and will use translation, which might be seen as literary exercise or public duty, to speculate, as do Stapleton and the modern biographers, about the mind of the writer and the unknown relationship between the translator's reading and his writing.

Molière's *L'Avare* as scripted
commedia dell'arte

Richard Andrews

Despite a relatively long tradition of relating Molière's plays to the *commedia dell'arte*, the details of this relationship have not yet been fully displayed. In previous generations, views of what 'Italian comedy' was actually like were (at least among French scholars) somewhat romanticized, and based to an excessive degree on eighteenth-century French sources rather than earlier Italian ones. It is symptomatic that what is still the best-known study in this field relates Molière's work to the 'spirit' of *commedia dell'arte*,[1] rather than seeking out a concrete inheritance in the form of theatrical practice and dramaturgical method. There has for some time been a need for the work of the French master to be examined by Italianists, who can base their enquiries on a thorough direct acquaintance with the techniques historically used by the *commedia dell'arte*, and in particular on the revised view of the whole genre which has been made available by the past thirty years of scholarship.

However, claims to break new ground in the new millennium have to be tempered by a recognition of recent researches by a Swiss scholar. Claude Bourqui has published an impressively comprehensive study of Molière's sources,[2] covering scientifically demonstrable ones, probable ones, and also those which have been proposed but need to be rejected. Prior to that, at a conference in 1995, he delivered from his own point of view a paper on *L'Avare* which, by its title and its actual content, might seem to make the present study unnecessary.[3] We shall be quoting, and accepting, some of his principal conclusions towards the end of this essay. Nevertheless, I would propose that there are still some fresh considerations to be made which can complement Bourqui – observations which are primarily of theoretical and methodological import. They have a bearing on the general theme of this collective tribute to Corinna

---

1 Gustave Attinger, *L'Esprit de la commedia dell'arte dans le théâtre français* (Neuchâtel: La Baconnière, 1950). 2 Claude Bourqui, *Les Sources de Molière* (Paris: SEDES, 1999) [henceforth: '*Sources*']. 3 Claude Bourqui, '*L'Avare* de Molière à la lumière de la *commedia dell'arte*', in *La Commedia dell'Arte tra Cinque e Seicento in Francia e in Europa*, ed by E. Moselle (Fasano: Schena, 1997), 277–89 [henceforth: '*L'Avare*'].

Lonergan, in so far as it addresses notions of 'translation' and of movement of material between cultures.

In Appendix I to this essay, we offer a list of the moments and elements in Molière's *L'Avare* which can be considered 'derivative', with a bias towards those which derive or might derive specifically from Italian sources. But the word 'derivative' does not really express the criteria or the purpose of the present analysis, because we are not here engaged in a sterile exercise of source-hunting. It is more important to establish points of method – our own research methodology on the one hand, and Molière's dramaturgical practice on the other.

When Bourqui embarks on a study of Molière's '*Sources*', he makes it clear in his introduction that he understands that term in a very strict sense. His definition of a source is 'a text – in its entirety or in one or more fragments of it – about which we can prove that it was used directly and deliberately by [Molière] when composing his own work'.[4] He goes on to define all his terms carefully, including the words 'text', 'directly' and 'deliberately', using criteria which belong to traditional literary history with a 'scientific' or positivistic bias. He knows perfectly well (to judge by his later detailed proposals) that in the theatrical tradition to which Molière belonged, pragmatism may tell us that all kinds of other influences and borrowings – less 'textual', less 'direct' and less 'deliberate' – are highly likely; but he is not prepared in his compendium to give such links a status higher than that of speculation. We now wish to propose here that in this kind of field we cannot afford to be quite so particular, and that to insist on purely literary concepts of demonstrable textual sources is to denature or distort the object of our study. As it happens, this throws up in addition some considerations on the concept of 'translation' as applied to theatre texts and theatre material.

In effect, our Appendix I which describes itself as a 'Summary of repertoire components' is doing two separate jobs at once. On the one hand, it does list some of the most obvious places where Molière, in *L'Avare*, might have drawn 'directly and deliberately' on an identifiable 'text' which has survived to this day. But it is more interested, ultimately, in trying to list elements and units in *L'Avare* which might have existed as separate and transferable 'theatergrams', to use the word happily coined by Louise George Clubb[5] – pieces of text, or formats, or simply ideas which would be re-usable in other plays, which might in

---

4 'Par «source» d'une pièce de Molière, nous entendons un texte – dans son intégralité ou dans un ou plusieurs de ses fragments – dont nous pouvons démontrer qu'il a été utilisé directement et délibérément par l'auteur au moment de la composition de son oeuvre.' (Bourqui, *Sources*, p. 16).   **5** L.G. Clubb, *Italian Drama in Shakespeare's Time* (New Haven and London: Yale UP, 1989), pp. 1–26.

fact already have been used in other plays, and which have the potential to
become items in the repertoire of an improvising *commedia dell'arte* company or
of a single *commedia dell'arte* performer. The reason why this latter analysis
becomes combined and confused with a listing of 'sources' or 'derivations' stems
from a particular view, which this essay aims to propound, about how a dramatic author, in seventeenth-century France would experience and identify
material which he could then re-use or adapt.

Even Claude Bourqui, having first proposed very rigorous rules for accepting or rejecting proposed sources, moves in practice to using more fluid and
more truly 'theatrical' (rather than 'literary') criteria. In particular, he is prepared to make serious reference to *commedia dell'arte* scenarios many of which
(though not all) are impossible to date firmly as being anterior to the work of
Molière. There are critics who have wanted to play down the influence of Italian
theatre on Molière; and they have argued whenever they could that where similarities appear between a Molière play and a scenario, then the scenario is likely
to have been copied from Molière rather than vice-versa. Bourqui recognizes
that the probabilities run the other way, even when he cannot prove it. He is
prepared to take the existence of 'families' of scenarios which appear in various
manuscripts, and which attest to the traditional survival in the *arte* of certain
stories and scenes, as good evidence for the existence of this material in a form
on which Molière is likely to have drawn. In the case of *L'Avare*, he raises particularly strongly the cases of a group of six scenarios most of which bear titles
including the word 'Tradito'; and another group of four whose title varies but
is represented here in Appendix I by the title *Le case svaliggiate* (in relation to
L'Avare II, 5). One version of *Il tradito*, from the Locatelli collection, is actually
datable at 1617, which helps; but the others are generically from the seventeenth
or even early eighteenth centuries, and as surviving 'texts' cannot figure in a
provable chronology antecedent to Molière's own plays. Bourqui nevertheless
accepts that these scenarios represent, and even demonstrate, the existence of a
long period during which the material they contain was part of a common pool
available to the theatre profession. He does not find it possible or sensible to
reject their cumulative weight, or to attempt to insist that they all post-date
Molière and are therefore influenced by him. He finds it more likely, even by
his meticulous criteria, that they are related to, or express, material which influenced Molière – even if Molière never actually set eyes on the particular manuscript texts which happen to have come down to us.

By accepting this Bourqui is adopting, quite rightly, an extension to his own
methodology, which impinges on his initial definition of a 'source'. He is no
longer insisting that, in that particular theatrical climate, he can limit his search

to 'a text'. He is noting that texts which happen to have survived must be taken as evidence of other texts which have not survived, and of unscripted performances which could not possibly survive. And he is saying that Molière is likely to have come across at least some of his material in one of those non-survivable forms. He might have seen a different copy of a scenario containing roughly the same material; or, even more probably, he could have seen the material performed, and absorbed what it had to offer him without the intervention of any text, written or printed. In the strict language of traditional textual criticism, a large body of comic theatre material – surviving scenarios, surviving texts both Italian and French, and Molière's own plays – can at best be said all to derive from a common source; but that source has not itself survived for our study, and in many cases it never took the form of a single identifiable text or version on which a scholar could now focus. The point may appear obvious, in terms of the common sense of theatre history; but in the world of Molière scholarship it represents an approach which still seems controversial, and which is still not adopted as frequently as it might be.

As well as seeking 'derivations', therefore, we must look for other ways in which two pieces of theatre can reflect one another. In particular, when dealing with Italian improvised theatre, we must look for 'structures' – for methods of building a scene or a dialogue which favour the mnemonic techniques of improvisation, or which would give improvising actors an easy chance of playing off one another. When we find such structures, then we may be lucky enough in some cases to know of a parallel example in a surviving theatre text; but even if we are not so lucky, we still ought to recognize that the existence of the structure in itself is a sign of a kind of 'derivation' from previous *commedia dell'arte* practice. It is an indirect derivation rather than a direct one, the redeployment of a compositional method rather than the copying of a text.

In a previous study published in 1989,[6] I highlighted the close similarities between a sequence in *L'Avare* (stretching over Act IV scenes 4–5) and a scene from the comedy entitled *Li diversi linguaggi* by Virgilio Verucci, printed in Venice in 1609. *Li diversi linguaggi* belongs to an early seventeenth-century genre which Italian critics have (rather unaccountably) dubbed 'Commedia ridicolosa'. This term refers to a body of plays written by and for gentlemen amateur performers who were unable or unwilling to risk improvisation, and who there-

6 R. Andrews, '*Arte* dialogue structures in the comedies of Molière' in *The Commedia dell'Arte from the Renaissance to Dario Fo*, ed. by C. Cairns (Lampeter: Edwin Mellen Press, 1989), pp. 141–76. See also R. Andrews, 'Shakespeare, Molière et la Commedia dell'Arte', in *La Commedia dell'arte, le théâtre forain, et les spectacles de plein air en Europe, XVIe–XVIIIe siècles*, ed. by I. Mamczarcz (Paris: Klincksieck, 1998), pp. 15–27.

fore had a demand for fully scripted versions of typical *commedia dell'arte* shows. These plays are therefore stuffed with *arte* material and methodology, on a level of detail which the professionals always avoided putting on to paper in their scenarios. In Act III scene 1 of this particular comedy, we have Zanni trying to make peace between Pantalone and his daughter Lavinia, who are quarrelling (of course) over the matter of whom Lavinia is going to marry. Zanni separates the two combatants, and treks back and forth between them, negotiating his services and sorting out what each of them actually wants. He then stands centre stage and proclaims that he has reconciled them – which the audience, having heard all the conversations, knows is simply not true. Father and daughter each believe that the other has given in, and conduct a predictable dialogue starting with joy and forgiveness, and then reverting to the quarrel with which the scene started when they perceive that in fact nothing has changed. Exactly the same sequence, minus a few details, is offered in Act IV of *L'Avare*, where the servant Maître Jacques tries the same technique to reconcile Harpagon and his son Cléante. There is nothing in Molière's French version which could be seen as a direct verbal translation of the scene in *Li diversi linguaggi*. The important thing is that exactly the same things happen, in the same order. For an improvising actor, this is enough to make the two scenes identical. The servant simply has to remember that he *first* approaches the parent, *then* approaches the child (perhaps more than once, to prolong the suspense), establishes what each of them wants, does not try to change either of their minds, but *then* nevertheless proclaims centre stage that they now agree with each other. What he actually says comes as a matter of course, as if he were doing these things unrehearsed in real life – he has no need to memorize a text. Similarly, the actors playing the parent and the child have each to remember what their own character wants, in a style of comic plot which is driven almost entirely by conflicting desires. On the strength of their motivations they just 'behave naturally', say the obvious things, at each stage of the sequence. There is a kind of 'translation' here, but of actions or events, not of words.

In this case, we happen to have an earlier version of the sequence used by Molière, actually preserved in print. So here we can talk in a more direct way about 'derivation'; though we might prefer to see this in terms of both Verucci (in 1609) and Molière (in 1668) 'deriving' from a unit of performance material which was common theatrical property, in an oral tradition – rather than Molière *necessarily* 'deriving' from Verucci in particular. If we turn to other scenes from *L'Avare*, the situation is more mixed. As an example, we could focus on Act I, scene 4, which is the scene in which Harpagon first confronts his son, and then his daughter, with his plans for their marriages. (Some selected

passages from this scene are transcribed below in Appendix II, with alphabetical markers to separate out particular sequences of dialogue.) Here too both I
and Claude Bourqui have spotted sequences which duplicate or reflect moments
from Italian 'Commedia ridicolosa' plays. Young Cléante has fallen in love with
Mariane; and in an amusingly prolonged sequence which is marked as **(G)** in
the Appendix, father and son first agree totally on her suitability as a wife. They
work together through a conventional list of her good qualities, and Cléante
gets more and more excited at the notion that his chosen bride is actually
approved by his father. He is then crushed by the revelation that Harpagon
approves of her so much that he intends to marry her himself. This classic and
standard piece of comic suspense also appears in essence in a 'commedia ridicolosa' called *Pantalone imbertonao* by Giovanni Briccio, first printed in 1617.[7]

In our scene from *L'Avare*, Cléante leaves in despair, and Harpagon turns his
attention to his daughter Élise in the sequence marked as **(H)** below. His desire
that she should marry an old man, Seigneur Anselme, is rejected by her point
blank, first in terms which attempt to be polite, and eventually in what amounts
to a straight shouting match in which Harpagon says 'You will!' and Élise says 'I
won't!'. Similar exchanges are to be found in *Li diversi linguaggi*, III, 1, in the scene
which then turns into Zanni's attempts at diplomacy which we have already considered. So far, so apparently 'derivative'; but there are also other features here
to consider. These sections **(G)** and **(H)** are structured as a fundamentally repetitive formula, which I have characterized on other occasions as 'the elastic gag'.[8]
Cléante and Harpagon agree on Mariane's qualities in speeches which mirror one
another and could in theory go on indefinitely. In Élise's case, one character saying 'Yes' and the other saying 'No' is even more repetitive and open-ended; and
in fact Molière has written it so that there is always a deliberate verbal echo from
father to daughter, or vice-versa. These are structures which improvising actors,
without a written script, can fall comfortably into and prolong for as long as they
like: one simply has to listen to the other's form of words and repeat it, or twist
it, in response. They then judge by sheer rhythmic instinct and audience response
the moment at which the repetition has to be terminated and the punch-line, or
simply the next stage of the action, has to follow.

The two examples **(G)** and **(H)** just highlighted happen to have parallel
Italian examples preserved in print. The conversations between father and children earlier in the same scene of *L'Avare* have no such obvious 'derivation' and

7 See also Bourqui, *Sources*, pp. 234–5.   8 R. Andrews, 'Scripted Theatre and the Commedia
dell'Arte', in *Theatre of the English and Italian Renaissance*, ed. by R. Mulryne and M. Shewring
(London: Macmillan, 1991), pp. 21–54: also R. Andrews, *Scripts and Scenarios: the Performance
of Comedy in Renaissance Italy* (Cambridge: CUP, 1993), chapter 5, pp. 169–203.

yet are clearly structured along the same lines. In section **(A)** below, Harpagon is surprised at the end of a monologue about his hidden money, which he wanted no one, even his children, to hear. His suspicious back-and-forth exchanges, in which Élise and Cléante alternate mechanically as his interlocutors, constitute another 'elastic gag' ('Did you hear …?' – 'No.' – '*Did* you …?' – 'No', potentially *ad infinitum*). The same applies to section **(B)**, in which he keeps protesting his poverty, and interrupting the attempts of the other two at polite denials ('I really could do with …' – 'Yes, but …' – 'I really could, you know …' – 'But …', and so forth).

There are sequences like this in most of Molière, but some plays are much more stuffed with them than others. No one has yet checked whether their frequency is higher in the plays regarded by critics as more 'farcical' and less psychologically penetrating, or whether it is higher in plays written in prose rather than in verse. Both these things might be true, but they have yet to be proved. But where a text is constructed principally around such repetitive exchanges (an excellent example would be the whole first act of *Le Médecin malgré lui*), then one must speak of a greater use of *commedia dell'arte* technique, because these are the structures and shapes favoured by improvising actors. There are also longer speeches or dialogues which can be conceived as standard repertoire numbers, transferable from one play to another. Such items also strengthen the impression of a dependence on *commedia dell'arte* material, or of a desire to reflect *commedia dell'arte* style. I could refer here, in the case of *L'Avare*, to Harpagon's reproaches about his son's extravagance in that same Act I scene 4 (omitted from Appendix II, between sections **(D)** and **(E)**); to the device of reading a document on stage in II, 1 (one actor reads, the other comments: neither of them has to learn lines in advance); to platitudinous speeches, again stemming from parent–child relationships, in I, 2 and V, 4; and to the whole extended 'romanesque' narrative of Seigneur Anselme in Act V, in which a long adventurous story establishes the real family relationship between three of the characters and provides the dénouement of the play.[9]

In the end, though, analysing a few slected passages in an essay of limited length is not going to carry this argument, because the case being made is cumulative. A substantial number of moments in this play appear to have been taken from a theatrical stock cupboard: it is their quantity, rather than anything else, which leads both Claude Bourqui and myself to characterize *L'Avare* as a scripted *commedia dell'arte* show adapted for a French audience. It is the total contents of

9 The earliest example of this 'theatergram' in modern vernacular drama comes in Ariosto's *Negromante* of 1520: by Molière's time it was such a cliché that actors could perform it with their eyes shut, after memorizing a few essential details of the story to be told this time.

Appendix I which must convince, or not, that this is the case: the present essay can only examine selected examples. But if the case is regarded as proven, then *L'Avare* (along with some other Molière comedies) emerges as a play in many ways similar to its 'Commedia ridicolosa' Italian predecessors in the early part of the seventeenth century. In both cases, large parts of the play are a kind of 'translation' into fixed dialogue (first written and then printed) of material which did not exist previously in the form of scripted words, but in the form of plot units, of structures, of sequences, of *events on stage*. A theatrical 'text', especially at that moment in history, did not have to consist of words. Molière has 'translated' a selection of non-verbal texts into French, just as Briccio and Verucci 'translated' similar material into Italian dialects.

If we accept this description, then it has some quite large repercussions on our view of what kind of theatrical experience is constituted by Molière's *L'Avare*. This is recognized and explored by Bourqui, in a set of conclusions which there is no alternative but to quote in full:

> Nous voilà plongés en plein centre d'un débat fameux sur le sens de l'oeuvre de Molière. Faut-il considérer avec René Bray que l'oeuvre de Molière est, dans son ensemble, dépourvu de contenu et n'est en quelque sorte que forme artistique – sans que cela n'empêche pour autant que Molière ait une vision du monde qui transparaisse parfois au détour de l'une ou l'autre scène de ses pièces – ou faut-il être d'avis, avec beaucoup d'autres, que cette oeuvre est le reflet d'une idéologie, fruit d'une croyance dans la capacité du théâtre comique à changer le monde?
>
> Ce que nous avons mis en évidence au cours de cette communication tendrait à nous rapprocher de la première position. Et si d'aventure on devait pencher pour cette vision des choses, peut-être serait-on mieux armé pour comprendre la réception mitigée qu'a reçue la comédie de *L'Avare* dans la critique moderne. En effet, rapidement la pièce fut sacrée comme comédie de caractère qui n'en est pas un bon exemple. De Fénelon à Schlegel, on a voulu mettre en évidence les incohérences de *L'Avare*. D'autres critiques, bien intentionnés, ont voulu au contraire démontrer la cohérence du personnage et de l'oeuvre. Jusqu'à un Américain, qui déclarait tout simplement que l'unité de la pièce est celle de la victoire de la vie sur la mort.[10]
>
> Tout ce débat est fondé sur l'attente d'une cohérence dans la *fabula*, et partant dans le personnage principal. À considérer que Molière, antiaris-

---

10 Marcel Gutwirth, 'The Unity of Molière's *L'Avare*', *Publications of the Modern Language Association of America*, 76 (1961), 359–66.

totélicien dans *L'Avare*, n'a aucun intérêt pour ce critère de cohérence de la *fabula*, le problème s'évanouit.

Peut-être est-il trop facile de tirer un trait ainsi sur près de trois siècles de critique littéraire. Mais peut-être aussi sommes-nous en mesure de voir plus clair que nos devanciers, ayant l'avantage de bénéficier d'une meilleure connaissance du phénomène de la commedia dell'arte, par les travaux italiens de ces trente dernières années. Une étude de grande envergure de l'influence de la commedia dell'arte sur Molière devrait permettre d'affiner ce jugement et de vérifier s'il est transférable à d'autres oeuvres a priori peu italianisantes de Molière, voire à l'ensemble d'un parcours marqué par des choix et des stratégies de carrière étrangers à leur milieu et à leur époque.

(Bourqui, '*L'Avare* ...' (1995), pp. 283–4)

But there are more extensive implications even than those expressed here. It is certainly arguable, as Bourqui has argued, that we should not try to judge this play on criteria of psychological consistency or plot coherence. In fact audiences of all types and epochs are remarkably willing to ignore the absence of both these qualities, if a comedy is sufficiently full of laughs arising from grotesque caricature and sheer energy. During a theatrical performance, one is not in a position to turn the pages back to previous scenes and check exactly what was expressed before. But our considerations must go beyond cool aesthetic judgments, and also take in matters of emotion and sensibility.

A number of critics, over the past 150 years, have been torn when assessing *L'Avare* between its comic tones and what they see as potentially tragic ones. 'It is dreadful, isn't it' – or so many have argued – 'to think what awful things Harpagon's miserliness can make him say and do, and the equally awful feelings he can then inspire in his own children. A family is torn apart and denatured by one person's obsessive vice. What can have happened to a man to reduce him to such a state? Such things are surely not funny at all.' I have heard that a French production of the play once seized on the two very brief references to the fact that Harpagon's wife is dead, put a shrine to that woman at the back of the set, and indicated in every way possible that it was her disappearance which unhinged him and led to such unnatural behaviour. The famous monologue in Act IV scene 7 has often been analysed as an essentially painful portrayal of the disintegration of a human personality. In an introduction to a British edition of the play for school students, published in 1949, the editor asks in all seriousness: 'What comic scene ever ended with the words "I want to have everyone hanged, and if I do not retrieve my money I shall hang myself afterwards"?'[11]

11 *L'Avare*, ed. by Ronald A. Wilson ('Harrap's French Classics', London 1949), p. xlvii.

The answer to that question might be that we are dealing with a play by Molière and not with a novel by Balzac (who, in *Eugénie Grandet*, certainly did analyse seriously the devastating effects of avarice on family relationships). The reactions and directorial strategies quoted above are based on a response which Molière and everyone of his time would (arguably) have found quite incredible. Characters in comedy, who are being laughed at for their ludicrous and unreasonable behaviour, do not have inner lives. We are not supposed to subject them to sympathetic psychological analysis: we are just supposed to find them ridiculous. Feeling pain on their behalf is an attitude which began to inform comedy from the eighteenth century onwards, and which was certainly sought and even required from Romantic and post-Romantic fictions composed in the nineteenth century. Some may wish to argue that in some plays, for example *Le Misanthrope*, Molière was making his comic writing more complex, and asking rather more awkward questions about human behaviour and motivation than had been asked by any of his predecessors. Maybe he was beginning to point the way towards eighteenth-century *sensibilité* – in some of his work. But according to our proposed analysis, *L'Avare* cannot belong to that category, if it exists. The overwhelming derivation of this comedy, in its detailed technique, is from the *commedia dell'arte* tradition. Along with the similarities of technique, which would be blatantly obvious to an audience of the time, goes a similarity of tone. The theatrical world of *L'Avare* is one of insistent derision, in which miserly old men who fall in love with young women deserve all the humiliation they can get, and in which even outright insanity in principal characters is used as an excuse to invent absurd verbal nonsense and make people laugh. Harpagon's famous monologue is not tragic at all: it is, apart from anything else, deeply metatheatrical, constantly playing off the audience's acknowledged presence and assuming that the spectators will be falling about with laughter. (And it is in this characteristic most of all that the speech reflects its most distant ancestor, the monologue of Euclio in Plautus's *Aulularia*.)

There is no such thing as an inherently tragic or serious subject. Everything depends on the writer's choice of how a subject will be treated; and so matters like family disharmony, derangement, and even death, can be made comic if we so choose (and if we can present them in a way which works). Carlo Goldoni tells us, in his preface to *I due gemelli veneziani*,[12] that he and his principal actor between them managed to make an audience laugh by the way in which they presented and performed the death on stage of a principal comic character. One of the much-loved 'Tom & Jerry' cartoons – aiming as much

12 The play is usually dated 1747/48: as well as appearing in standard anthologies of Goldoni's plays, it has been edited separately by Guido Davico Bonino (Turin: Einaudi, 1975).

as anything at a children's audience, and certainly not intending to undermine its own comic appeal – risked ending the story with Tom's execution by beheading.[13] Having recognized this, we may still have questions to face regarding how to stage *L'Avare* in an incurably post-Romantic age. For some practitioners, and some potential spectators, it may now be inconceivable to offer a play in which characters are not supposed to have an inner life. Alongside 'translations' from unscripted action into scripted words (and, in some contexts, from Molière's French into another language), we may have to consider questions of 'translation' from one type of sensibility to another. Nobody, after all, is now prepared to present *The Taming of the Shrew* or *The Merchant of Venice* in the brutal anti-feminist or anti-semitic spirit which an Elizabethan audience probably expected. If we feel the same now about *L'Avare*, then so be it. But as with those two Shakespearean examples, if we choose to make a 'translation' to a different sensibility, we ought in conscience to know what we are doing.

APPENDIX I

MOLIÈRE: *L'Avare* (1668)
Repertoire components: summary, scene by scene

References to the work of Claude Bourqui are to his *Les Sources de Molière* (Paris: SEDES, 1999) ['*Sources*']; and '*L'Avare* de Molière à la lumière de la *commedia dell'arte*', in E. Mosele (ed.): *La Commedia dell'Arte tra Cinque e Seicento in Francia e in Europa* (Fasano: Schena, 1997), 277–89 ['*L'Avare*']. See also R. Andrews: '*Arte* dialogue structures in the comedies of Molière', in C. Cairns (ed.): *The Commedia dell'Arte from the Renaissance to Dario Fo* (Lampeter: Edwin Mellen Press, 1989), 142–61 ['Andrews 1989'].

A full account of detailed similarities to Plautus's *Aulularia* is found in W. Knörich: 'Die Quellen des *Avare* von Molière', in *Neue Zeitschrift für Französische Sprache und Literatur* 8 (1886), 51–87. The relationship to Plautus is indisputable; but one also has to note that individual scenes and gags which originate in *Aulularia* may have been (and sometimes demonstrably were) also taken up in Italian plays and scenarios. Scripted *commedie erudite* which were clearly based on *Aulularia* (but which then could act as independent sources for *arte* theatergrams) were Lorenzino de' Medici: *Aridosia* (1536), and Gelli: *La sporta* (1543). In French, a first adaptation was Chappuzeau: *L'Avare dupé* (1663). The gen-

13 *The Two Mousketeers*, released in March 1952. Evidence from memory has been confirmed by a website: www.lafn.org.

eral plot situation of a miserly father obstructing an amorous son or daughter was so diffuse in classically-derived scripts and scenarios as to be totally banal, whether or not there was a thematic focus on avarice as such.

ACT I

1. Lovers Valère and Élise: plot exposition, but also a dose of standard *concetti* in their prose, typical of repertoire of Innamorati [Bourqui: *L'Avare*]. (The first ten speeches are non-specific, transferable to other plays and contexts.) The situation of the lover taking post as a servant in his beloved's household has a long ancestry, starting with Ariosto's *I suppositi* (1509): it appears insistently in no fewer than six manuscript *scenari* mostly entitled *Il tradito* [Bourqui: *Sources*], and in the *commedia ridicolosa* by Verucci: *Li diversi linguaggi* (1609). Valère's speech on the power of flattery has the potential to become a separate repertoire number.

2. Brother Cléante and sister Élise: more plot exposition. Cléante rehearses a speech typical of a comedy father, to dispose of those arguments quickly: a neat Molièresque trick, but the content of the speech is in itself banal.

3. Harpagon and servant La Flèche: actions to establish the character, with some antecedents in Plautus's *Aulularia* vv. 40–52; and vv. 632–54; cf. *La Sporta*, I, 1; also *L'Avare dupé*, II, 6.

4. Élise, Cléante, Harpagon. Reproaches by a father about his son's expensive life-style appear in *La sporta*, II, 1, and then in French scripted comedies. The repetitive suspense sequence between father and son, revealing their rivalry over Mariane, is an 'elastic gag' – possibly generic, but compared by Andrews [1989] and by Bourqui [*L'Avare; Sources*] to a scene in a *commedia ridicolosa*, Briccio: *Pantalon imbertonao* (II, 6 in the 5-act version of 1616; I, 15 in the 3-act version of 1617 quoted by Bourqui). There is then another repetitive elastic routine between father and daughter, likened [Bourqui (*Sources*) quoting Andrews] to Verucci's *Li diversi linguaggi* (III, 1). Even before these more recognizable sequences, the dialogue breaks down into easily memorizable stages or units, and the whole scene seems particularly structured around improvisation technique.

5. Valère, Harpagon, Élise. In *Aulularia*, vv. 238–260, the miser anxiously checks more than once that no dowry will be required for his daughter's marriage. The Molière scene has a different emphasis; and the mechanistic repetitive sequence around the phrase 'sans dot' is a classic elastic gag structure [Andrews 1989].

ACT II

1. Cléante, La Flèche. The reading of a document by one character (in this case a contract for a loan of money), interlarded with comments by another, is an easy format for improvisation, and recurs frequently in *commedia ridicolosa*. (This specific loan document, substituting a load of junk for actual money, comes from Boisrobert: *La Belle plaideuse* (1655), IV, 2. Cf. *Li diversi linguaggi* IV, 6, where Pantalone proposes leaving similar junk to Zanni, in his will, instead of money.)

2. Maître Simon, Harpagon, Cléante, La Flèche. The situation of two groups of people conversing separately on opposite sides of the stage is a standard technique traceable back to Roman comedy. The 'agnition' that moneylender and client are father and son has a classical/Italian feel, in its echoing repetitive exchanges: the situation as such is explicitly traceable to *La Belle plaideuse*, I, 4–8.

3. Arrival of Frosine. **4.** La Flèche, Frosine. Exposition, but with 'miser gags' (cf. *Aulularia* vv. 296–320) about Harpagon in his absence.

5. Harpagon, Frosine. Frosine's flattery and playing-down of Harpagon's age, in the context of his intended marriage, has been likened by critics to Ariosto's *Suppositi* (1509) I, 2; and the general 'flattering' sequence to an *arte* scenario, *Le case svaliggiate* [Bourqui: *Sources*]. Frosine's speech explaining how much money Mariane will save reads like a repertoire number (but also has antecedents in *Aulularia* vv. 474–536). The mechanistic closing sequence (Harpagon looks 'sévère' whenever Frosine mentions money, switches to looking 'gai' when she speaks again of Mariane) is a repetitive elastic gag. It is followed by another one whereby Harpagon refuses to respond to Frosine's hints, each time talking about something quite different.

ACT III

1. Harpagon with family and servants. The series of instructions which Harpagon gives to his servants, with regard to the coming reception, can be seen as discrete 'miser gags' put into the mouth of the miser himself. It is followed later by more of them from Maître Jacques, in the form of 'what people say'. Maître Jacques being encouraged to speak freely, and then being beaten for doing so, is a basic sequence from farce (of all ages and provenances?).

2. Maître Jacques, Valère. The rivalry between the superior 'false' servant and the lower-class 'real' servant dates at least from the anonymous *Gli ingannati* (1532), and is the basis of all the scenari entitled *Tradito* [Bourqui: *Sources*]. The threat of one (cowardly) character to administer a beating, his retreat, and his being beaten by his adversary, is a standard improvisable sequence used particularly by *arte* Capitani: it appears even more pertinently, betweeen characters analogous to these, in one of the *Tradito* scenari as a '*lazzo di dare le bastonate*' [Bourqui: *Sources*]. In this case it is composed of two brief elastic sequences of dialogue.

3. Frosine arrives. **4.** Mariane, Frosine. Some echoes of standard sixteenth-century dialogue between the young innocent and the bawd, though toned down because of *bienséance*.

5. Harpagon, Frosine, Mariane. An attempt by Harpagon to speak 'lover's prose' is made ridiculous by the preconceptions planted by Frosine.

6. Élise joins them. **7.** Cléante joins them. His elaborate speeches to Mariane, understood one way by her and another way by Harpagon, echo tricks played in Molière's own *Le Dépit amoureux* and *L'École des maris*. An improvising actor might practise such equivocal prose as an exercise for different plots. The proxy gift of the ring, which Harpagon dares not revoke, is related by Bourqui [*Sources*] to a scene in the *arte* scenario *Le case svaliggiate*; and it leads to some repetitive elastic exchanges.

8. Interruption. **9.** Pratfall in the doorway. The party breaks up.

ACT IV

1. Cléante, Mariane, Élise, Frosine. With the young people planning further intrigues, this scene is mainly plot. But it has been noticed that Frosine (converted to the side of the young lovers) comes up with a scheme of which we do not hear again; and in fact Frosine is written out of the play from this point on. A theatergram borrowed from another source, and then discarded?

2. Harpagon spots his son acting suspiciously. **3.** Harpagon, Cléante. Harpagon wheedles out his son's true feelings by gross cynical deception.

4. Maître Jacques, Harpagon, Cléante. The sequence in which Maître Jacques pretends to reconcile the two (in a series of 'actions' easily memorizable without a written script) also appears in Verucci's *Li diversi linguaggi* [Andrews, 1989]; and something similar in an *arte* scenario, *La cameriera nobile* [Bourqui: *Sources*]. The simpler situation of a third party – in this case Dottor Graziano – expressing agreement with both sides of an argument appears in *Pantalone imbertonao* (II,1 or I, 15, in the different versions).

5. Cléante, Harpagon. Father and son work through the discovery that Maître Jacques hasn't reconciled them at all. This reflects the closing part of the Verucci scene, and is larded with repetitive elastic exchanges.

6. La Flèche, Cléante. La Flèche has stolen the money. (cf. *Aulularia* vv. 616–623; *La sporta* V, 4.)

7. Harpagon's soliloquy, having lost his money. Many echoes of *Aulularia* (713–26); and of *Aridosia* (III, 6). But the self-conscious absurdity, with direct appeal to the audience, is (arguably) played up more than in those sources, under the influence of *commedia dell'arte* meta-theatricality. (Cf. also *Li diversi linguaggi*, IV, 6; but here Zanni is on stage throughout, and Pantalone's proposal to hang himself develops into a different gag: see *Avare* II, 1 above.)

ACT V

1. Harpagon, Commissaire, Clerc … **2.** … plus Maître Jacques. The off-stage *équivoque* about killing the pig may relate to *Aulularia* vv. 390–8. Maître Jacques's accusation of his hated adversary Valère comes as an opportunistic off-the-cuff response: this may not be the case in the '*Tradito*' scenario sources. His extraction of circumstantial information from Harpagon, in order then to relay it himself, is likely to be a known gag.

3. Valère enters, to be accused. The extended *équivoque* in which Harpagon is speaking of his money and Valère of the 'treasure' which is Élise is recorded as a regular feature of the '*Tradito*' series of *scenari* [Bourqui: *Sources*], as well as of *Aulularia* (vv. 734–783) and *La sporta* (V, 6). Here the sequence is drawn out to really improbable length, a piece of virtuosity on the part of the dramatist.

4. The whole family crowds in. Élise's plea for mercy has the feel of a repertoire speech: the situation is a common one in plays and scenarios.

5. Arrival of Anselme, lost father of Valère and Mariane. The long narrative of the romanesque adventures of this family, accompanying the agnition which will solve all the problems, is a 'theatergram' dénouement of many comedies – and also of derived *scenari* – starting with Ariosto's *Negromante* (1520).

6. Final resolution, in which the 'cassette' full of money is traded off against the marriages of the young people. Harpagon retires alone with his money (cf. *L'Avare dupé*), his monomania remaining without a cure.

APPENDIX II

MOLIÈRE : *L'Avare*, Acte I scène 4[14]
(extracts: all 'paragraphing', and labelling of sections, is by RA)

Harpagon: [*Monologue … entrance of children*]
O Ciel! je me serai trahi moi-même: la chaleur m'aura emporté, et je crois que
j'ai parlé haut en raisonnant tout seul.

(A)
Qu'est-ce?
Cléante: Rien, mon père.
Harpagon: Y a-t-il longtemps que vous êtes là?
Élise: Nous ne venons que d'arriver.
Harpagon: Vous avez entendu …
Cléante: Quoi, mon père?
Harpagon: Là …

14 I have used the anthology of Molière's plays edited by Robert Jouanny (Paris: Classiques Garnier, 1962): the complete scene appears in II on pp. 248–55.

Élise: Quoi?

Harpagon: Ce que je viens de dire.

Cléante: Non.

Harpagon: Si fait, si fait.

Élise: Pardonnez-moi.

Harpagon: Je vois bien que vous en avez ouï quelques mots. C'est que je m'entretenois en moi-même de la peine qu'il y a aujourd'hui à trouver de l'argent, et je disois qu'il est bienheureux qui peut avoir dix mille écus chez soi.

Cléante: Nous feignions à vous aborder, de peur de vous interrompre.

(B)

Harpagon: Je suis bien aise de vous dire cela, afin que vous n'alliez pas prendre les choses de travers et vous imaginer que je dise que c'est moi qui ai dix mille écus.

Cléante: Nous n'entrons point dans vos affaires.

Harpagon: Plût à Dieu que je les eusse, dix mille écus!

Cléante: Je ne crois pas ...

Harpagon: Ce seroit une bonne affaire pour moi.

Élise: Ce sont des choses ...

Harpagon: J'en aurois bon besoin.

Cléante: Je pense que ...

Harpagon: Cela m'accommoderoit fort.

Élise: Vous êtes ...

Harpagon: Et je ne me plaindrois pas, comme je fais, que le temps est misérable.

Cléante: Mon Dieu! mon père, vous n'avez pas lieu de vous plaindre, et l'on sait que vous avez assez de bien.

(C)

Harpagon: Comment? j'ai assez de bien! Ceux qui le disent en ont menti. Il n'y a rien de plus faux; et ce sont des coquins qui font courir tous ces bruits-là.

Élise: Ne vous mettez point en colère.

Harpagon: Cela est étrange, que mes propres enfants me trahissent et deviennent mes ennemis!

Cléante: Est-ce être votre ennemi, que de dire que vous avez du bien!

Harpagon: Oui: de pareils discours et les dépenses que vous faites seront cause que l'un de ces jours on me viendra chez moi couper la gorge, dans la pensée que je suis tout cousu di pistoles.

(D)

Cléante: Quelle grande dépense est-ce que je fais?

[*Long tirade from Harpagon, over Cléante's protests, about the latter's extravagance.*]

(E)

[*Skirmishings about who is going to speak first about what.*]

(F)

Cléante: C'est de mariage, mon père, que nous désirons vous parler.

Harpagon: Et c'est de mariage aussi que je veux vous entretenir.

Élise: Ah! mon père!

Harpagon: Pourquoi ce cri? Est-ce le mot, ma fille, ou la chose, qui vous fait peur?

Cléante: Le mariage peut nous faire peur à tous deux, de la façon que vous pouvez l'entendre; et nous craignons que nos sentiments ne soient pas d'accord avec votre choix.

Harpagon: Un peu de patience. Ne vous alarmez point. Je sais ce qu'il faut à tous deux; et vous n'aurez ni l'un ni l'autre aucun lieu de vous plaindre de tout ce que je prétends faire.

(G)

Et pour commencer par un bout: avez-vous vu, dites-moi, une jeune personne appelée Mariane, qui ne loge pas loin d'ici?

Cléante: Oui, mon père.

Harpagon: Et vous?

Élise: J'en ai ouï parler.

Harpagon: Comment, mon fils, trouvez-vous cette fille?

Cléante: Une fort charmante personne.

Harpagon: Sa physionomie?

Cléante: Toute honnête, et pleine d'esprit.

Harpagon: Son air et sa manière?

Cléante: Admirables, sans doute.

Harpagon: Ne croyez-vous pas qu'une fille comme cela mériteroit assez que l'on songeât à elle?

Cléante: Oui, mon père.

Harpagon: Que ce serait un parti souhaitable?

Cléante: Très-souhaitable.

Harpagon: Qu'elle a toute la mine de faire un bon ménage?

Cléante: Sans doute.

Harpagon: Et qu'un mari auroit satisfaction avec elle?

Cléante: Assurément.

Harpagon: Il y a une petite difficulté: c'est que j'ai peur qu'il n'y ait pas avec elle tout le bien qu'on pourroit prétendre.

Cléante: Ah! mon père, le bien n'est pas considérable, lorsqu'il est question d'épouser une honnête personne.

Harpagon: Pardonnez-moi, pardonnez-moi. Mais ce qu'il y a à dire, c'est que si l'on n'y trouve pas tout le bien qu'on souhaite, on peut tâcher de regagner cela sur autre chose.

Cléante: Cela s'entend.

Harpagon: Enfin, je suis bien aise de vous voir dans mes sentiments; car son maintien honnête et sa douceur m'ont gagné l'âme, et je suis résolu de l'épouser, pourvu que j'y trouve quelque bien.

Cléante: Euh?

Harpagon: Comment?

Cléante: Vous êtes résolu, dites-vous …?

Harpagon: D'épouser Mariane.

Cléante: Qui, vous? vous?

Harpagon: Oui, moi, moi, moi. Que veut dire cela?

Cléante: Il m'a pris tout à coup un éblouissement, et je me retire d'ici.

Harpagon: Cela ne sera rien. Allez vite boire dans la cuisine un grand verre d'eau claire. Voilà de mes damoiseaux flouets, qui n'ont non plus de vigueur que les poules.

(H)

C'est là, ma fille, ce que j'ai résolu pour moi. Quant à ton frère, je lui destine une certaine veuve dont ce matin on m'est venu parler; et pour toi, je te donne au seigneur Anselme.

Élise: Au seigneur Anselme?

Harpagon: Oui, un homme mûr, prudent et sage, qui n'a pas plus de cinquante ans, et dont on vante les grands biens.

Élise (*Elle fait une révérence*): Je ne veux point me marier, mon père, s'il vous plaît.

Harpagon (*Il contrefait la révérence*): Et moi, ma petite fille, je veux que vous vous mariiez, s'il vous plaît.

Élise: Je vous demande pardon, mon père.

Harpagon: Je vous demande pardon, ma fille.

Élise: Je suis très-humble servante au seigneur Anselme; mais avec votre permission, je ne l'épouserai point.

Harpagon: Je suis votre très-humble valet; mais, avec votre permission, vous l'épouserez dès ce soir.

Élise: Dès ce soir?

Harpagon: Dès ce soir.

Élise: Cela ne sera pas, mon père.

Harpagon: Cela sera, ma fille.

Élise: Non.

Harpagon: Si.

Élise: Non, vous dis-je.

Harpagon: Si, vous dis-je.

Élise: C'est une chose où vous ne me réduirez point.

Harpagon: C'est une chose où je te réduirai.

Élise: Je me tuerai plutôt que d'épouser un tel mari.

Harpagon: Tu ne te tueras point, et tu l'épouseras. Mais voyez quelle audace! A-t-on jamais vu une fille parler de la sorte à son père?

Élise: Mais a-t-on jamais vu un père marier sa fille de la sorte?

Harpagon: C'est un parti où il n'y a rien à redire; et je gage que tout le monde approuvera mon choix.

Élise: Et moi, je gage qu'il ne sauroit être approuvé d'aucune personne raisonnable.

[...]

Some of the theoretical propositions contained in this essay have now also been explored in R. Andrews, 'Molière, *Commedia dell'Arte*, and the questions of influence in Early Modern European theatre', *Modern Language Review*, 100–2 (April 2005), pp. 444–63.

Theatre of revolt and *Teatro grottesco**

Joseph Farrell

It would be perverse to deny the gesture of revolt against the moral and social orthodoxies of the time in the bitter words spoken at the climax of Luigi Chiarelli's *La maschera e il volto* by Paolo, protagonist of the play: 'Ah, no! [...] Io non voglio più rendere conto a nessuno della mia vita, alla società, agli amici, alla legge, niente, basta: voglio diventare [...]'.[1] In isolation, these lines could suggest that Paolo has achieved a profound *dérèglement* with social customs, and that an abyss between the claims of the individual and the responsibilities of the citizen has been opened. The centre, it would seem, no longer holds, and the dissenters, represented by Paolo, are engaged on inviting the public to turn a sceptical or ironic eye on the standards which have held sway in the society they inhabit. However, any crisp view of this sort requires to be nuanced. Chiarelli's play plainly struck a chord and was a great success both in Italy and abroad, but in the caution he always displayed, Chiarelli can be viewed as a representative man of the culture of his time. It is interesting that for all his disdain for 'bourgeois theatre', he wrote for commercial organizations, and understood the cultural as well as financial nexus that had to obtain between consumers and purveyors of drama.

There are other speeches in the same key, some spoken by Paolo, others by Cirillo, a banker who has the role of *raisonneur* in the piece. After his release from jail for the supposed murder of his wife – a murder which never in fact occurred – Paolo explains the sad wisdom he has acquired during his months of solitude:

> Accortezza! Non bisogna mai costringere le persone a trovarsi faccia a faccia con i propri convincimenti [...] bisognerebbbe che gli uomini avessero più coraggio, e annullassero le convenzioni che essi hanno pattuito con le loro

* I am grateful to the Carnegie Trust for the Universities of Scotland for a research grant in the preparation of this article.
1 The play was first performed at the Teatro Argentina, Rome, 29 May 1916, with the celebrated *capocomico* Virgilio Talli as director. All quotations refer to Gigi Livio, *Teatro grottesco del novecento; antologia* (Milan: Mursia, 1965) hereafter cited as Livio. The anthology contains a critical text of Luigi Chiarelli, *La maschera e il volto*, Rosso di San Secondo, *Marionette, che passione!*, Luigi Antonelli, *L'uomo che incontrò se stesso*, and Enrico Cavacchioli, *L'uccello del paradiso*. Lines quoted, p. 65.

vanità e con il loro orgoglio, bisognerebbe che dimenticassero di aver mentito con gli altri per cercare di essere unicamente, religiosamente sinceri con se stessi: ma questo non è facile [...] allora si segue quello che si chiama il programma della nostra vita, e che, come tutti i programmi, essendo perfettamente logico, è completamente inadatto alla vita. (Act II, p. 32)

This play dramatizes more than a theatrical clash between the old and new genres. Chiarelli adopted in his title the mask-versus-face formula later identified with Pirandello, but the social conflict adumbrated is at the same time both more profound and more superficial than the formula implies. It is more profound in the sense that the work, which was written during World War One, indicates a crisis in the mores underwriting a civilization, and is the expression of a moment when the previously accepted hierarchy of values, those which can be broadly termed Victorian, are no longer judged valid. It is more superficial inasmuch as Chiarelli seems himself baffled by the contradictions of which his play is an expression.

Paolo calls for an end to exhausted conventions and talks of a *programma* which is now in conflict with life itself and, as invariably occurs in periods when such conflicts come to the fore, issues an imprecise call for a return to 'sincerity', or to 'nature'. Neither nature nor sincerity are, however, self-explanatory, existential concepts: the appeal to 'nature' may mask a cultural discontent with the social, cultural or philosophical status quo, but it also implies that a more authentic, natural order exists ready-made in the cosmos, and that the complex task of creating a new order in society can be avoided. In Freudian terms, the conflict is between the superego which has lost its hold and the ego which makes new demands. It was only a decade later that Freud gave definitive shape to this discord with the work known in English as *Civilization and Its Discontents,* where he discussed the nature of the super-ego of a cultural epoch and even suggested that civilization is born of the conflicts between the superego and ego, adding that such conflict engenders of necessity a sense of guilt:

> The superego is an authority that we postulate, and conscience a function we ascribe to it, along with others – this function being to supervise and assess the actions and intentions of the ego, to exercise a kind of censorship. The sense of guilt [...] is the ego's perception of being supervised in this way, its assessment of the tensions between its own strivings and the claims of the superego.[2]

2 Sigmund Freud, *Civilization and Its Discontents* (London: Penguin, new edition 2004), p. 94.

Paolo, and the grotesque theatre of which he is one of the strongest representatives, operates at a moment when the relationships between the ego and the superego have broken down, when the ego claims authority to pass judgement on the superego and to dispute its right of control over human activities. The *programma* the superego seeks to impose now seems to the rebellious ego inadequate, deficient, irrelevant or simply absurd. Such moments are normally expressed in theatre by the ironical, satirical or comic approach. In the speeches quoted, Paolo, in his small way, arrogates to himself a role similar to that played in theatrical history by Figaro, the scoffing servant created by Beaumarchais, but it is such a comparison that will make the work appear slight. Paolo, or Luigi Chiarelli, experienced an uncertainty unknown to Figaro, or to such genuine contemporary rebels as Ibsen or Shaw. Having fearlessly declared himself an outsider and a rebel against the status quo, Paolo stuttered to silence when he sought to declare what he wanted to become. He and the wife with whom he had been reconciled know that remaining in society is now for them impossible, but when he comes to the point where he has to declare what he would like to become, the speech quoted above trails off into a series of faltering dots. Conveniently, his voice is at that point drowned out by a band striking up 'una marcia funebre di Chopin' in the street below. The march apparently breaks the flow of his thought and alters his mood. He and Savina, his wife who had betrayed him years before and who had returned after a long period of guilty exile in London, are moved by the music and when it dies away in the distance, Paolo turns to her in a gesture of forgiveness and renewed love. The two speak only each others' names, but this moment of tense emotion means that the grand declaration Paolo was about to make can plausibly evaporate, allowing for a pleasingly happy and melodramatic ending. Even the institution of marriage can be reinstated, but the audience is left wondering what Paolo would have liked to become after he had made clear his dissatisfaction with his society, its laws, his friends and their ways. But did Paolo know? Did Chiarelli?

In questions of this sort lie elements of the dissatisfaction many critics then and now have felt with the whole phenomenon known as *teatro grottesco*. It has become fashionable among contemporary Italian critics to talk of it with a certain condescension, or even to consider it unworthy of autonomous treatment. In her admirable work on Italian theatre in the early years of the twentieth century, Franca Angelini refers to the grotesque drama only *en passant*. She makes her only mention of it while discussing the *sintesi drammatiche* of Rosso di San Secondo: 'Siamo nell'ambito di quel "teatro in rivolta" che da noi va sotto il nome di "grottesco", che ci riconduce a quella immagine marionettistica dell'uomo tanto invisa ai critici [...]'.[3] Grotesque theatre deserves more detailed study than Angelini is prepared to grant it, but her words suggest two interesting lines of inquiry, the one involving the centrality of the 'immagine marionettistica dell'uomo' and the other the suggestion that grotesque theatre, while specific to Italy, can be regarded as part of a wider 'theatre of revolt', (to use the title of Robert Brustein's celebrated book),[4] a connection few Italian theatre historians have been willing to make. It is commonplace to establish the rebellion of the grotesque writers against bourgeois drama and the *pièce bien faite*, but the theatrical and moral parallels with the roughly contemporary Edwardian theatre of Arthur Wing Pinero, Henry Arthur Jones and even Oscar Wilde in Britain have been overlooked.[5] Chiarelli's admirers have always insisted both on the novelty of his enterprise, and also of his adherence to a purely Italian genealogy: '*La maschera e il volto* segna una data nella storia del teatro italiano. Non si tratta soltanto di un grande successo ma anche, e soprattutto, d'una svolta decisiva nel cammino della nostra letteratura drammatica, pur restando nei limiti della più pura tradizione italiana.'[6] The play, and grotesque theatre as a whole, can best be considered not in isolation but as part of a questioning theatre which, post-Ibsen, flourished in various European countries. The main issue for critics is to determine the nature and limits of the revolt that grotesque theatre represented. Gigi Livio, editor of the anthology of works which has attained canonical status, was oddly unencouraging: 'i grotteschi hanno messo sotto accusa il dramma borghese senza, d'altra parte, aver qualcosa di nuovo da contrapporgli [...]'.[7] The *dramma borghese* – and there is another critical cliché due for reconsideration – was undoubtedly a target of the grotesque writers, but Livio surely understates the innovative force of the new drama. For Livio, while the historical conditions denoted by the 'espressione sovrastrutturale' of the age, by which he means 'la decadenza del naturalismo e del dramma borghese', permitted the grotesque playwrights to sweep away the relics of the old styles, the conditions were not ripe for fundamental change.[8] The sub-Marxist jargon of superstructures and pre-revolutionary conditions no longer has the self-evident authority it had at the time Livio was writing, but his view that the grotesque writers were at best half-hearted reformers is widely held.

There is a curious clash between the current neglect of grotesque writers and the esteem in which they were once held, as shown by the vivacity of the debates

---

3 Franca Angelini, *Teatro e spettacolo* (Bari and Rome: Laterza, 2001), p. 25. **4** Robert Brustein, *The Theatre of Revolt: An Approach to Modern Drama* (Boston: Little Brown, 1964). **5** Ian Clarke, *Edwardian Drama* (London: Faber, 1989). **6** Domenico de Vic Beamish, *Introduzione* to *La maschera e il volto* (Milan: Treves, 1931), pp. xi–xii. **7** Livio, p. xiii. **8** Livio, p. xiii.

unleashed by them in their own time. Indeed, it may be that there is a fuller contemporary record of their productions than, perhaps, of those in any other period of Italian playwriting. Critics and reviewers of keen insight included Silvio D'Amico (1887–1955), tireless theatrical reformer, Adriano Tilgher (1887–1941), the philosophical critic who influenced Pirandello by his interpretation of his plays, the poet Vincenzo Cardarelli (1887–1959), and the playwright Marco Praga (1862–1929). All were regular reviewers for periodicals, as were such political-philosophical thinkers as Antonio Gramsci (1891–1937), and Piero Gobetti (1901–26), the theorist of Liberal Revolution. Journalists who were also critics of high talent and who commanded attention in the world of theatre included Ettore Albini (1891–1925) and Renato Simoni (1875–1952). And of course the old jibe can be repeated that no country erects statues to critics, but at that time the division between creativity and criticism was more finely drawn than would be the case in successive ages. Such grotesque playwrights as Rosso di San Secondo, Antonelli and Chiarelli were later to earn their living as critics.

It may or may not have been to their advantage that their works were premièred in what now looks like a golden age of theatre criticism in Italy, but it is a fact that these critics fell on the new drama with zeal. Precisely because of their intellectual authority, they each departed from a *parti pris* of their own and saw in the new playwrights representatives of the reforms they most eagerly advocated or of the defects they most thoroughly abominated. The stance of Marco Praga, a playwright normally classified as a representative of Victorian age *teatro borghese* and certainly no proponent of radical change in theatrical matters, is hardly surprising but he spoke for many contemporaries when in a review of Enrico Cavacchioli's *L'uccello del paradiso*,[9] he dismissed not only him but the aims of the grotesque dramatists in general. Speaking in tones of weariness, he wondered how genuinely innovative they were:

> [...] è una vecchia, assai vecchia commedia. Vecchia nella favola, nelle vicende, negli episodi, nella costruzione, nella tecnica: vecchia nei tipi e nei caratteri [...]; io sono qui a domandare come mai il Cavacchioli, senza trasformare di molto una vecchia favola, senza avere osservato da un punto di vista nuovo una vecchia situazione drammatica, senza aver nulla innovato nella tecnica [...] sia riuscito [...] ad apparire un innovatore, a mettersi nella schiera di coloro che si presentano a noi quali i riformatori della scena italiana.[10]

9 First performance, Carignano, Turin, 19 March 1919. First publication, with introduction by Renato Simoni, Milan, Mondadori, 1920. 10 Marco Praga, review dated 24 June 1919,

Enthusiasts included Gramsci and Gobetti, but while it is interesting to revisit old battlefields, it is more important to enquire whether the grotesque playwrights are due for revision in their own right, not merely as interesting contemporaries of Pirandello. In the first place, they were genuine theatre reformers. The period around World War One was a moment of renewal and innovation in Italian theatre. Succeeding years saw lively debates between writers and critics over the (variously denominated) new and the old. In addition to the emergence of grotesque theatre, other signs of vitality included the Futurist manifestos, notably the 1913 manifesto on Variety Theatre, and the Futurists' own anarchic performances, or *sintesi,* in various Italian cities in 1915–16. The main exponents of the 'Theatre of Revolt' in Europe were plainly Ibsen and Strindberg, whose impact was felt deeply in Italy, but the grotesque writers, while not having the depths of the Scandinavians, advocated innovation in theatre while also giving voice to a malaise in social custom which was being made apparent on the stages of all Europe. They may not have had the iconoclastic boldness of the early *avant-garde,* preferring to remain within more familiar parameters, but they were innovators.

By general consent, the *teatro del grottesco* was born on 29 May 1916, the date of the premiere in Rome of *La maschera e il volto*. It did not have a long life, and has more than once been referred to as a 'meteor' whose brightness was extinguished by the middle of the following decade. The description 'grotesque' was arbitrary, although no more so than now accepted terms used for other aesthetic movements such as the Baroque or Romantic. It has no connection with the Renaissance sense of the word, deriving from the discovery in the days of Raphael of bizarre paintings in the *grotte* under the Domus Aurea of the Emperor Nero, nor even with that richer and deeper meaning where it indicates misalliances and distortions of convention, reason and expectation in, for example, Shakespeare's comedies. Bottom was a grotesque character in an older sense of the word. At a later stage, Victor Hugo used the term polemically in his preface to *Cromwell* to denote a rejection of romantic ideas of the sublime. Chiarelli adopted the word much more casually. At a time when dramatists were reluctant to use the standard word *commedia*, Chiarelli subtitled his work 'a grotesque in three acts', and the term became generic.

There was never any manifesto of grotesque theatre, nor is there any agreed definition nor, as is the case with virtually all artistic movements excepting the Pre-Raphaelite Brotherhood, any canonical list of exponents. It was never a school, nor did it have designated bars or haunts where the zealots met. While

now reprinted in *Cronache teatrali del primo Novecento* (Florence: Nuovedizioni Enrico Vallecchi, 1979), pp. 20–1.

there is no doubt that what divides them is at least as significant as what unites, Luigi Chiarelli (1880–1947), Enrico Cavacchioli (1885–1954), Luigi Antonelli (1882–1942) and Pier Maria Rosso di San Secondo (1887–1956) are commonly identified as demonstrating the grotesque approach, with Massimo Bontempelli (1878–1960) and Luigi Pirandello (1867–1936) having, it is thought, a more tenuous connection with a club whose existence was in any case purely imaginary. None of the writers in question was 'grotesque' for his entire career, most obviously in the case of Pirandello, but also with Antonelli whose first major production, *La campana d'argento* was staged in 1909, and who had a long, commercially and aesthetically successful career in theatre. The same could be said of Bontempelli, who was described as displaying traits of 'magical realism' in the 1920s, long before the term was applied to South American writers. Enthusiasts for the theatre of Rosso di San Secondo are anxious to underline the idiosyncratic nature of his poetic theatre and his debts to the Sicilian tradition, while Antonelli did the job of dissociation for himself: 'io non ho mai partecipato a gruppi, non mi sono mai messo insieme con altri, ho fatto tutta la mia strada da solo. E chi mi ha messo tra gli scrittori del grottesco e chi mi ha assegnato ad altri gruppi, non ha seguito, né letto, né capito il mio teatro.'[11] These words were written very much as a post-factum act of self-aggrandizement. Antonelli elsewhere claimed to have been the genuine 'onlie begetter' of the complex of attitudes and ideas that later was known as 'grotesque'. In a letter of 13 March 1942 to Silvio D'Amico he requested him to bear in mind 'ciò che io rappresentai quando non c'era Pirandello e cominciai con un lavoro che scombussolò una quantità di gente (*Il convegno,* 1914) quando era di là da venire *La maschera e il volto'*. It is true that Antonelli went his own way and developed a style of his own, but at the time of the staging of his masterpiece, *L'uomo che incontrò se stesso,* he accepted being viewed as a 'scrittore grottesco'.[12] He did, however, have some reservations over the interpretation of the play by the *capocomico,* Antonio Gandusio. In the same letter to D'Amico, he made the point: 'Così che al mio *Uomo che incontrò se stesso* hai attribuito atteggiamenti e deviazioni farsesche perchè l'hai visto rappresentare da Gandusio.'[13]

Gandusio was a celebrated *brillante* of the time, and the use of the reproachful term 'deviazioni' raises the question of the intended role of laughter in the vision of Antonelli and other grotesque writers. However, any attempt at a definition of what constituted the grotesque would have to contain many caveats

11 Luigi Antonelli, *Lo scrittore si confessa,* introduction to *L'uomo che incontrò se stesso e altre commedie* (Rome: Edizioni italiane, 1942), p. 270. 12 First performance in *Teatro Olympia,* Milan, 23 May 1918. First publication, Milan, Treves, 1919. 13 The letter is now in the Fondo D'Amico in the Civico Museo Biblioteca dell'Attore del Teatro Stabile di Genova.

and lists of exceptions, as is the case with definitions of other cultural movements, but Giorgio Pullini, a sympathetic and perceptive commentator of the phenomenon, made a valiant effort:

> Con 'grottesco' si intende indicare una visione deformata della realtà in cui, sulla legge della verosomiglianza assoluta, regolata dal principio dell'esperienza quotidiana e della sua credibilità, prevale la forza ironica, ora critica ora parodistica, di una tesi anticonformista dell'autore. Si scavalca, cioè, il canone pressoché imprescindibile dell'oggettività come impersonalità [...] per portare in primo piano la voce del drammaturgo [...] addirittura attraverso l'ammissione sulla scena di un personaggio che commenti l'azione e la svisceri dall'interno nelle sue contraddizioni [...].[14]

If it is acceptable to offer a summary, and necessarily inadequate, list of the characteristics of grotesque drama, these would include: a visceral distaste for Victorian or bourgeois drama in all its manifestations, leading to a demand for reform in theatre as well as in society; a dissatisfaction with naturalist or *verista* theatre, in particular for the invisibility of the author theorized by Zola, and in consequence a desire to put the author centre-stage, at least via the figure of the *raisonneur*; a preference for – mild – irony or satire; a wish to abolish the distinction between tragedy and comedy leading to the attempt to treat putatively tragic subjects as comedy; an interest in the dramatic potential of the puppet; a focus on the clash between mask and face.

The grotesque writers are now considered to have operated under the benign shadow of Pirandello, but it is worth bearing in mind that it was only post-1916 that Pirandello's acknowledged theatrical masterpieces appeared. Pirandello's now universally accepted superior status was not always apparent to contemporary critics. Gramsci, who reviewed theatre regularly for *L'Avanti,* referred in a 1918 piece to the 'gruppo degli innovatori: Pirandello, Chiarelli, Antonelli'.[15] *Pensaci, Giacomino!* and *Liolà* were staged in 1916, the same year as *La maschera e il volto.* The premiere of *Così è (se vi pare)* took place the following year. It was not until 1921 that *Sei personaggi in cerca d'autore* was produced, but it is with *Pensaci, Giacomino!* that Pirandello first dramatizes the clash between private convictions and public convention, or between mask and face or even between ego and superego, that was to be characteristic of both his more mature work, and of grotesque theatre.

14 Giorgio Pullini, *Teatro contemporaneo in Italia* (Florence: Sansoni, 1974), pp. 4–5. See also his *Teatro italiano fra due secoli, 1850–1950* (Florence: Parenti, 1957), pp. 269–313. 15 Quoted by Guido Davico Bonino, *Gramsci e il teatro* (Turin: Einaudi, 1972), p. 84.

If there is much, for instance, in the fascination with the concept of masks and the conflict between the 'face and the mask', that links Pirandello with the others, the differences are equally profound. In Pirandello, the mask/face clash indicates a deep existential dilemma, since behind the mask there is no more than another mask, meaning that it will never be possible to reach any authentic face, or personality. Personality is a series of guises, some assumed by the individual, others imposed on him by the circles who surround him, but none can be judged any more genuine or definitive than the other. This is the tragedy of the Father in *Sei personaggi*, haunted not by guilt but by the 'injustice' that his mask, and therefore his being, was determined by one demeaning encounter in a brothel with a woman who turned out to be his stepdaughter. For the writers of grotesque theatre, on the other hand, the mask is a more contingent matter. It denotes primarily the dominance of social convention, the enforced deference to society's civic code, etiquette and attitudes, but it leaves open the possibility that underneath the mask an authentic face expressing 'sincere' private conviction is concealed. As Gramsci wrote: 'La maschera: il complesso degli atteggiamenti esteriori che gli uomini assumono sotto lo stimolo della realtà sociale che li circonda. La maschera è la patina superficiale del costume, della moda, dello *snob,* il precipitato tra tutte le reazioni tra la vita individuale e la vita collettiva [...].'[16] The clash is deeper than the mere recognition and denunciation of hypocrisy, but characters in grotesque theatre who recognize the falseness of their situation lack the radical dissenting vision or capacity for heroic revolt of Ibsen's or Shaw's rebels. Grotesque and Edwardian theatre was tolerant of those who wished to continue to live in society and who were in consequence prepared to defer outwardly to its canons, an attitude displayed by the *habitués* of society salons in Oscar Wilde's *Lady Windermere's Fan* or *A Woman of No Importance.* They know that new standards are being proposed, especially for women, but they cannot quite comply with them: their dilemma over the conflicting pull of both the mask and the face is real and urgent.

Pirandello also shared the distaste for nineteenth-century, or bourgeois, playwriting which is perhaps the most immediately identifiable trait of grotesque theatre. The decorum, the gentility, the endorsement of codes of ethical, political, social and sexual assumptions which marked plays such as *I mariti* (1867) by Achille Torelli (1841–1922), where Emma learns her obligations to her husband, were in those years the subject of ironic treatment. The rebelliousness of the grotesques should not be overstated. G.K. Chesterton spoke of the culture of the turn of the century as the 'Victorian compromise', and that remains per-

---

16 Quoted by Guido Davico Bonino, p. 92.

haps the best description of a theatrical output based not on corrosive satire, scorn or rejection but on a detached irony and disbelieving humour that suggested that old attitudes are passing but have not entirely disappeared. The self-assured Victorian patriarchs who ruled their homes like their factories may have given way to a more irreverent breed without the dogmatic convictions of their forebears, but the characters who represent the new generation on stage were unsure of how to rid themselves of old nostrums. The mood marks such English plays as Arthur Wing Pinero's *The Second Mrs Tanqueray* as much as Italian grotesque drama.

The 'woman question' dominated grotesque theatre as it did English Edwardian theatre. The conflict in Chiarelli's *La maschera e il volto* concerns the eternal triangle of husband-wife-lover and the appropriate treatment of the wife guilty of infidelity, this being a more serious problem in Mediterranean society than in Edwardian England. The wronged husband is Count Paolo Grazia, and it is worth underlining his aristocratic status. None of the grotesque playwrights shared the ambition of Shaw or Ibsen to expand the range of social classes considered suitable for the stage. There is once again a parallel with the Edwardian Pinero: 'I think you would find, if you wanted to write drama, not only that wealth and leisure are more productive of dramatic complications than hard work, but that if you want to get a certain order of ideas expressed or questions discussed, you must go pretty well up the social scale.'[17] The characters in grotesque drama are indeed 'pretty well up the social scale'. None of them has to bother himself with the demands of industrial society. The arena in which the clash between new and old moralities is to be contested is the field of sexual ethics, or the attitudes to be adopted by the husband towards the errant wife. It may be worth noting that all the grotesque writers were, like Pirandello, from Sicily or the Mezzogiorno, where the *delitto d'onore* was more commonly sanctioned by wont and habit, as well as by law. Paolo, under no provocation, makes the wholly casual statement that if Savina, his wife, were caught *in flagrante* with another man, he would of course kill her: 'd'altronde, è una cosa che si sa, questa' (Act I, p. 4). He offers no further defence of his beliefs or of his intended conduct. This is, in other words, the code to be followed, the code followed on Italian stages throughout the Victorian age. However, Paolo's motivation is not an adherence to the code of honour as such, but a fear of ridicule: 'un marito che perdona è ridicolo, cento volte ridicolo. Non esiste nulla di peggiore del ridicolo' (Act I, p. 5). Almost by accident, he discovers that his wife had been in fact betraying him with his closest friend, but when faced with this cri-

17 William Archer, *Real Conversations* (London: John Murray, 1904), pp. 21–2.

sis, he cannot bring himself either to carry out his threats or to face the loss of prestige in public. The couple connive to allow Savina to flee to London, leaving him free to claim that in a fit of passionate jealousy he had drowned her in Lake Como. No jury is willing to convict a man for a crime of passion, so after a period in jail awaiting trial, Paolo returns home a hero, to discover that a woman's body, presumed to be that of Savina, has been found in the lake. The body is duly identified by Paolo, but at that point Savina herself returns. Having been cleared of murder, Paolo now finds himself facing imprisonment for having made false reports of murder to the police. The couple rediscover their old love, and run off together, and so in however paradoxical a way, family values are upheld even if the iron demands of the honour code are undermined.

Chiarelli is no Ibsen, so Savina is no Nora from *Doll's House,* nor is Paolo a Dr. Stockmann who in *An Enemy of the People* comes to relish standing wholly alone. The originality of the play lies in part in the questioning of previously held social standards, but also in the merger of dramatic genres and categories. (Strangely enough, Ibsen had written to Hegel in 1882 that he was unsure whether to call *An Enemy of the People* 'a comedy or simply a play: it has much of the character of a comedy, but there is also a serious basic theme.)[18] Comedy and tragedy came together in Chiarelli's work, but there are elements of compromise in this position, which is far from 1950s black comedy. There are even doubts over whether Chiarelli really aimed at that mixture of genres. Marco Praga wrote in his memoirs that Chiarelli had written *La maschera e il volto* as a work of serious drama, and wished it staged as such until Virgilio Talli drew his attention to the vein of iconoclastic comedy present in his writing.[19] This anecdote, which indicates the same dilemmas Antonelli had over Gandusio's staging of his work, has been challenged, but it does seem likely that Chiarelli sleepwalked into the new mixed style. However, he caught the mood of the moment with a humour which conceals seriousness and is deep enough to accommodate what were once seen as tragic themes and impulses. Rosso di San Secondo too would insist that the plight of the characters of *Marionette, che passione!* should not 'dar luogo al comico, bensì a un sentimento di tragico umorismo'.[20] There is no need to labour the fact that Pirandello's theory on *umorismo* was of the same stamp.

This authorial control was itself innovative, and grotesque theatre can be viewed as the one of the rare moments in Italy's theatre history when power was in the hands of playwrights, rather than of actors or directors. A reaction to the undue power of actors had been in the air, and it is not surprising to find

---

18 Michael Meyer, *Ibsen* (London: Penguin, 1985), p. 520.   **19** The anecdote has been often retold, and is quoted in Livio, p. viii.   **20** Livio, p. 73.

that Silvio D'Amico, who was to call for the passing of that power in his pamphlet *Tramonto del grande attore,* was an enthusiast, even if a critical one.[21] Antonelli saw limits to his enthusiasm, and much later, in the already mentioned letter of 13 March 1942 to D'Amico, he rebuked him for giving inadequate weight to the script, expressing mock concern for D'Amico whose busy life as a critic meant that, he complained to D'Amico, 'non hai tempo di leggere i testi'. It may have been the merest banality applied to any other European stage, but in Italy with its specific, actor-centred traditions, those confident words on authors and scripts were novel, even revolutionary. While the grotesques were the only 'school' of authors Italy has produced, the paradox is that it emerged in the same period as the figure who was destined to eclipse the author in the theatrical hierarchy, the director.

The plays themselves show a self-conscious theatricality which was in line with what would later be tagged 'metatheatricality'. The characters are conscious of playing roles, of being part of some fiction and of acting out parts in a life-comedy which is not altogether coherent. Attention is also very deliberately drawn to the writer's perspective. The *raisonneur,* a figure borrowed from French theatre, made his appearance, but was more of the on-stage *motor immotus* than merely an ironic commentator. Cavacchioli's *L'uccello del paradiso* (1919) contains a character known simply as *Lui,* a creator figure who moves in salons among men and women, offering advice and judgements but seemingly detached, in a dimension of his own. The ubiquity of the *raisonneur* is another symptom of the impatience and knowing irony with the theatrical conventions the grotesques demonstrated. Cavacchioli is given to the use of heavy imagery and overblown poetic diction to express this sense of bewilderment of characters in an unfamiliar cosmos. In *L'uccello del paradiso,* there is no avoiding the obvious symbolism of the activities of Giovanni Ardeo, the taxidermist who lives in a museum surrounded by stuffed birds and other artificial creatures. Life, as Pirandello would express it, has been forced into inappropriate forms, and this inappropriateness weighs heavily on Ardeo's estranged wife as she visits him and their daughter once a week. On one occasion Ardeo recounts the legend of the bird of paradise, an exotic creature in some oriental island, whose feet have been ripped off to prevent it touching ground, but which can fly above storms. Cavacchioli started his literary career with volumes of Futurist verse, but his characters in his grotesque period are not so much supermen as superior beings, continually striving for poetic effects.

21 Silvio D'Amico, *Tramonto del grande attore* (Milan: Mondadori, 1929). See also the same author's *Il teatro dei fantocci* (Florence: Vallecchi, 1920).

This sense of estrangement contributes to the puppet-like characterization which is another aspect of much grotesque drama. Interest in puppets and their potential use in theatre was widespread at the time, encouraged by the Futurists and by Edward Gordon Craig, who settled in Florence in 1908 and whose writings were enormously influential in this regard. He founded and edited a journal with the significant title *The Mask* (1908–29), propounding ideas which were given definitive form in his book, *The Marionette* (1918). The notion that theatrical character could really aspire to no more than the status of puppets was reinforced by the reaction against the quest for psychological depth which had been one of the cornerstones of nineteenth-century theatre. In some ways, the new characters, and not only in the theatre of the grotesque, were fashioned in accordance with the principles laid down by the Cubists in painting, for whom a painting was a work painted on a flat surface, hence bereft of any sense of depth or perspective. The figures who people the drama of Cavacchioli and Rosso di San Secondo are robotic, like puppets on a string, responding to stimuli they do not fully comprehend. Silvio D'Amico wondered if the new dramatists were no longer capable of believing in their own creatures.

This robotic quality is most evident in Pier Maria Rosso di San Secondo's *Marionette, che passione!*.[22] Rosso di San Secondo, as well as trying to create a poetic theatre, drew on German Expressionism, and in a prefatory 'note to the actors', felt it necessary to insist: 'Pur soffrendo, infatti, pene profondamente umane, i tre protagonisti del dramma, specialmente, sono come marionette, e il loro filo è la passione. Sono tuttavia uomini: uomini, ridotti marionette. / E dunque profondamente pietosi' (p.73). None of the characters is given a name. The three principal figures are identified only as *La signora dalla volpe azzurra, Il signore in grigio* and *Il signore a lutto*. While still strangers to each other, the three gather in a telegraph company office, where the first two strive in vain to compose messages to the errant partners who have abandoned them. They propose forming a new relationship with each other, but are roundly mocked for this idea by the third. All three remain together, ending up in a restaurant where in addition to their own table, they have the waiters set a table for 'i tre invitati che non verranno'. The woman's husband does come and she is uncomplainingly led off by him, an act which causes the *signore in grigio* to choose suicide over a desolate life. Inner motives are sketched out with the imprecision of a Punch and Judy show, for if these characters have an inner life, it is not one which is knowable to others. They act, they perform in ways which are mysterious and unaccountable, all the while speaking in forced lyrical tones. The

22 First performance, 4 March 1918, Teatro Manzoni, Milan, directed by Virgilio Talli. First publication, Treves, Milan, 1918.

themes, the pain and anguish the characters suffer may have been those experienced by figures in naturalist theatre, but naturalism and *verismo* have been
consigned to the past.

The most theatrically interesting and deftly imagined work, which was also
an attack on received ideas, came from Luigi Antonelli. One of his later works,
Il maestro, was directed by Pirandello with Marta Abba as female lead.[23]
However, his leading work of the grotesque period was undoubtedly *L'uomo
che incontrò se stesso*. In this play, Antonelli removed the conventional topics from
the expected context to place them in a wholly original fantasy dimension. The
play carries the subtitle, *Avventura fantastica in tre atti,* and is set *in un'isola al di
fuori della geografia*. His subject too was adultery but the touch of fantasy in his
writing recalls J.M. Barrie's drama: critics have likened the magic island where
the action evolves to Prospero's island, but the resemblance to an adult version
of Never-Never-Land is striking.[24] Dr Climt presides over an island outside
time, and there Luciano meets Sonia, his now dead wife, whose infidelity he
had discovered only when her body and that of her lover were dragged from
the wreckage of a building. His efforts to warn his younger self of the impending adultery are futile, although the elder Luciano had himself managed to seduce
the younger Sonia after their first meeting on the island.

Antonelli has a lightness of spirit and an imaginative panache which none
of the others achieved. The social questions the writers of grotesque theatre
debated belong now to another age, and they themselves look like adventurers
on the road to an El Dorado they had not quite the stamina to reach. However,
the theatrical fantasy linked to emotional pain in their work remains intriguing,
as does their use of comedy, whether that was due to them or to the collaboration with directors who enlarged the impact of their work. The respect they
commanded in their own lifetimes was not misplaced.

23 First performance, 19 December 1933, at Teatro Argentina, Rome. First publication,
Edizioni Italiane, Rome, 1939. 24 Luciano Paesani, *Luigi Antonelli e l'arte dell'attore* (Pescara:
Edizioni Campus, 2001), p.69. This work, in addition to an informative introduction, also
contains the text of *L'uomo che incontrò se stesso, La casa a tre piani* and *Il maestro*.

Eliot, Dante and *Four Quartets*: a pattern behind the pattern in 'Burnt Norton'

Doug Thompson

Ever since Eliot's first essay on Dante, in 1920,[1] critics have invariably felt obliged to signal their awareness of the latter's influence on his work. Where comment has been incisive it has tended to focus on ways Eliot borrowed from, cited, echoed, or emulated Dante's style, a trend established in Mario Praz's 'T.S. Eliot and Dante' (1937)[2] – an essay which preceded the composition of the *Quartets*, of which only 'Burnt Norton' had as yet been published.[3] There we learn that 'Eliot's indebtedness to Dante ranges from the quotation and the adaptation of single lines or passages to the deeper influence in concrete presentation and symbolism'. A little later, Praz offers half a dozen or so examples of 'actual quotations', before concluding

> But such passages need not detain us for long: one can find similar deft insertions in dozens of other poets. The shock of surprise they give us adds no doubt to the effect of the poem, but it is not from them that we can learn what Dante's influence has meant for Eliot.
>
> That influence is closely connected with Eliot's interpretation of Dante's allegory [...]. Clear visual images, a concise and luminous language: these are the two qualities of Dante Eliot has in mind.[4]

1 T.S. Eliot, 'Dante', in *The Sacred Wood: Essays on Poetry and Criticism* (London: Methuen, 1920 [1967]), pp. 159–71. 2 The essay was first published in *The Southern Review*, 2, 3 (1937); later in *The Flaming Heart: Essays on Crashaw, Machiavelli and Other Studies* (Gloucester, MA: Peter Smith, 1966). 3 A propos of 'Burnt Norton', Eliot wrote: 'There were lines and fragments that were discarded in the course of the production of "The Murder in the Cathedral". [...] However, these fragments stayed in my mind, and gradually I saw a poem shaping itself round them: in the end it came out as "Burnt Norton"'. The poem was published in his *Collected Poems, 1909–1935* (1936). He further explained: 'Even "Burnt Norton" might have remained by itself if it hadn't been for the war, because I had become very much absorbed in the problems of writing for the stage [...]. The war destroyed that interest for a time: [...] "East Coker" was the result – and it was only in writing "East Coker" that I began to see the *Quartets* as a set of four' (*New York Times Book Review*, 29 November 1953). Both cited in *T.S. Eliot, Four Quartets: A Casebook*, ed. by B. Bergonzi (London: Macmillan, 1969), p. 23. 4 Praz, p. 361, pp. 364–5.

There is no intention of contesting the validity of this argument, merely of underlining its overriding concern with aspects of poetic technique as the proper focal point for any investigation into the nature of the influence of the earlier poet upon the later.[5] In his 1950 lecture, 'What Dante means to me', Eliot himself confirmed and elaborated on these views, stressing Dante's supreme mastery of his 'craft' and his refinement and extension of the possibilities of expression of his 'language'. In this latter question he echoes 'Little Gidding', where he had used Mallarmé's notion of 'purifying the language of the tribe', of passing on to posterity 'one's own language, more highly developed, more refined, and more precise than it was before one wrote in it'.[6] In his 1929 essay, he had already made the connection between Dante and 'universal Latin', the 'highly developed literary Esperanto' of the Middle Ages which had put so much at Dante's disposal;[7] while in 1944, in 'What Is a Classic?' he had shown Virgil to be a parallel case, 'constantly adapting and using the discoveries, traditions and inventions of Greek poetry [...] this development of one literature, or one civilization, in relation to another, which gives a peculiar significance to the subject of Virgil's epic'.[8]

However, in his 1950 lecture, Eliot had also emphasized Dante's 'exploration of sensibility', by which he meant principally his ability to illuminate the whole range of human emotions. The poet, he argues, is essentially 'an explorer beyond the frontiers of ordinary consciousness [who] will only be able to return and report to his fellow-citizens, if he has all the time a firm grasp upon the realities with which they are already acquainted',[9] by which he means the realities of the material world. It is to this last characteristic, as much as to those identified by Praz, to which in *Four Quartets* Eliot himself aspires, the authoritative voice of the poet-seer, who reaches beyond the myriad accidents in the flow of time, to approach and illuminate the universal design whose patterns furnish the key to understanding the meaning and functions of all human experience within it.

In the final chapter of his *Dante and English Poetry*, dedicated to Eliot, Steve Ellis uses a quotation from Eliot's essay on John Marston as an epigraph: 'We perceive a pattern behind the pattern' and it is this which immediately alerts us

5 Before proceeding to an analysis of 'Burnt Norton' (of which the reader should ideally have a copy to hand), some of Eliot's own views on the importance (and influence) of Dante will be reviewed. **6** Originally, a talk given at the Italian Cultural Institute in London, 4 July, 1950, and subsequently published in *To Criticize the Critic, and Other Writings* (London: Faber and Faber, 1965), pp. 125–35 (p. 133). **7** See T.S. Eliot, *Selected Essays* (London: Faber and Faber, 1932 [1972]), pp. 237–77 (p. 239). **8** Originally, the Presidential address to the Virgil Society in 1944. First published by Faber in 1945 and subsequently in T.S. Eliot, *On Poetry and Poets* (London: Faber and Faber, 1957), pp 53–71 (p. 61). **9** Eliot, *To Criticize the Critic*, p. 134.

to his very different approach from that epitomized by Praz to defining the relationship between Dante's and Eliot's poetry.[10] We shall, in due course, return to this central tenet of 'pattern'. Ellis shows how both poets pursue the same essentially classical road, following a tradition first established by Virgil, speaking a universalizing language whose ultimate goal is the reconciliation of all apparently contradictory parts in the One.

It is axiomatic that a radical shift in our common perception of the relationship of 'spiritual' to 'natural' has taken place in the six centuries that separate Dante and Eliot, and although this shift is emphasized in Eliot's own experience of the contemporary world and his presentation of it, Ellis makes no attempt to explain it, indeed berates Eliot for his presumed failure to take proper account of the concerns of this world, as Dante had done. Dante, however, was writing for an age in which few seriously doubted the temporal and physical continuities between this world and that which followed physical death, and Dante himself saw that continuum as a seamless whole, whereas Eliot saw his context as an 'immense panorama of futility and anarchy',[11] in which spiritual matters were the serious concern of an ever-diminishing minority. The psychological gap his persuasion had to leap was emphatically much wider than that which faced Dante, for whom the Church and the Empire (at least, in theory) together embraced the spiritual and the temporal in their complementary tutelary roles. What Dante could safely take for granted, Eliot had to seek to rehabilitate – that unity which Dante well understood but which, in Eliot's view, Humanism (and its concomitant 'dissociation of sensibility') had sundered. Eliot argued that it is not 'the method of Dante [which] is obsolete [rather] that our vision is perhaps comparatively restricted'.[12] Like Dante, Eliot wishes to 'reach / into the silence [...] reach / the stillness' of the Eternal, and like Dante, he is continually bringing us back to this earthly life, recognizing that that is our point of departure and must be lived through as the only available, uncompromising road to Beatitude, because life itself is a 'refining fire' in which we, at best, will move from love as desire to Love as peace and harmony. 'In my beginning is my end', he acknowledges, as he resumes the concerns of 'Burnt Norton' in 'East Coker', where 'end' carries the dual significance of physical death and beyond that, the ultimate goal, which is the Eternal.

The starting point of Eliot's 1920 essay on Dante is a reproof for a quasi-Crocean Valéry who, among other things, had recently affirmed that 'Parler

10 S. Ellis, *Dante and English Poetry, Shelley to T.S. Eliot* (Cambridge: Cambridge UP, 1983). 11 The statement comes from Eliot's review of Joyce's *Ulysses*: 'Ulysses, Order and Myth' in *The Dial*, 75, 5 (November 1923), pp. 480–3 (p. 483). 12 Eliot, 'Dante' (1920) in *The Sacred Wood*, p. 171.

aujourd'hui de poésie philosophique [...], c'est naïvement confondre des conditions et des applications de l'esprit incompatibles entre elles.' It was, rather,
according to Eliot's reading of Valéry, the poet's task to endeavour 'to produce
in us a *state*' – and by 'state' Eliot clearly understood 'emotional state'.[13] Dante
is called upon to illustrate the utter unacceptability of both these assertions, since
in Dante (Eliot counters) 'the philosophy is essential to the structure [while] the
structure is essential to the poetic beauty of the parts'. What Eliot finds is that

> no emotion is contemplated by Dante purely in and for itself. The emo-
> tion of the person, or the emotion with which our attitude appropriately
> invests the person, is never lost or diminished, is always preserved entire,
> but is modified by the position assigned to the person in the eternal
> scheme, is coloured by the atmosphere of that person's residence in one
> of the three worlds. [...] If the artistic emotion presented by any episode
> of the *Comedy* is dependent upon the whole, we may proceed to inquire
> what the whole scheme is [...]. This structure is an ordered scale of
> human emotions [...]. Dante's is the most comprehensive, and the most
> *ordered* presentation of emotions that has ever been made.[14]

To justify the necessity of this 'ordering' of human emotions in art, Eliot explains
that the reader's 'state' is *not* the emotions evoked in the poem but rather his
own particular mode of perceiving 'what the poet has caught in words'.[15] Those
words, at least in Dante, imply a whole philosophy in which emotions are precise indicators of moral positions within a universal hierarchy. Eliot is also very
clear about Dante's motivation – 'certainly the *Comedy* is in some way a "moral
education"', he affirms, citing Dante's own coupling of poetry and didacticism
in the *Convivio*: 'the principal design [...] is to lead men to knowledge and
virtue'.[16] Already, by 1920, Eliot is affirming the subordination of emotion to
an all-embracing philosophy which, in its turn, provides the structure of a didac-
tic poem, and in this he is citing Dante as supreme authority and exemplar. In
his 1929 essay, Eliot was to return to this idea of the displacement of emotion-
for-its-own-sake as the central concern of the poet: 'From the *Purgatorio*', he

---

13 Eliot, 'Dante', in *The Sacred Wood*, pp. 159–60 for this and for the following quotation.
14 Ibid., pp. 167–8.   15 In 'Tradition and the Individual Talent' (*The Sacred Wood*, pp. 47–59),
Eliot affirms that 'Poetry is not a turning loose of emotion, but an escape from emotion; it
is not the expression of personality, but an escape from personality' (p. 58). In 'The Possibility
of a Poetic Drama', in the same volume (pp. 60–70), he addresses the question of the balance of 'intellect' and 'feeling' in a work of literature, arguing for the essentially purifying
function of the former (pp. 64–65).   16 Quoted by Eliot in English, *The Sacred Wood*, p. 164.

observes, 'one learns that a straightforward philosophical statement can be great poetry; from the *Paradiso*, that more and more rarefied and remote *states of beatitude* can be the material for great poetry'.[17] Here, we have in essence, not only Eliot's view of Dante's unerring purpose and method, but the future framework of *Four Quartets*.

Four Quartets, Steve Ellis suggests, 'project temporality as a necessary evil, and seem [...] to adopt a more or less uncompromising non-humanist, non-vitalist and non-immanentist position',[18] which is not wholly wrong with regard to Eliot and not wholly right in the case of Dante. Natalino Sapegno's perspective, I think, comes much nearer the mark:

> It is clear that Dante's position, his starting point, contains a fundamental dichotomy. On the one hand, there is an attitude of antithesis and rejection regarding the world he sees in decay, cast into disorder and chaos,[19] be it from the viewpoint of doctrines or from the viewpoint of institutions. On the other hand, there is an attitude of intense participation because Dante clearly does not base his rejection on disinterest or indifference. His rejection is passionate and engagé; there is always implicit in it the desire for renewal, the quest for some way of changing the pattern of decadence.[20]

Eliot's position is not dissimilar. Sapegno continues:

> If we wished to draw up a kind of chart of the diverse evolution of these two attitudes of rejection and participation, we could say that the sense of participation and commitment, the outspoken invectives against the reality of his time, while strongest at the beginning and constituting the first stimulus and basis from which the inspiration arose, becomes gradually mitigated. In the last *cantica*, it gives place to an attitude not of indifference but of authoritative detachment, in virtue of which the invectives of the *Paradiso* (for we find them there, too) have a different accent. They are voiced by saints and therefore are characterized by a tone of

---

17 Eliot, *Selected Essays*, p. 252.   **18** See Steve Ellis, *The English Eliot: Design, Language and Landscape in 'Four Quartets'* (London: Routledge, 1991), p. 68.   **19** Compare Eliot's own observation on his times, cited in note 3.   **20** For the entire quotation see Natalino Sapegno, *Introduzione alla 'Divina Commedia'. Le lezioni di Cambridge e di Yale*, ed. by Bruno Germano, introduced by Giuseppe Mazzotta (Torino: Aragno, 2002), pp. 74–5. The original Italian precedes on pp. 45–7. The editor has changed 'confuse' to 'correlate', the former being a misleading translation of Sapegno's *confondersi*.

authority, severity, and remoteness. They no longer have the violence and impetus of the invectives of the *Inferno*, where Dante comes to correlate the reality of the Infernal life with the reality he was witnessing around him on earth [something which Eliot does, as we shall see, in the third movement of 'Burnt Norton']. In the framework of the passions and Infernal disorder, Dante saw mirrored exactly the confusion and anarchy of the contemporary conditions of Italy and Europe. [...] It is therefore in the *Paradiso* that we see this refusal [Dante's rejection] assume its most precise and marked form – that of detachment from the ephemeral world. [...] With this growing detachment come the pages of the *Paradiso* where Dante contemplates from on high this little globe, this wretched earth that is nothingness compared to celestial reality and yet is so bloodied by human strife, ' the threshing floor that makes us so ruthless' ('*l'aiuola che ci fa tanto feroci*').

The further Dante's journey draws him away from the Earth the less he is concerned with its particularities, becoming ever more involved in understanding the larger patterns – physical and doctrinal – which govern it and the Universe of which it is a part. It is this detachment from the transient, in order to seek the wholeness of the design, that Eliot quite deliberately emulates.

Eliot, however, does not try to rewrite the *Commedia*. *Four Quartets* has nothing like its scope, even if written with its vast panorama very much in mind. *Four Quartets* does not represent a first-person, narrative journey nor does it have that sense of physicality nor heavy emphasis on sin which the first part of Dante's allegorical journey, in particular, necessarily imposes. The *Quartets* are rather a series of linked meditations upon the relationship of spiritual exile in the physical, post-Edenic world, which is subject to the seemingly linear movement of time, with Eternity, which lies beyond the physical and which is therefore not subject to time's laws. Time is a process of endless flux (and, for the vast majority of human beings, of movement and desire, literally of rest-less-ness); Eternity is endless fixity-in-motion, and it is from this apparently contradictory, irreconcilable difference that the two principal, informing sets of images in the *Quartets* are derived – images of motion and images of stillness. Human kind, caught by its dual nature – the Aristotelian-medieval notion of *anima naturalis* and *anima rationalis* – between the physical and the instinctive on the one hand, and the ideational on the other, constantly seeks assurance that the afterlife is not merely idea but has its own, very special kind of reality. As an exercise in Christian exegetics – which the eventual *Four Quartets* consciously became – part of its function is to propose and illustrate the likelihood of the reality of Eternity in

God through different manifestations of the intersection of the timeless with time, the supernal with the natural; through events which are so untypical of the total worldly context in which they occur that they may be taken as 'signals' from, and evidence of, that other world. For Dante too, nature and natural things are no less rooted in, and orientated towards, God than is the supra-natural. Theologically speaking, in order to exalt grace it is a mistake to scorn nature, since with the Incarnation, which is central to Eliot's final sense of reconciliation in 'Little Gidding', the two are made one. 'The *Paradiso*', in particular, as Christopher Ryan observes, 'frequently couples these two sources of the human being's [...] fulfillment, creation and the Incarnation.'[21]

'Burnt Norton', which was written as entire and complete in itself, is a poem which, in Sapegno's scale of values, comes much closer to the Dante of the *Paradiso* than of the *Inferno*. There is neither the intense passion nor the sense of drama of the first *cantica*; that had belonged, of course, to the much earlier 'infernal' phase in Eliot's writing, encompassed by particularly *The Waste Land* and *The Hollow Men*. 'Burnt Norton' – and subsequently the whole of the *Four Quartets* – assumes the possibility of salvation at the outset, so that the poet's principal task is to show how that possibility is signalled in the flow of time, and to seek out a pathway, a *diritta via*, from time to the Timeless, which will speak to the contemporary world in crisis.

The poem begins, quite unlike the *Commedia*, with no direct reference to the poet's present (albeit allegorized) circumstances, but rather with a characteristic ten lines of impersonal philosophizing on the nature of the relationship between time and experience – lived or unlived. Logic would seem to tell us that if there is no time other than the present, then 'All time is unredeemable' – it can never be recovered and never be compensated for. This is arguably the most arid, because the most pessimistic, moment in the whole poem. Yet, in 'Ash Wednesday' (1930), which parallels, draws on, and finally admits as possible the processes which Dante describes in the *Purgatorio*, Eliot had already come upon a formula which did indeed seem to 'Redeem the time, redeem the dream' (Part IV). What could 'Burnt Norton' add to this?

There then follows a sequence of eight lines ('Footfalls echo in the memory') which, though using 'we', 'your', 'I', and 'my', might well nevertheless uphold the impersonal, generalized nature of the discourse hitherto, between the poet and his unknown readers. Yet these pronouns and possessives could equally well be personal references, a parallel discourse between the poet and another person (or persons), who had shared the possibility of an unrealized

---

21 See Christopher Ryan, 'The Theology of Dante', in *The Cambridge Companion to Dante*, ed. by Rachel Jacoff (Cambridge: Cambridge UP, 1993), pp. 136–52 (p. 149).

experience with him at some unstated time in the past. Eliot's visit to the garden at Burnt Norton, probably in the late summer of 1934, in the company of Emily Hale, with whom years earlier he seems to have had a close, perhaps even loving relationship, may – as Lyndall Gordon has suggested – provide a key to a deeply personal vein running through this first poem, even though it is never revealed overtly.[22]

Dante's *Commedia* explores what *did* happen as a result of the choices individuals actually made in their earthly lives, and the eternal consequences of those choices in very different kinds of life-in-death. Eliot, however, embarks on an admittedly unpromising recollection and examination of what, though declared 'unredeemable', are the choices *which could have been made, but were not*, 'the what might have been', a form of death in life, of which 'a bowl of rose leaves' is a singularly impressive image, whose symbolic features will reverberate back and forth in the rest of the opening sequence – indeed, throughout the eventual *Quartets* as a whole. Like Dante, Eliot has suddenly transported his poem into another world that lies beyond the physical, and it too, like Dante's, is a 'world of speculation'.

What is the nature of the experience in the garden? We are lured in by a guide, impersonal though animate, a thrush, often regarded as the sweetest singer of all birds, in search of 'other echoes'; though we are reminded that this sweet sireing is itself a 'deception'. But then, with the movement into the garden, the discourse takes on the studied ambiguity of allegory and myth. In what sense are we entering 'our first world'? Is it that of 'general' childhood or that of two individual, earlier selves, or the period of an initial relationship between two individuals, or is it possibly that of mankind as a whole, the world of the Edenic Earthly Paradise, or indeed all of these reflected together?[23]

The following sequence tells us what is found there and something of the character of this garden of missed opportunities (17–39). The mysterious 'they' would seem to represent the 'other echoes' additional to the 'footfalls', and are perhaps the choices which could have been made but were not, the ghosts of

22 Lyndall Gordon, *Eliot's New Life* (Oxford: Oxford UP, 1988), pp. 45–50 in particular.
23 Dominic Manganiello suggests that this 'excursion into a world of speculation marks [...] a return to [Eliot's] original state as a child of Adam'. Like Dante in the Garden of Eden, the poet attempts to find his real self as 'it might have been', [see *T.S. Eliot and Dante* (London: Macmillan, 1989), p. 102], which seems likely enough, though more so for 'Burnt Norton' as an integral part of the *Quartets* than for the same poem in isolation, in 1935. It should also be noted that Eliot, in a letter to John Haywood dated 5 August 1941, suggested that 'our First world' was the world of childhood, and that it is not used with the theological implications which attend its use later in the *Quartets*. See Helen Gardner, *The Composition of Four Quartets* (London and Boston: Faber and Faber, 1978), p. 83.

past possibility. Nothing there is apparent to the senses – 'they' are 'invisible', the 'music' is 'unheard', the 'eyebeam' is 'unseen' – yet though the autumnal 'leaves' are 'dead', as the world of the *Commedia* is dead, the 'air' is strangely 'vibrant', energized and full of expectation, and the thrush-guide 'responds' to the silent music of possibility, while there is the strong *feeling* that the 'roses' are 'looked at'. This garden is enchanted; it is a place of transformations. Despite the earlier warning that 'all time is unredeemable', a connection is made between the 'what might have been' and the present – the moment of reading or remembering – through the mediation of words, especially description of the compulsions emanating from the 'music' and the 'roses', both of which will figure centrally in the conceptual transfigurations to follow throughout the whole of the *Quartets*, to bring us to redemption. Something resembling this oblique garden experience had already occurred in *The Waste Land*, and echoes both its language and its inability to grasp the lived experience sufficiently to give it a name:

> Yet when we came back, late, from the Hyacinth garden,
> Your arms full, and your hair wet, I could not
> Speak, and my eyes failed, I was neither
> Living nor dead, and I knew nothing,
> Looking into the heart of light, the silence.
>
> (*The Waste Land*, I, 37–41)

One text which may lie behind 'Burnt Norton', especially the first and second movements, is the twenty-third canto of *Paradiso*, that in which Beatrice brings Dante to the vision of 'le schiere / del triunfo di Cristo e tutto 'l frutto / ricolto del girar [delle] spere!' (19–21). Certainly, this canto is the origin of the 'crowned knot of fire' with which the *Quartets* will triumphantly end.[24] Nardi's gloss on this notion of 'frutto ricolto' is of particular interest for our purposes, for it points to the recurring pattern of generation on Earth, and its determining power:

> I cieli servono all'uomo, regolando con i loro movimenti la periodica generazione delle cose di quaggiù, predisponendo il corso della vita umana, iniziando i moti dell'animo, provvedendo con le varie influenze alla varietà degli ingegni e delle indoli.[25]

24 '[…] non ebber li occhi miei potenza / di seguitar *la coronata fiamma* / che si levò appresso sua semenza.' (118–20) Italics mine. **25** See B. Nardi, *Dante e la cultura medioevale* (Bari: Laterza, 1942), pp. 256–7, quoted in *La divina commedia, Paradiso*, ed. by N. Sapegno (Firenze: La Nuova Italia Editrice, 1985), p. 290. (The heavens are useful to man, as they regulate with

The concepts of heavenly influence through the whole scheme or pattern of the Universe and of man's life in time as a suffering exile,[26] are both of capital importance in the *Quartets*. But there are other points of possible influence; for example, Beatrice admonishes Dante, demanding to know:

> 'Perché la faccia mia sì t'innamora,
>   che tu non ti rivolgi al bel giardino
>   che sotto i raggi di Cristo s'infiora?
> Quivi è la rosa in che 'l verbo divino
>   carne si fece; quivi son li gigli
>   al cui odor si prese il buon cammino.'
>
> (*Paradiso*, XXIII, 70–5)

The connections made here, between the garden, the rose, the Word and the incarnation, are central to the structure and theology of 'Burnt Norton' and the *Quartets* as a whole.

The movement within the garden seems predetermined by its formal lay-out, bringing 'we' and 'they' to a point suggestive of a theatre, the 'box circle' (as Hugh Kenner first suggested – but which also evokes the evergreen of box-wood,[27] then the endlessness of the circle) in which movement itself is 'in a for-mal pattern', 'without pressure, over the dead leaves', indeed, 'in measure, like a dancer', as Eliot later expresses it in 'Little Gidding' (146), the intricate pat-terns which link us throughout our earthly lives with all that we might have done or been. Then the miracle occurs, made up of 'water out of sunlight', where 'the lotos rose' in 'the heart of light' – a hallucinatory experience, where in reality there was no water, no lotos, only 'dry concrete, brown edged', emphasizing yet again the 'deadness' of this garden of unfulfilled memories. Yet, what is described here is the central experience of this first movement, the first indication that the initial 'All time is unredeemable', though logically arrived at, may nonetheless have been too hasty a conclusion. The nature of time is more complex than the simple concatenation of past, present, and future will allow; the nature of reality more complex than the merely material or experi-ential. The transformations which take place are verbal but the experience they describe can be real enough, an experience which is determined by light, light

their movements the recurrent generation of things on earth, predisposing the course of human life, moving the spirit, and ensuring with their various influences the variety of human minds and inclinations.) **26** See 133–5 of this canto: 'si vive e gode del tesoro / che s'ac-quistò piangendo ne lo essilio / di Babillòn'. **27** Hugh Kenner, *The Invisible Poet: T.S. Eliot* (Methuen: London, 1960), p. 252.

seeming to be water which, through 'The surface glittered out of heart of light',[28] directly connects the manifestation of the mirage (the accident in time) with its source, the sun. Out of the deadness, through the mediation of a not uncommon experience of mirage, comes a reminder of the essential life-giving forces of water and sunlight, and furthermore, these together act as a mirror which reflects the *actuality* of 'they', the unrealized choices, and the growing suspicion that they may still remain as options. But then, for both Dante and Eliot, following the teaching of St Bonaventure, the whole universe is a mirror through which God may be seen and known.

This whole sequence seems to echo the 'river of light' passage in *Paradiso* XXX. 61–9, the 'river' itself a mirage, as Beatrice explains; but more importantly, Dante has the impression of a pool of light which is reflected from the very centre of the Heavenly Rose of the Empyrean, and in this pool he sees reflected 'quanto di noi là sù fatto ha ritorno' (114). Added to this mirroring of possibility is the symbolic further indication of the nature of that possibility in the coupling of 'lotos' and 'rose', firstly in expressing the surfacing of the lotos (noun + verb), secondly in juxtaposing two symbols of love, but of very different kinds (noun + noun).

The 'rose' has long symbolized sexual love in the Western poetical tradition, but the 'lotos' too has a very full history as a symbol, particularly in eastern religions and philosophies (of which Eliot was a knowledgeable student). In ancient Egypt, it emerged from the primeval ooze and from its calyx came the divine creator. Its blossoms, which opened at the touch of sunlight, were linked with the Sun god and the mythical emergence of light from the slime in which the universe began. In India, the lotos blossom is the most important symbol of spirituality and art, while Padma, its goddess, is closely linked with the conceptual world of water and fertility. In Buddhism, one of its manifestations, *Padma-nartesvara*, is literally 'the lord of the dance'; it is also a symbol of knowledge which leads out of the cycle of reincarnation to Nirvana. In all of this, like the rose in Dante – as he journeys from the *Vita nuova* to the Heavenly Rose of the *Paradiso* – the lotos is essentially an emblem of transformation from one state of being to another, which is purely spiritual in character, and is thus a particularly apt and

---

28 Note the expression 'the heart of light' which links this passage with that quoted earlier (p. 162) from *The Waste Land*. The origin of the expression is, of course, Conrad's 'heart of darkness'. Eliot's appropriation of the phrase is not merely an example of Praz's notion of the 'deft insertion', however. Its use here, in 'Burnt Norton', has particular purpose in underlining a pivotal moment, an epiphany. The aridity of the 'drained pool', its 'nothingness' and 'hope-lessness', is a moment at the 'heart of darkness'. The sudden appearance of the sun and its mirage instantaneously establish its opposite.

powerful image here, where Eliot, like Dante before him, is concerned to show how mankind is not the prisoner of time nor of physicality. More than this, he shows that it is principally through the non-physical aspects of our humanity that we are connected with the determining forces of all life.

It is more than likely that Eliot's personal relations, with Emily Hale and with the wife he had recently deserted,[29] hover over 'Burnt Norton'. Given Eliot's strong Christian convictions, he could not but feel that that desertion intensified his spiritual exile, and in these circumstances the stirrings of an old love, which seemed to promise consolation, though likely to be real enough, could no longer be physically realized since additionally, he had taken a vow of celibacy. His former relationship with Emily Hale, though not named, may therefore also be among the unrealized choices 'reflected in the pool' (of light).[30]

For Lyndall Gordon, the moment in the garden at Burnt Norton represents 'a replay of Dante's reunion with Beatrice on the verge of Paradise' – in a gar-den-like setting beside the river Lethe'.[31] Textually, the presence of 'water out of sunlight' may indeed hint towards the baptism into the 'new life' which fol-lows Dante's crossing of Lethe and his first meeting with Beatrice. Indeed, it appears that Eliot once discussed with William Force Stead 'the way that Dante's love for Beatrice passed over into love of God in the *Vita Nuova*' and that on that occasion he had confessed 'I have had that experience'.

However – and we must look at the words of the poem rather than specu-late beyond it – 'a cloud passed, and the pool was empty'. The moment is gone in which past possibilities seemed almost to flicker into present realities.

The bird-guide urges immediate departure and the reason given for this is that 'the leaves' (formerly described as 'dead') 'were full of children / Hidden excitedly, containing laughter'. The image is one of happy anticipation, so why is it then followed by the observation that 'human kind / Cannot bear very much reality', itself occasioning an even greater sense of urgency in the bird? It would seem to be a defining moment; the 'reality' we fear is perhaps double-sided: that we must relinquish the past as we would have had it then, if we had

---

29 On 17 September 1932, Eliot sailed for the USA to take up a one-year appointment as Norton Professor at Harvard. Effectively, this was the date of his separation from Vivienne. He had already planned to set in motion the legal proceedings for such a separation during his stay in America. It was during that same year that he re-established relations with Emily Hale.   **30** Here, incidentally, the notion of 'perpetual possibility / Only in a world of spec-ulation' (7–8) takes on, in retrospect, another sense, suggested by that of the Latin etymon, *speculum*, mirroring or reflecting or coming face to face with. As we shall see, the multiple possibilities of meaning inherent in individual words provide Eliot with one of his chief means of transforming states of being.   **31** For this and the further quotations in this para-graph see Lyndall Gordon, pp. 12–13.

chosen it, but that that very past can nevertheless point us to a different future from that which our present, lived experience would seem to promise, for the true nature of time itself has been exposed, not as sequence but as simultaneity. Eliot is indicating, I think, that the conjectural nature of the poem's opening statement (present and past 'Are both *perhaps* present in time future') has resolved itself into certainty – that the past and the future are *always* present, where 'present' is no longer merely the threshold between past and future, but rather an indication of the sempiternal. The 'end' to which the original statement 'pointed' was a terminus, a point of arrival, whereas the 'end' to which this final statement 'points' is a goal, the eternal which is constantly with us. Through the transformations effected in this first movement, Eliot makes us question our notions of time and reality, to make us see that time is only apparently linear and sequential, is rather, as it were, an eternal present, in which (as he will tell us in the next movement) there is 'concentration / Without elimination'; it is the same view Dante arrives at in *Paradiso*, XVII, for example, where we learn that God is 'il punto / a cui tutti li tempi son presenti' (17–18). What Eliot does in this first movement is to draw on a nucleus of myth – that of Man's 'first state' – and by filtering it through a selection of (chiefly) Dante's myths and symbols, he creates his own myth of the discovery of spiritual enlightenment and enrichment, already available to us in this material world.

The second movement begins with a fifteen-line lyric in a symbolist style, 'Garlic and sapphires in the mud', whose significance has been much debated. What it does is to demonstrate that there is an ever-recurring order within the natural flux, an order which, whatever its apparent existential discords, functions according to predetermined patterns in which everything is 'reconciled among the stars'. This, it need hardly be said, is a central theme in the *Commedia*, where the physical structure of the three realms of the afterlife is composed of concentric circles which, in their turn, both act as separate 'compartments' whose different categories of inhabitants are arranged according to theologically determined hierarchies, and impose on those same inhabitants a cyclic, not a linear mode of time and being.

The first two lines are dense with symbolic significance which breaks through the somewhat bizarre surface texture to offer confirmation of the direction the poem has taken in the first movement. The 'axle-tree' suggests both the chassis of a wheeled vehicle and the mythical tree which, because rooted in the earth but pointing towards the heavens, was widely interpreted in Medieval cosmology as the *axis mundi*, around which the cosmos was organized and rotated. This notion is continued a few lines further on with the suggestion of moving 'above the moving tree'. But the first sense too reinforces the notion of turning circularity, since the wheels each rotate on their own axle. The concept is soon to be picked up again in the second part of this second movement, in the conceit of the 'still point of the turning world', but perhaps it was already there in the first movement too, in the guise of time rather than space, with all time concentrated at a point, that of the eternal present. In these opening lines, the 'sapphire' too ought not to pass without comment since its blue colouring has traditionally been associated with the heavens and especially with the planet Venus. The sixteenth-century scientist Lonicerus maintains it makes people 'joyful, fresh, and devout', whereas Albertus Magnus, one of Dante's spiritual mentors, says it brings peace and harmony and makes those who have contact with it 'devout and pure in their relationship with God'.[32] The *Quartets* are full of examples of this sort of echo, though it does not matter overmuch if we fail to identify a significance in them all. Nevertheless, for each one whose correspondences we do recognize, the poem's direction and purpose become clearer still, its coherence being further confirmed.

It is perhaps worth pausing briefly to comment on Eliot's mode of discourse in these opening movements of 'Burnt Norton'. Ronald Bush's observations here seem particularly helpful:

> Entering the rose-garden, we are continually aware of an intrusive arrangement of words that resist the pull of the dream. [Its] syntax is elaborately controlled [and] is never allowed to break down. Instead [...] its disorder is simply a disorder of reference. That is why its language constantly asks us to cast a cold eye on experience and why we never have the sense of becoming part of a drama.[33]

There is indeed a certain disjointedness about the sense, as though the poet is talking about an 'absent' or withheld centre, but doing so in terms of fragments of worldly realities of whose cohesive relevance we, as yet, remain unaware. The sure, indeed powerful movement of the verse, with its emphatic four-beat stress, is disconcerting, paradoxical, continually hinting, perhaps, that we are 'having the experience but missing the meaning'.[34] As so frequently happens with the highly methodical Eliot, clues to his own technique are often found in his comments on other people's writing, and in a Preface written in 1931, he explained that:

---

32 See entry *Le Saphir* in <http://www.demeure-alanon.net/precieux.htm>, p. 7. 33 Ronald Bush, *T.S. Eliot: A Study in Character and Style* (Oxford: Oxford UP, 1984), p. 200.
34 Compare 'The Dry Salvages', line 93: 'We had the experience but missed the meaning'.

> Symbolism is that to which the word tends both in religion and in poetry;
> the incarnation of meaning in fact; and in poetry it is the tendency of
> the word to mean as much as possible. To find the word and give it its
> utmost meaning, in its place; to mean as many things as possible, to make
> it both exact and comprehensive, and really to unite the disparate and
> remote, to give them a fusion and a pattern with the word, [...] this is
> the mastery at which the poet aims.[35]

It is precisely Dante's 'polysemy' that is here described and which is so magi-
cally at work in 'Burnt Norton'.

The second part of the second movement (62–89) begins with an attempt
to express the notion of the ever-turning, ever-changing universe, and more
particularly the Earth within it, in terms of a revolving wheel, with its theoretical 'still point' around which all else turns. If, indeed, Eliot is thinking of Dante's
cosmography, then that 'still point' must be Love or God, since it is God's Love
which, in Dante's scheme, is the great driving force in the created world and
universe ('at the still point, there the dance is ...'). In *Paradiso* XXIV, 130–2, we
find Dante's profession of faith expressed in these terms:

> [...] Io credo in uno Dio
> solo ed etterno, che tutto 'l ciel move,
> non moto, con amore e con disio.

There is also a tentative explanation of the sort of experience we would find at
the 'still point' (70–8). Everything would fall into place, there would be 'release
from action and suffering, release from the inner / And the outer compulsion
[...] both a new world / And the old made explicit',[36] and so on; the transformation of life's anxieties into peace and harmony; just such an experience as Dante
had as he stood within that other 'wheel', the Heavenly Rose, in the Empyrean.

Following this conjecture, in line 79, comes an attempt to link this hypo-
thetical ecstasy (or 'consciousness', as Eliot prefers to call it) with the world of
sense, reminding us again that 'human kind / cannot bear very much reality':

> Yet the enchainment of past and future
> Woven in the weakness of the changing body,
> Protects mankind from heaven and damnation
> Which flesh cannot endure.   ('Burnt Norton', II, 79–82)

35 See the third edition of Harry Crosby, *Transit of Venus* (Paris: Black Sun Press, 1931), pp.
viii–ix. 36 This final line is possibly an echo of the penultimate line of *Paradiso*, XXIII: 'e
con l'antico e col novo concilio', which also suggests the later 'folded in a single party' of
'Little Gidding' (191).

Building on this idea of 'the enchainment of past and future' in the 'changing body', Eliot explains that the living of life in time 'allow(s) but a little consciousness' since 'To be conscious is *not* to be in time' (italics mine). This, of course, shifts the whole focus of the poem and its purpose, since it effectively affirms that reality (that of which we *would* become conscious at the 'still point') is not, after all, the temporal but the a-temporal or better, supra-temporal. Nevertheless, 'only in time can the moment in the rose-garden [...] / be remembered'. In order to reach reality it is necessary to live in, and through, time, since 'Only through time time is conquered'. Whatever emphasis Dante might place on the temporal in relation to the supra-temporal – and the question has been much discussed – it is unlikely he would have disagreed with these assertions of Eliot's. There is no rejection, then, of the temporal, but it necessarily takes second place to the non-temporal whose character, as yet, remains undefined. Yet specific recollection, at this point, of 'the moment in the rose-garden', seems to be suggesting a 'special' meaning for that moment, which, though remaining grounded in temporal experience, lifts it above the merely temporal.

Perhaps more than any other passage in *Four Quartets*, the third movement of 'Burnt Norton' brings to mind the 'infernal' passages of *The Waste Land*: the

> Eructation of unhealthy souls
> Into the faded air, the torpid
> Driven on the wind that sweeps the gloomy hills of London,
> Hampstead and Clerkenwell, Campden and Putney,
> Highgate, Primrose and Ludgate   ('Burnt Norton', III)

is not far away, in spirit or, indeed, in inspiration, from 'A crowd flowed over London Bridge, so many, / I had not thought death had undone so many',[37] itself a reworking of Dante's description in *Inferno* III ('io non averei creduto / che morte tanta n'avesse disfatta') of the souls waiting to cross Acheron into Limbo, the first zone of Hell. Eliot's, in 'Burnt Norton', is 'a place of disaffection / Time before and time after / In a dim light', a place of neither light nor darkness, an in-between-state, life – yes – but purposeless, going nowhere, a 'twittering world', characterized by aimless movement. To escape it, to find meaning, the poet here proposes and seeks *real* darkness, 'to purify the soul', after the manner of the so-called 'negative way' of the great Medieval mystics, who sought the

> [...] destitution of all property,
> Desiccation of the world of sense,

---

37 *The Waste Land*, I, 61–2.

> Evacuation of the world of fancy,
> Inoperancy of the world of spirit.   ('Burnt Norton', III)

Every bit as much as the ordered active life, this way of contemplation implies a rejection of 'this twittering world'.

Like Dante (though not nearly so vehemently, nor so often), Eliot attacks what he sees as a prevailing decadence, which is paralysing moral, political and intellectual life, in an atmosphere of indifference. To argue, as Ellis does,[38] that this is tantamount to a rejection of life *per se*, is to misunderstand the life and the poet. Certainly, Eliot was attracted by both mysticism and asceticism in a way that Dante was not. Though precluded from participation in public life, after his exile in 1302, Dante continued to advocate it strongly for those in a position to contribute to the common good, and seems always to have veered towards the active by preference, though forced to the contemplative, by necessity, and as exile and as writer he must have been no stranger to solitude. Eliot was temperamentally unsuited to prominence in public life, his manner was awkward, detached, perhaps too self-consciously elitist, and while in theory he would – did, indeed – agree with Dante's insistence on living this life usefully, and for others, he was too much the twentieth-century professional man of letters to be distracted for long by any active sense of social duty. Yet, he worked for many years in Lloyds' Bank, he committed himself to long, tiring and dangerous hours as a 'fire-watcher' during the London Blitz, and was active both in the Church of England and as an encouraging, painstaking publisher and journal editor. Yet he was rarely at ease with people outside his own circle of friends and did not generally find it difficult being alone. I am not sure these characteristics diminish him overmuch.

The beautiful short lyric of the fourth movement of 'Burnt Norton', 'Time and the bell have buried the day', plays upon the notions of night and darkness, suggested in the previous movement by the 'internal darkness' pursued in the purification of the soul. But here, the burying of the day, the 'black cloud' that 'carries the sun away', hint strongly at the involuntary darkness of death. The series of three questions, surmising, in turn, a possible connection between 'us'

---

38 'Both *The Rock* and the *Quartets* [show] the world as 'a completely alienating or alienated existence in relation to God', and stressing in 'Burnt Norton's' phrase, 'the waste sad time' of historical exile [...]; rather than upholding the reality of the eternal *and* the temporal, 'Burnt Norton' is explicit in its devaluing of the latter to the status of the unreal. Thus throughout Eliot's work there is no approach to the Creator through His creation, or if there is it is only in those visionary intrusions of the supernatural into the natural which act as reminders of the negligibility of the latter.' (Ellis, citing in part V.A. Denant, *The English Eliot*, pp. 124–5).

and the sunflower, the clematis, or the yew tree, after death, is answered obliquely in the assertion that:

> [...] After the kingfisher's wing
> Has answered light to light, and is silent, the light is still
> At the still point of the turning world. ('Burnt Norton', IV)

The connection between the lyric and the 'dark night of the soul' of the third movement, lies perhaps in the intuition that the latter is a parody of death from which new life is assured in much the same way that the new eternal life or 'light' is already figured in the kingfisher's 'brief transit' from darkness through light back to darkness.[39] Later in the eventual *Quartets*, particularly in 'The Dry Salvages' (III, 6), the Heraclitian notion that 'the way up is the way down, the way forward is the way back' seems to echo the medieval-Aristotelian view, reflected in the *Commedia*, that (as Kenelm Foster expressed it) 'the upward path from the many to the One [from creatures to God] implies a prior downward path. *Eros* moves in a circle; through *eros* things return to God because they came through *eros* from God.'[40] Something resembling this doctrine is perhaps dimly perceived in the flashing of light to light in the material sphere, being eternally present at the 'still point', the source of the *true* light, which is Love, in the Heavenly.

In the final movement ('Burnt Norton', 37–75), Eliot returns to the idea of constancy in flux, dealt with at the start of the second, but here he is concerned with the reflection of the principle as it is manifested in words, in the plastic arts and in music. Spoken words and music are lost as soon as they are uttered, they 'reach / Into the silence'. However, if they are given a material form (in writing or musical notation) then they too are capable of reaching that 'stillness' which, like the stillness of 'the Chinese jar [...] moves perpetually' through time, and can ever be recreated and re-experienced at any point in time (and, of course, place). Form is thus the vehicle of the salvation of words and of music; 'form' and 'performance' coexist, so that, in a manner of speaking: 'the end precedes the beginning', indeed, there is now no beginning and no end, 'And all is always now'. The finite, through form, has become the infinite. The analogy

---

39 On a personal note, I have only ever seen kingfishers twice in these islands, and on both occasions, as chance – or was it more likely the habit and habitat of kingfishers – would have it, Eliot's description sprang immediately to mind. The birds came out of the darkness of overhanging trees along the river, crossed a brief patch of sunlight, then re-entered the dark trees further along the river, and were gone. **40** See Kenelm Foster, *The Two Dantes and Other Studies* (London: Darton, Longman and Todd, 1977), p. 43.

here is in the relationship of ephemeral to perpetual, with that already observed in the momentary flash of the kingfisher's wing being 'still / At the still point of the turning world'.[41] They are both representative of an eternal continuum in which materiality is no obstacle to spirituality and temporality is no obstacle to infinitude. If the reasoning is right here, then the idea expressed by Beatrice, in *Paradiso*, I. 103–5, that

> [...] Le cose tutte quante
> hanno ordine tra loro, e questo è forma
> che l'universo a Dio fa simigliante

would seem to be very much in Eliot's mind at this point.

In this relationship of the ephemeral part to the constant, timeless whole, Eliot was reworking St Augustine's teaching and, in his introduction to Valéry's *The Art of Poetry*, he further elaborated the point:

> [...] I find that I enjoy, and 'understand', a piece of music better for knowing it well, simply because I have at any moment during the performance a memory of the part that has preceded and a *memory* of the part that is still to come. Ideally, I should like to be able to hold the whole of a great symphony in my mind at once.[42]

Eliot now returns to a consideration of the fate of words in the contemporary world: he catalogues a whole series of 'assaults' on, or abuses of, language, the end result of which is invariably non-communication. Then, abruptly, he moves from 'words' to the 'Word' – 'The Word in the desert': the *saving* Word which emerges from 'the empty desolation' as does the purified soul from the world of 'internal darkness' in the ascetic 'dark night of the soul'. This 'Word', Christ, who is the earthly language of God's saving Grace, is also under 'attack' like language, the chief medium of *human* communication. The nature and potential result of both 'assaults' is identical, distraction from the word's primary function – communication and communication of Grace. Eliot was (as we have seen) a great admirer of the precision and clarity of Dante's language which, according to him, always fulfilled its function – and in the *Commedia* it too is a compass pointing constantly towards Grace.

41 Although not wishing to labour the point, it is perhaps worth noting the pivotal importance of the word 'still' here, in its sense of 'continues to be', but also in its sense of 'unmoving', whereby it suggests again the notion of the 'unmoved Mover'. 42 Paul Valéry, *The Art of Poetry*, translated by Denise Folliot, Introduction by T.S. Eliot (London: Routledge & Kegan Paul, 1958), p. xiv. Italics mine.

The closing seventeen lines of 'Burnt Norton' take up, once more, the uni-fying principle of specific detail prefigured in universal patterns or rhythms. Present here is the Aristotelian notion of matter in a state of continuous flux, seeking its rest, the 'stillness', which represents perfection and signals reunifica-tion with the Creator: 'the light is *still* at the still point of the turning world'. Not surprisingly, it is Dante (as well as St John of the Cross) who provides the image with which the sequence begins: 'The detail of the pattern is movement, / As in the figure of the ten stairs'(159–60) where, in the movement of sinners up through the terraces of Purgatory and in their upward progress through the planetary heavens, the whole of human life is mirrored in the final stages of the search for perfection through reunification with God. There then follows a con-trast between 'Love' and 'Desire':

> Desire itself is movement
> Not in itself desirable;
> Love is itself unmoving,
> Only the cause and end of movement,
> Timeless, and undesiring [...]   ('Burnt Norton', 161–5)

Following Aristotle, Dante underlines the essentially passive element present in all experience, in the sense, that is, that all knowledge starts in sensation, as does all desire.[43] The human capacity for love must always, therefore, be awakened by an external stimulus. The whole argument begins (in Canto XVII of *Purgatorio*) with Virgil's explanation of the origins of sin, but *desire* is the necessary impulse from which the spiritual journey begins, that journey which can lead from a wish to possess any object of desire to a desire to be possessed by Love, which is God. Love only *desires* when it is 'Caught in the form of limitation / Between un-being and being' (67–8), that is, during the period of earthly life. As Foster has suggested, with *Convivio* III. ii. 8 in mind – 'As appetitive we are attached to God directly and from the start; as cognitive, we must approach him indi-rectly through the piecemeal medium of experience in time – that is, as Dante puts it, through the 'showings' of God which are the forms of goodness which we apprehend in external nature or in our minds'.[44] The last seven lines, illus-trating what for Eliot are '"showings" of God' again bring together the idea of

43 See *Purgatorio*, XVIII, 19–26: 'L'animo, ch'è creato ad amar presto, / ad ogne cosa è mobile che piace, / tosto che dal piacere in atto è desto. / Vostra apprensiva da esser verace / tragge intenzione, e dentro a voi la spiega, / sì che l'animo ad essa volger face; / e se, rivolto, inver' di lei si piega, / quel piegare è amor, quell'è natura / che per piacer di novo in voi si lega.'
44 Foster, p. 47.

the potential unity of the moment and the eternal, the material and the spiritual, when, 'Sudden in a shaft of sunlight' –

> Even while the dust moves
> There rises the hidden laughter
> Of children in the foliage
> Quick now, here, now, always –

in which 'quick' is both imprecation to immediate recognition and affirmation of eternal, vital presence. And, convinced of the openness and continuous availability of this passage between the temporal and the eternal, Eliot closes (as a believer must) with the observation: 'Ridiculous the waste sad time / Stretching before and after' each of these epiphanies.

'Burnt Norton' was very much the model for 'East Coker' and it was only during the writing of the latter that the idea of *Four Quartets* came to Eliot.[45] Thus the poem with which his *Collected Poems, 1909–1935*, had ended, became the starting point for a whole new poetic venture – 'in my end is my beginning'. The meaning inherent in each of the poems, taken separately, is cumulative, as is that for the *Quartets* as a unified whole, but in the 'new life' become possible through a sudden awareness – not an extraneous 'intrusion' of one order of being upon another – we have the central theme of the whole work. Just as Dante, in the *Vita Nuova,* begins with sexual love and ends in the *Commedia* with love etherealized, so too Eliot seeks out a similar path in which Love, Divine Love, becomes the motive force and the end of all human endeavour.[46]

---

45 'East Coker' was published on Good Friday, 1940. 'The Dry Salvages' followed in 1941, and 'Little Gidding' in 1942.   **46** For a more general reading of all *Four Quartets* see Andrew Thompson and Doug Thompson, *Transfiguration and Reconciliation in Eliot's 'Four Quartets'* (Genoa: Cideb Editrice, 1995).

Joycean translations of *Anna Livia Plurabelle*: 'It's translation, Jim, but not as we know it.'

Carol O'Sullivan

The adjective 'untranslatable'[1] has almost achieved the status of a Homeric epithet in relation to *Finnegans Wake*. Few untranslatable texts, however, can have been translated as many times as the *Wake*. The book has been translated, in whole or in part, into Italian, French, Japanese, German and Plain English among a number of other languages. The lure of the 'untranslatable' text has operated on many translators, including the book's own author, James Joyce.

Joyce collaborated on two translations, into French and Italian, of sections of the chapter of *Finnegans Wake* known as 'Anna Livia Plurabelle' (hereafter ALP), which features two washerwomen washing clothes on the bank of the Liffey and discussing Humphrey Chimpden Earwicker. These two translations will be referred to below as self-translations inasmuch as Joyce worked on them and his collaborators all modestly played down their own involvement, declaring that Joyce was the driving creative force behind the translations. Certainly his collaboration and appending of his name to the results seems to demonstrate that he was happy with them.

The ALP fragment of what was at the time still known as *Work in Progress* was first published separately under the title *Anna Livia Plurabelle* in 1928. In 1931 a French translation appeared credited to Samuel Beckett, Alfred Péron, Ivan Goll, Eugène Jolas, Paul L. Léon, Adrienne Monnier, Philippe Soupault and James Joyce. The composition of this committee is slightly misleading, because the text was first translated in 1930 by Samuel Beckett and Alfred Péron, and only subsequently worked on later that same year by the other named writers in a group which did not include Beckett or Péron. The earlier draft by Beckett and Péron had however reached the proof stage, and was eventually published in 1985 by Cahiers de l'Herne.

The other translation on which Joyce worked was into Italian. It was carried out in collaboration with Nino Frank and was the last major piece Joyce worked on before his death. The tale of the development of the Italian ALP is more than

---

1 Fritz Senn invokes the work's 'generally acknowledged untranslatability' in 'The Tellings of the Taling', *James Joyce Quarterly* 4:3 (spring 1967), 229–33 (p. 229). See also Umberto Eco, 'Ostrigotta, ora capesco' in James Joyce, *Anna Livia Plurabelle*, ed. Rosa Maria Bollettieri Bosinelli (Torino: Einaudi, 1996), pp. v–xxix (p. xi).

a little involved. For a long time, the version which was known was in fact a second draft edited by Ettore Settanni. In the beginning, as Frank tells the story, he was approached by Joyce with a request for collaboration on a translation of ALP into Italian. They worked on it a couple of afternoons a week for about three months. Frank is careful to insist 'que Joyce est au moins pour trois quarts dans ce texte italien, moi-même lui tenant surtout lieu de cobaye et de compagnon de travail'.[2] A second collaborator, Ettore Settanni, subsequently became involved – or involved himself, according to Frank – and made a number of changes that were unauthorized by Joyce. Joyce called these changes 'addolcimenti' and Risset's examination of them shows that some can even be seen as improvements. Others, however, 'expressed intended censure both political and sexual' and 'there are other changes which reveal simple incomprehension of the allusions, Irish and other, to be found in the text'.[3] When the fragment was published in 1940, Settanni also failed to credit Frank for the translation, on the grounds that Frank's name would have hindered publication because he was a Jew and a known anti-fascist. The translation, signed Joyce and Settanni, was published in two parts under the titles 'Anna Livia Plurabella' and 'I fiumi scorrono' in *Prospettive* in 1940. In 1955 the two texts were reprinted in *Solaria* signed Joyce, Frank and Settanni. This was the only known version for more than twenty years. The earlier version by Joyce and Frank alone was not published until 1973.

Joyce himself only worked as a translator on sections of ALP, not attempting the rest of the *Wake*. There is a complete French version of the *Wake* and half an Italian *Wake*, by Philippe Lavergne and Luigi Schenoni respectively, both first published in 1982. Further volumes of Schenoni's translation were published in 2001 and 2004.

The Joyce/Frank translation was first brought to critical attention in an article by Jacqueline Risset published in the late 1970s. The other major critic to address the question of Joyce's self-translations is Rosa Maria Bollettieri Bosinelli. Both Risset and Bollettieri Bosinelli characterize the translation as something which is not, in fact, translation. Risset and subsequent commentators have argued for the status of this text as an original work and Rosa Maria Bollettieri Bosinelli has remarked that 'as a "translation" it would pose serious theoretical problems'.[4] Umberto Eco observes in his introduction to the parallel text edi-

---

2 Nino Frank, 'L'Ombre qui avait perdu son homme', in *Mémoire brisée* (Paris: Calmann-Lévy, 1967), pp. 29–64 (p. 53).   3 Jacqueline Risset, 'Joyce translates Joyce', translated by Daniel Pick, in *Comparative Criticism* 6, ed. by E. Shaffer (Cambridge: Cambridge UP, 1984), pp. 3–21 (pp. 5–6) (first published as 'Joyce traduit par Joyce' in *Tel Quel*, 55 (autumn 1973), 47–62).   4 Rosa Maria Bollettieri Bosinelli, 'Anna Livia's Italian Sister', in *Transcultural Joyce*, ed. by Karen Lawrence (Cambridge: Cambridge UP, 1998), pp. 193–8 (p. 195).

tion of ALP in the Einaudi series 'Scrittori tradotti da scrittori' of both versions worked on by Joyce that 'se dovessimo attenerci all'esperienza di FrJoyce e ItJoyce, tutte le teorie della traduzione andrebbero in crisi'.[5] This, in other words, is a dangerous translation. Why?

Past comments by critics that *Finnegans Wake* is untranslatable because it has no identifiable source language can be quickly dismissed as facetious – it is obvious from its syntactic structure as well as from its vocabulary that the *Wake* has a core language and that that language is English overlaid with scores of other languages, wordplay and intertextual and cultural reference.

Finnegans Wake is in fact an operation upon language, rather than a text, as the Polish translator Maciej Slomczynski recognized. He suggested that 'since 'Wakese' is distorted English, it should be possible to translate the English component and mould the target language so as to include the necessary distortions'.[6] This had, in fact, been very similar to Joyce's 'technique of deformation'. Slomczynski was speaking at a panel in Trieste on the translation of *Finnegans Wake*. We are told that the response of the rest of the panel to his suggestion was rather negative: 'The majority felt that this procedure would result in the creation of what might almost be called an original work, which can no longer be called derivative (as a translation should be), except in the sense that it was inspired by *Finnegans Wake*'. Here 'translation' becomes an antonym of both creativity and originality. The above statement almost seems to be saying that the definition of translation is that it is bad.

The question of the translator's autonomy as a decision-maker is crucial here. Polysemy requires choice of the translator, and this is perhaps the most difficult aspect of the process. The necessity to identify priorities in translation is often forgotten in the compulsion to convey every element of the source text, for which the only comfortable alternative is an authorial instruction outlining what to include and what to omit (ironic when we consider that as soon as the author makes that decision for us, the result is classed as something 'other' than translation): 'Translation is sometimes described as an art of choices and sacrifices. Since *Finnegans Wake* is characterized by a refusal to choose (between different words in a single position), sacrifices are particularly costly and an authoritative guide pointing at what is expendable and what should absolutely be retained would be invaluable.'[7] Jacques Derrida has reflected at length over a period of fifteen years on the difficulty of translating polysemy, repeatedly[8] returning to focus on the

---

5 Umberto Eco, 'Ostrigotta, ora capesco', p. v. 6 Leo Knuth, 'The *Finnegans Wake* Translation Panel at Trieste', *James Joyce Quarterly* 9:2 (winter 1971), 266–9 (p. 268). 7 Daniel Ferrer & Jacques Aubert, 'Anna Livia's French bifurcations' in *Transcultural Joyce*, ed. by Karen Lawrence (Cambridge: Cambridge UP, 1998), pp. 179–86 (p. 183). 8 E.g. Jacques Derrida,

phrase 'he war'(*Finnegans Wake*, 258. 12) which includes the English and German third person perfect tenses of the verb 'to be' and the English noun 'war'. This phrase torments Derrida with its multiplicity of languages and associations:

> Le *he war* ne noue pas seulement, en ce lieu, un nombre incalculable de fils phoniques et sémantiques, dans le contexte immédiat et dans tout ce livre babelien; il dit la déclaration de *guerre* (en anglais) de celui qui dit: 'Je suis celui qui suis' et qui ainsi fut (*war*), aura été intraduisible en sa performance même, *au moins dans ce fait* qu'il s'énonce en plus d'une langue à la fois, au moins l'anglais et l'allemand.[9]

The problem, for Derrida, seems to be that one must translate even polyglot source texts into one target language,[10] and he quotes Lavergne's French translation: 'Et il en fut ainsi' saying, 'Ce n'est plus la guerre.' He points out that the translator must choose one of the languages, English or German, and that thus 'la confusion entre le *war* anglais et le *war* allemand ne peut que disparaître, en se déterminant, à l'écoute. Il faut choisir et c'est toujours le même drame. La confusion, dans la différence, s'efface'.[11] Derrida sees the translation of this kind of wordplay as at once imperative – recognizing the strong call to translate that the text exerts on readers – and impossible.

Ultimately, Derrida's approach is sterile, as his awareness of the double-bind of translation, the 'necessary and impossible task',[12] causes him to yearn for translation, but not achieve it. Though translation remains a recurring presence in his work, he never surrenders entirely to the call of the text.[13] How do real translators, who do not have the luxury of failing to find a solution, approach the polysemy of the *Wake*? The phrase 'And how long was he under loch and neagh?' is translated by Lavergne 'Et combien de temps resta-t-il enfoui sous clé a double-tour' with a footnote referring to the legend of Loch Neagh. This is very similar to Schenoni's policy of explicative translation, searching for what he calls the 'livello base di significato':

La Carte postale: de Socrate à Freud (Paris: Flammarion, 1980), p. 257; Jacques Derrida, *The Ear of the Other: Otobiography, Transference, Translation,* translated by Peggy Kamuf, ed. by Christie McDonald (Lincoln/London: University of Nebraska Press, 1985), pp. 98–9. The conversations reported in *The Ear of the Other* took place in 1979, showing that at this point Derrida was already preoccupied by the phrase. **9** Jacques Derrida, 'Des Tours de Babel', in *Psyché: Inventions de l'autre* (Paris: Éditions galilée, 1987), pp. 202–35 (p. 207). **10** Jacques Derrida, *Ulysse gramophone: Deux mots pour Joyce* (Paris: Éditions galilée, 1987), p. 45. **11** Ibid., p. 47. **12** Derrida, *The Ear of the Other*, p. 98. **13** This tension between translation and non-translation is perhaps best illustrated in Derrida's guest lecture at the Assises de la Traduction Littéraire in Arles in 1998. Cf. Jacques Derrida, 'Qu'est-ce qu'une traduction "relevante"?' *Quinzièmes Assises de la Traduction Littéraire (Arles 1998)* (Arles: Actes Sud, 1999), pp. 21–48.

tutte le parole di *Finnegans Wake*, anche quelle polivalenti, hanno un senso predominante, che non è poi altro che trasmette la 'trama' del libro. [...] tra tutti i significati che stanno al di sotto di quello base e le innumerevoli allusioni di ogni genere, che rappresentano una delle ricchezze di *Finnegans Wake*, ho privilegiato [...] quelli più importanti con riferimento alla trama e a quei motivi principali che ricorrono per tutto il libro come dei veri e propri *leit-motive*.[14]

This policy can be read as an attempt to tidy up the ludic chaos of the text and reduce it to recognizable meaning, acting antagonistically to the text's explosion of semantic redundancy. The distrust of puns clearly goes very deep, as Derek Attridge has observed in *Peculiar Language*: 'The pun remains an embarrassment to be excluded from "serious" discourse [...]. It survives, tenaciously, as freak or accident, hindering what is taken to be the primary function of language: the clean transmission of a pre-existing, self-sufficient, unequivocal meaning.'[15] Schenoni's translation of the pun on Lough Neagh, though it goes further than Lavergne's in its attempt to render the multiple levels of the text, is the infelicitous 'e per quanto tempo è stato sotto loughiave e neaghratura?' which attempts to bring together 'lough neagh' and 'chiave e serratura,' willy-nilly; Schenoni's undervaluing of the phonic elements of the phrase dooms the attempt to failure.

A comparison between the Beckett/Péron version, and the later collaborative French translation reveals that Joyce is extremely sensitive to potential puns, and systematically embeds more and more puns within individual lexical items in the previous translation, as in the following examples:

> Tuck up your sleeves and loosen your talk-tapes.[16]
> Retrousse tes manches et délie ta langue.[17]
> Retrousse tes manches et délie ton battant.[18]

> I know by heart the places he likes to saale, duddurty devil![19]
> Je sais par coeur les endroits qu'il aime à saalir, le mymyserable.[20]
> Je sais paroker les endroits qu'il aime à seillir, le mymyserable.[21]

---

14 Luigi Schenoni, 'Nota del traduttore', in James Joyce, *Finnegans Wake*, Libro Primo, I–IV, trans. Luigi Schenoni (Milano: Mondadori, 1993), pp. lxxv–lxxviii (p. lxxvi). **15** Derek Attridge, *Peculiar Language: Literature as Difference from the Renaissance to James Joyce* (Ithaca, NY: Cornell UP, 1988), p. 189. **16** *Finnegans Wake*, 196. 8–9. **17** Alfred Péron & Samuel Beckett, 'Anna Livia Pluratself' in Joyce, *Anna Livia Plurabelle*, ed. Bollettieri Bosinelli, p. 155. **18** James Joyce et al. in Joyce, *Anna Livia Plurabelle*, ed. Bollettieri Bosinelli, p. 3. **19** *Finnegans Wake*, 196. 14–15. **20** Alfred Péron & Samuel Beckett, p. 155. **21** James Joyce et al., p. 3.

The second French version is a revision of the first, and we can see Joyce punning on argotic and archaic French, intensifying swear words, doubling syllables and increasing the wordplay in individual expressions: thus *par coeur* acquires the sense of 'to parrot' as well as to know by heart. Concision is also an important criterion for Joyce:

> Tuck up your sleeves and loosen your talk-tapes.
> Rimbocca le maniche e sbriglia la raganella.[22]
> Rimboccamaniche e sciolilinguagnolo.[23]

> I know by heart the places he likes to saale, duddurty devil!
> Conosco ad hartmemoria i punti che gli piace insaalezzare, a quel
> duddondino di darteggiante diavolo![24]
> So ben io cosa quel macchiavuol. Lordo balordo![25]

Where polysemy proves difficult to translate, on the other hand, Joyce cuts the Gordian knot, refusing the status of authoritative guide to the text. He offers for the 'lough neagh' line the translation 'e quanto rimase dai frati Branca?' a reference to the Fratelli Branca of Fernet fame. The image of immersion in liquid remains and the rest is radically reset. This is typical of Joyce's strategy throughout the translation, as Risset demonstrates, transforming a famously polyglot text including more than sixty languages into a monoglot text working almost exclusively with the wide-ranging resources of Italian. Earlier he translates 'you'll die when you hear' as 'Roba da chiodi!', and in his translation of the following series of mock proverbs he cannot resist a Dantesque reference, just as an English translator might be moved to include Polonius with this collection of wise saws:

> But toms will till. I know he well. Tamp untamed will hist for no man.
>   As you spring so shall you neap.[26]
> Ma chi fa il rio paga il fio. Chi se mena vanto, raccatta trambusto. E ciò
>   sa il suo dottore.[27]

This would seem to be exceeding his brief a little, as all that was wanted was a translation which overloaded an Italian structure with polysemy, punning and culturally specific items. In an article on Joseph Brodsky's self-translations Michael Molnar declares that 'Writers who translate themselves enjoy the advan-

---

22 Schenoni translation in Joyce, *Anna Livia Plurabelle*, ed. Bollettieri Bosinelli, p. 89. **23** Joyce/Frank translation in Joyce, *Anna Livia Plurabelle*, ed. Bollettieri Bosinelli, p. 2. **24** Schenoni translation, p. 89. **25** Joyce/Frank translation, p. 3. **26** *Finnegans Wake*, 196. 22–3. **27** Joyce/Frank translation, pp. 4–5.

tage of privileged access to the intellectual activity behind the work. This grants them "noetic licence", namely the right denied the ordinary translator of alter- ing the original.'[28] This is the right invoked by critics in order to preserve an inadequate and constraining definition of translation by labelling any translation which 'alters the original' either bad or, if authorial activity is suspected, a trans- lation which takes advantage of noetic licence.

Bollettieri Bosinelli categorizes or indeed writes off Joyce's ALP as 'transla- tion as a creative process which only the author can successfully achieve',[29] and which adopts 'strategies that one would hardly recommend a translator to fol- low'.[30] True, because if a translator were to follow them, all our assumptions about translation and creativity would come tumbling down. Risset, too, argues for the self-translation's status as original work, rather than as a brilliant trans- lation which can offer a model for other translators.

There is, usefully, an example of a translator following Joyce's example, in the most recent German translation of ALP from the 1993 parallel text version by Dieter H. Stündel entitled *Finnegans Wehg: Kainnäh Übelsätzung des Werkeß vfun Schämes Scheuß* which declares its translated status even as it denies it. Here, according to Fritz Senn, the translator is proceeding 'by free semantic expan- sion from which not even passages of pointedly foreign origin are exempt'.[31] Stündel 'does not choose the easy path (he sometimes comes on like Sisyphus taking on a complimentary order of stones for the next ascent)'. Senn's exam- ple is the translation of 'ordovico or viricordo' (*Finnegans Wake*, 215. 23) which should come under the heading of phrases in a polyglot text which belong nei- ther to the source text nor to the target text (when the target text is German) and which can therefore remain as they are. Senn points out that most transla- tors would merely translate the 'or' which belongs to the base language and leave the Italianate terms unchanged. However, in Stündel's translation the phrase becomes 'Greis Vico oder E rinnerung'. Senn considers the relationship between the two texts, concluding that 'What is clearly lost in the extra effort is the phonetic and literal implementation of 'the same anew': out of 'ordovico' we can rescramble 'viricordo' by simply adding another r. Just as in Joyce we move from an initial *ordo* to a final one in the kind of circle Vico talks about'.[32] This loss is conclusive for Senn despite the several additions to the phrase in translation, with the detached E of Erinnerung resonating with Earwicker, with

---

28 Michael Molnar, 'Noetic Licence in Brodsky's Self-Translation', *Russian Literature* XXXVII: 2–3 (1995) 333–7 (p. 333). **29** Rosa Maria Bollettieri Bosinelli, 'Introduction: Anna Livia Plurabelle's Sisters', in *Transcultural Joyce*, ed. by Karen Lawrence (Cambridge: Cambridge UP, 1998), pp. 173–8 (p. 176). **30** Bollettieri Bosinelli, 'Anna Livia's Italian Sister' p. 197. **31** Fritz Senn, 'ALP Deutsch: ob überhaupt möglich?', in *Transcultural Joyce*, ed. by Karen Lawrence (Cambridge: Cambridge UP, 1998), pp. 187–92 (p. 191). **32** Ibid.

'rinnen' echoing the *riverrunning,* and with a suitably occluded 'Kreis' referring to the Viconian circle. These enrichments cannot offset the loss for Senn because the lost chords are Joyce's, and the additions are merely of the translator. Another German translator, Wollschläger the translator of *Ulysses,* comes under fire in a review because he often tries to compensate for such unavoidable loss by providing a similar effect in the immediate context. 'Unfortunately, this practice may overstimulate the translator's creative energy and develop into a tendency to improve on the text', says Manfred Jahn apocalyptically.[33]

Bollettieri Bosinelli says that 'only the "original" author could afford the liberty of stretching beyond the limits imposed by the source text'.[34] It becomes obvious that in this world view the cardinal sin of translation is not loss, but gain. In fact, the gain which is in question in Joyce's Italian ALP is not stretching beyond the limits imposed by the source text, but stretching beyond the limits imposed by the definition of a target text, which is expected to be lacking, no matter how accomplished. ALP is a text which appeals to the translator to engage with it, to compete with it. The *Wake* is the last text on earth to set limits on its translators. The limits of which Bollettieri Bosinelli is speaking are imposed from outside by cultural expectations, by the investment in the laws and *tendances* which we have seen in operation and the uneasiness when translations (and translators) seem to get too big for their boots. Critics, including Joyce scholars, frequently imply their belief in a fantasy translation, which would be identical with the original (a fantasy which is in no way limited to Joycean texts). Senn declares that 'no translation can be expected to give us the full orchestration of Joyce's novel'.[35] Nevertheless he remarks elsewhere that 'it would be a unique stroke of luck if a translator could achieve the same depth and richness' as the original.[36] This despite the fact that Joyce's Italian ALP is, in my opinion, no less rich and deep than the English, and suggesting that Senn's criteria are not concerned with depth or richness, but with the preservation of links to referents in the 'real world'.

The author escapes censure, almost no matter what his strategy, but only at the cost of having it made clear that the exercise of noetic licence results in a text which is not a translation. According to the criteria of conservative translation theory, Joyce's text is indeed, because a self-translation, something completely different. However, if we consider Joyce's Italian ALP to be a translation, then the possibilities for growth and enrichment of the text are limitless.

---

33 Manfred Jahn, review of Andreas Gardt, *James Joyce auf Deutsch: Möglichkeiten der Literarischen Übersetzung* (Frankfurt: Peter Lang, 1989), *James Joyce Quarterly* 27:1 (fall 1989), 160–4 (p. 162). **34** Bollettieri Bosinelli, 'Anna Livia's Italian Sister', p. 195. **35** Fritz Senn, 'Seven against *Ulysses'*, *James Joyce Quarterly* 4:3 (spring 1967), 170–93 (p. 172). **36** Senn, 'Seven against *Ulysses'*, p. 178.

From waiting to coming: Beckett's *Waiting for Godot* and Titley's *Tagann Godot,* alias *Arriva Godot**

Rosangela Barone

First, some data and dates relevant to the two plays, and to a comparative analysis leading to a discussion of the translation of one of them, *Tagann Godot*, that is the subject of this paper.

I. BECKETT AND TITLEY

SAMUEL BECKETT (1906–89) – Dubliner/Parisian/Citizen of the Word, Nobel Prize for Literature 1969. After his early publications in English (1946), he wrote his first novel, *Mercier et Camier*, in French: the aim of that linguistic choice was to purge his style of the literalness that seemed to encumber his own English prose; his next step was to translate the text into English – an English that fully shows Beckett's penitential stark rigour. The novel was published in 1970. This became a habit for most of his successive works, including his first experiment with theatre, *En Attendant Godot* which was to become *Waiting for Godot.*

The text, written some time in 1948–9, was published in French in 1952, and the play was first staged at the Théâtre de Babylone, Paris (a nice symbolism in the name of the theatre, for those concerned with the Babel of languages), on 1 January 1953. The text in English was published in 1954, and the play was first staged at the Arts Theatre Club, London, on 3 August 1955. As to the playwright's native city, Dublin, it was first staged at the Pike Theatre, under the direction of Alan Simpson, on 28 October 1955.

Beckett's 'absurd' play goes to the core of modern Western philosophy. It deals with the moral and spiritual aridity of twentieth-century society and presents it in stark minimalist language, mainly shaped in the hardest form of questioning rather than in answers and statements.

ALAN TITLEY (1947–) – Corkman/cosmopolitan. He started his career as a

---

* This essay is dedicated to the Italian Department in Trinity College, Dublin, and to Corinna Salvadori Lonergan whose working life was identified with it for four decades.

teacher in Eastern Europe and Africa (while in Nigeria, he was gaoled for oppos-
ing the militarist government during the Biafrian war), and now he lives in
Dublin. He combines his activity as a lecturer at St Patrick's College of
Education, Drumcondra, with that of literary critic, cultural opinionist and creative writer (prose, poetry, drama) mostly in Gaelic, and also in English.

Tagann Godot is Titley's first experiment with theatre. It was written in 1987
and, that same year, it was awarded an Oireachtas Prize. It was first staged at
the Peacock Theatre, Dublin, on 15 February 1990, and published in 1991.

Titley's play is both a homage and a response to *Waiting for Godot*; it is an imaginative sequel to a play, now world-famous, by a great master of contemporary
theatre. Shaped as a surrealistic, bombastic burlesque, it draws upon, and questions, contemporary Ireland's mass-media culture and Hiberno-English *patois*.

II. 'WAITING FOR GODOT' AND 'TAGANN GODOT'

Titles

The name Godot appears in the title of each of the two plays. As to Beckett's
play, it has been documented that an abandoned early title for the original text
in French was simply: 'En attendant',[1] but the text was published and produced
with the name as part of the title. Beckett told Roger Blin, his first producer,
that the name was suggested to him by two slang words, *godillots* and *godasses*
(in French, meaning 'old army boots'). The playwright 'categorically denied
that Godot is God, but not that the possibility is suggested'.[2] In the play, Godot
is not mentioned immediately and he is to remain unknown up to the end.[3]

In the title, the name, *Godot*, is preceded by *Waiting for* – an impersonal '*ing*'
form that contains a paradox, that is, it indicates that an action is in progress
while in fact the situation (*waiting*) is static. What is more, that situation is destined to be permanent as Godot, originally envisaged by Beckett as a Charlie
Chaplin figure, never turns up, and the audience leaves the theatre with this
question in mind: 'What if Godot came?'

The title of Titley's play features the name of Beckett's elusive character
(*Godot*), which is made the subject of the action (*Tagann*); the verb is in the sim-

1 Cf. *The Theatrical Notebooks of Samuel Beckett – Waiting for Godot*, ed. by Dougald McMillan
and James Knowlson (London: Faber and Faber, 1993), I, p. 87. **2** Ibid., p. xvi. Here mention
is also made of the American director, Alan Schneider, who produced a list of over a hundred
suggestions. **3** In the Faber standard edition, the name first appears on p. 14 of the text which
starts on p. 9: Samuel Beckett, *Waiting for Godot* [henceforth *WG* followed by page number]
(London: Faber and Faber, 1956 [1965]). Cf. also *A Student's Guide to the Plays of Samuel Beckett*,
ed. by Beryl D. Fletcher and John Fletcher (London and Boston: Faber and Faber, 1978 [1985]).

ple present: *Tagann* as opposed to *Tá* Godot *ag teacht*, corresponding to the English '*ing*' form. Moreover, as announced in the title, in the course of the dramatic action Godot does come – he appears on stage at the very end of Act I and, again, in Act II.[4]

In dealing with the two titles, a first point about translation needs to be raised. In my Italian translation of Titley's play, *Arriva Godot*, the Gaelic word *tagann*, which occurs over a dozen times in the original text, is rendered by two different words: by the corresponding verb *venire* (to come) and, in the title and in several other occurrences, by the verb *arrivare* (to arrive), this latter choice being in order to render the exclamatory dimension, the sense of awe and surprise at the appearance of the long-expected figure of Godot.[5]

Structure, setting, characters

Waiting for Godot – Beckett's play in English is provided with a subtitle, *A Tragicomedy in Two Acts*, a definition this, '*tragicomedy*', that is not present in the original French version. The two Acts are uneven in length – the text of Act I (pp. 9–54) is eight pages longer than that of Act II (pp. 57–94). The setting in Act I is an undefined/undefinable landscape:

> *A country road. A tree.*
> *Evening.* (*WG*, 7.)

The darkness of the night will soon fall on that flat land (as in one of Yves Tanguy's paintings) 'animated' by a single slender tree (a Giacometti sculpture, in the 1961 production) and a simple road suggesting movement, progress, chance for an encounter and for company.

Act II has the same setting as Act I, yet with a slight difference:

> *Next day. Same time. Same place.* (*WG*, 55.)
> *The tree has four or five leaves.* (*WG*, 57.)

In that tree which has renewed itself (its boughs were naked before) there may be a reference to Dante's *Purgatorio*, XXXII. 58–60:

---

4 Cf. Alan Titley, *Tagann Godot – Coiméide Thraigéideach Dhá Ghníomh* [henceforth *TG* followed by page number] (Baile Átha Cliath: An Clóchomhar Tta, 1991). **5** Cf. Alan Titley, *Arriva Godot – Tragicommedia in due atti* [henceforth *AG* followed by page number], cura e traduzione di Rosangela Barone (Faenza: Mobydick–Cooperativa Tratti, 1999). 'Viene': pp. 17, 18, 19, 26, 28, 30. 'Arriva': pp. 25, 28, 30! (word followed by ! exclamation mark), 49!, 54! – twice, 58, 59.

Men che di rose e più che di vïole,
   colore aprendo, s'innovò la pianta,
   che prima avea le ramore sì sole.

In the Beckettian perspective, however, that is a deceptive mirage.

As to the Characters, in both Acts Vladimir and Estragon play the role of the protagonist: they are tramps ('wayfarers' would be a more apt definition, fellow-travellers, possibly), two inseparable companions complementary to each other. There are three secondary characters. There is the transient presence of the Boy, who enters towards the end of each Act just to deliver the message that Godot will not come that evening, but 'surely tomorrow' – in Act I that message is delivered 'in a rush', and in Act II it is dragged out of the young messenger by Vladimir (*WG*, pp. 50 and 92 respectively). Then there is the much less fleeting presence on stage, in both Acts, of Pozzo and Lucky, the master-slave complementary couple.

Waiting for Godot, 'a play in which nothing happens, *twice*',[6] opens with this statement:

> ESTRAGON – Nothing to be done. (*WG*, 9)

Act I and Act II end, respectively, as follows:

> ESTRAGON – Well, shall we go?
> VLADIMIR – Yes, let's go.
> *They do not move.*
> CURTAIN (*WG*, 54.)

> VLADIMIR – Well? Shall we go?
> ESTRAGON – Yes, let's go.
> *They do not move.*
> CURTAIN (*WG*, 94.)

The play, slightly asymmetrical in structure, and based on repetition with a difference and on *leitmotifs* in asymmetry, is as stark as a medieval morality play or a Japanese Noh play, yet it is sustained by a consistent sense of laughter. It is a play with no conclusion; even though Act II is more sombre than Act I, everything continues as in the past, and the key dimension of it all remains with the word: *perhaps*.

---

6 Vivian Mercier's lapidary definition in his review of the play for the *Irish Times*, 18 February 1956; also in V. Mercier, *Beckett/Beckett* (New York: Oxford UP, 1977; London: Souvenir Press, 1990), p. 242, note 1.

Tagann Godot — Titley's play, too, is '*A Tragi-Comedy in Two Acts*', but these two are almost equal in length – Act I is one page shorter than Act II (25 pages as opposed to 26).

The setting – as specified in the opening stage direction – is the same as in Beckett's play: the time of day is evening, there is a country road, there is a tree, *but* there is one apple on the tree and there is the specification that the setting is the same as in the *finale* of the play by Beckett:

> *Bóthar tuaithe. Crann a bhfuil úll amháin air.*
> > *Tráthnóna éigin.*
> *An stáitse mar atá ag deireadh* En Attendant Godot. *Estragon agus Vladimir ina seasamh. Rópa briste ar an talamh eatarthu. Cuma thuirseach thnáite orthu. Labhraíonn siad go fadálach traochta i dtús an dráma.* (TG, 7.)

This, in my Italian translation, reads as follows:

> *Strada di campagna. Albero con una sola mela.*
> > *Sera.*
> *Scena identica a quella del finale di* Aspettando Godot. *Estragone e Vladimiro in piedi. Fra i due, una corda spezzata. Entrambi hanno un aspetto stanco e sfinito. Inizialmente parlano con voce trascinata ed esausta.* (AG, 17.)

Act II has the same setting as Act I, *but thirty* seconds *before* the end of Act I:

> *An áit chéanna. Leathnóiméad roimh dheireadh an chéad ghnímh.*
> > *Estragon fós ar crochadh.* (TG, 33.)

In Italian:

> *Stessa scena. Mezzo minuto prima della fine dell'Atto I.*
> > *Estragone ancora appeso all'albero.* (AG, 51.)

Vladimir and Estragon, the two main characters, are the same, and in the same role of protagonist, as in Beckett's play. The Boy (Buachaill), too, is present in *Tagann Godot*, and he appears in both Acts to deliver the same message as in *Waiting for Godot* – early in Act I and nearly at the end of Act II. Here are his final words, addressed alternatively to Vladimir and to Estragon, just before his running away in order to escape further questioning from the two:

BUACHAILL – Tá brón orm, a dhuine uasail. Tá drochscéal agam duit, a
   dhuine uasail. Godot, a dhuine uasail. Bhí timpist aige, a dhuine uasail.
   Ní féidir leis teacht inniu, a dhuine uasail. […] Dúirt sé nach bhféad-
   fadh sé teacht inniu. […] Ach tiocfaidh sé amárach. Cinnte. (*TG*, 58.)

RAGAZZO – Scusami, signore. Ho una brutta notizia da darti, signore.
   Godot, signore. Ha avuto un incidente, signore. Oggi non può venire,
   signore. […] Ha detto che non può venire oggi, signore. […] Ma
   verrà domani, di sicuro. (*AG*, 83.)

Three other characters are introduced: Prograstaron, Mí-Ábha, and Momo.
Prograstaron is an imposing figure, pompously dressed, behaving like a circus
tamer or the presenter of a cheap television quiz show; Mí-Ábha is a faithful
dupe; Momo is the sprightly buxom assistant of bossy Prograstaron. Prograstaron
and Mí-Ábha replace – in the same hierarchical positions – Beckett's couple,
Pozzo and Lucky. Momo is not only an extra character, but indeed a female
one – as one might have expected from the apple hanging on the tree, at the
opening of the play. When the two starving tramps first see Prograstaron arrive
with his two assistants on a cart overloaded with goods and festooned with
many-coloured lamps – band music in the background – they take the new-
comer for Godot. That is an intriguing sequel to Beckett's 'absurd' play.
   Tagann Godot opens with the following dialogue:

ESTRAGON – Ní féidir liom dul ar aghaidh mar seo.
VLADIMIR – Sin is dóigh leatsa.
ESTRAGON – Dá scarfaimis? B'fhéidir go mbeimis níos fearr as.
VLADIMIR – Crochfaimid sinn féin amárach. (*Sos*) Is é sin, mura dtagann
   Godot.
ESTRAGON – Agus má thagann sé?
VLADIMIR – Beimid slán ansin. (*Baineann Vladimir a hata de, féachann
   isteach ann, cuireann a lámh taobh istigh de, craitheann timpeall san aer é,
   buaileann cnag ar a bharr agus cuireann ar ais ar a cheann arís é.*)
ESTRAGON – Voil, an imeoimid má sea?
VLADIMIR – Más maith leat.
ESTRAGON – Níl aon bhaint ag maith leis an scéal.
VLADIMIR – Voil, imeoimid mar sin.
ESTRAGON – Sea, imímis.
Ní bhogann siad. Sos.
VLADIMIR – An bhfuilimid imithe?
ESTRAGON – Ní shílim go bhfuil.
VLADIMIR – Caithfidh go bhfuilimid anseo fós, má sea.

ESTRAGON – Ní fhéadfainn a bheith cinnte.

VLADIMIR – Is cinnte go bhfuilimid áit éigin.(*TG*, 7.)

ESTRAGONE – Non posso andare avanti così.

VLADIMIRO – Questo è quanto pensi tu.

ESTRAGONE – Se ci separassimo? Forse ci guadagneremmo.

VLADIMIRO – Ci impiccheremo domani. (*Pausa.*) Lo faremo se Godot non verrà.

ESTRAGONE – E se verrà?

VLADIMIRO – Allora saremo salvi. (*Si toglie il cappello, ci guarda dentro, ci infila la mano, lo fa roteare in aria, poi gli dà un colpetto sopra e se lo rimette in testa.*)

ESTRAGONE – Allora, ce ne andiamo?

VLADIMIRO – Se ti fa piacere.

ESTRAGONE – Il piacere qui non c'entra.

VLADIMIRO – Beh, allora andiamo.

ESTRAGONE – Sì, andiamo.

Non si muovono. Pausa.

VLADIMIRO – Ce ne siamo andati?

ESTRAGONE – Non credo.

VLADIMIRO – Allora dovremmo essere ancora qui.

ESTRAGONE – Non ne sarei tanto certo.

VLADIMIRO – Quello che è certo è che siamo in un posto. (*AG*, 17.)

Act I ends with two shocking events – in sequence:

(a) Estragon is hanged for having lost the quiz competition with its extravagant prizes conducted by Prograstaron, and for having offended the latter's authority.

(b) At the very close of the Act, there is a bomb explosion and, out of the thick smoke, here comes Godot, featured as Charlie Chaplin, except for his long beard and a doctor's case in his hand. When he opens his mouth – an impish smile on his face – this is what he says:

(GODOT –) Agus bhí daoine ag rá nach dtiocfainn ar chor ar bith. (*TG*, 32.)

(GODOT –) E c'era gente che diceva che non sarei mai arrivato! (*AG*, 49.)

The opening stage directions of Act II are as follows:

An áit chéanna. Leathnóiméad roimh dheireadh an chéad ghnímh.
Estragon fós ar crochadh. (*TG*, 33.)

Stessa scena. Mezzo minuto prima della fine dell'Atto I.
Estragone ancora appeso all'albero. (*AG*, 51.)

Prograstaron, having got rid of Estragon, now tries to corner Vladimir with his quiz games. He does not succeed because Godot comes to Vladimir's help and turns Momo into a sow, Mí-Ábha into a cat, and Prograstaron into a dog. Actually, Godot also resurrects Estragon from the dead, much to the latter's regret and anger.[7] Estragon is so angry at having been brought back into this 'valley of tears' that he ties Godot onto the electric chair and kills him; then he drags his corpse into a fridge, reluctantly helped by Vladimir. The two tramps, once again alone, but now surrounded with all the extravagant prizes and abundant food that were on the cart, are excited at the idea of having become rich. Yet, Tantalus' experience is in store for them: as soon as they stretch their hands to fetch the object of their desire, that object moves away and disappears, until Godot suddenly pops out of the fridge – this time featured as Groucho Marx, a cigar in his hand – enters a luxurious car and, in front of the two dumbfounded tramps, drives off stage, uttering:

> (GODOT –) Agus shíl cuid agaibh nach raibh ionam ach seansaire! Pah!
> (*TG*, 57.)

> (GODOT –) E c'era qualcuno di voi che mi credeva nient'altro che un cialtrone! Puah! (*AG*, 82.)

The two wretched tramps start wondering whether all that they experienced was true. The Gaelic Tragi-Comedy in Two Acts ends with a question mark:

> ESTRAGON – B'fhéidir go mbeidh air teacht arís, má sea.
> VLADIMIR – B'fhéidir gurb é sin an freagra.
> ESTRAGON – Sea, ach cad í an cheist? (*TG*, 59.)

> ESTRAGONE – Forse dovrà tornare, allora.
> VLADIMIRO – Forse questa è la risposta.
> ESTRAGONE – Sì, ma qual è la domanda? (*AG*, 83.)

---

7 As well as the medieval tradition of Lazarus, this brings to mind the end of one of Oscar Wilde's *Poems in Prose*: 'The Doer of Good' ('But I was dead once and you raised me from the dead. What else should I do but weep?'), as well as W.B. Yeats's *Calvary* in *Collected Plays* (London: Macmillan, 1953), pp. 447–57 (p. 452).

In Titley's play, Beckett's 'tomorrow' is turned into 'today'. Godot does come, but only to disappear again, leaving those who remain 'on earth' with more questions than before.

If Beckett's 'absurd' play – with all its undercurrent laughter – is a stark existential play set in the land of 'everyman', Titley's surrealistic phantasmagoria tackles the existential question, but with a much lighter apparatus and in a well-defined setting, that is, present-day Ireland, consumeristic and televison-addicted, and, what is more, the Ireland of pseudo-*Gaeilgeoirí*, who make a mess of their own language, contributing to its pollution through lazy resort to cheap mass-media catch-phrases, Englishisms, absurd hybridisms, that is, a caricature of language, which communicates nothing and finally turns into cultural non-identity.

That last consideration brings us to consider language, and, with it, the problem of translation.

III. THE TRANSLATION

Beckett's language, distilled to the point of *reductio ad silentium* and with its increasing pauses, is basic language: at one and the same time it is daily and essential language, something to prove one's existence through elementary communication and to while away one's time – hence also the clichés, the vaudeville/music-hall/circus echoes, the catch-phrases and puns with which the text is crammed.

When it comes to translation, the more essential, that is, concentrated and distilled the language is, the more difficult it is to render it in the target language, not least because – as in Beckett's case – the rhythmical pattern created by mostly mono- and di-syllabic words is an integral part of the semantics of the text. Beckett's language is an agonizing strait jacket for any translator. Yet, the greater the challenge, the more rewarding is the effect.

In this respect, Titley's text presents a different type of difficulty. In opposition to Beckett's gaunt, naked, bare-boned language, Titley's is fleshy, luxuriant, pyrotechnical. What is more, its breath-taking dialogue paradoxically draws on a wide range of literary texts, folklore material, biblical and historical episodes, and events and characters in contemporary Ireland. The question mark with which the play ends is a warning against the pre-fabricated answers and statements with which the mass-media fob us off, and an invitation – made even more vibrant by the use of parody – to use our own heads, to query the ready-made solutions authoritatively or alluringly proposed from outside, and to exert our individual freedom of choice and responsibility in the decisions that we take. This process also involves the use of language – a particularly crucial point to Titley, who is a linguist, a creative writer, and a teacher. His play, *Tagann Godot*, abounds with jokes based on language hybridization.

Titley is deeply concerned with language and language awareness. He is far from being narrowly conservative in his attitude. He knows very well that inputs linked with exposure to other languages and cultures are an integral part of the evolution of a language. At the same time, he makes a stand against the non-use of Gaelic (in favour of English *tout court*), or – what he considers to be even worse – the use of spurious Gaelic, loaded with Englishisms, crammed with platitudes, and stuffed with mass-media slogans. Through *Tagann Godot*, he offers his compatriots a sample of the tragi-comic state of the Gaelic language as used today by the average speaker. A *leitmotif* in Titley's play is individual and collective identity being at stake in the non-use and/or misuse of language, and this theme he proposes mainly through laughter.

Laughter is a dimension which multiplies the problems of translation, as there is not only a block of language rooted in a specific socio-cultural *humus* to be transferred into another language nourished by, and nourishing, a different type of *humus*, but there is also the laughter to be aroused in the audience of the target language. As we know, jokes, allusions, puns, and wordplays are usually anchored in topical reality, that is, well-defined local events and/or characters. They propose – on a parodic level – contingent phenomena which a community (large or small) sharing the same specific spatial-temporal experiences, and, of course, the same language, has no problem identifying.

Tagann Godot is full of allusions to, and parodic echoes of, old sayings and literary texts as well as of contemporary ways of speaking and idiolects; it abounds with references both to old mythological and historical figures and to more or less prominent figures of today's Ireland. In the case of a play in translation, the audience must be put in a position of laughing as soon as a humorous cue is uttered on stage (there is no space for additional explanatory phrases bound to dilute the comic effect, let alone the use of footnotes). Consequently, on more than one occasion the literal translation must be abandoned in favour of a text that could make sense in the linguistic and cultural set-up of the foreign audience. In turning *Tagann Godot* into *Arriva Godot* I had to make several choices of that kind, which, without betraying the meaning and aim of the original Gaelic text, made sense, and even comic sense, in the mind of the Italian audience.

To conclude this paper, five examples representative of the solutions adopted in Italian follow:

1.

Prograstaron introduces Mí-Ábha to Vladimir and Estragon, enticing them to take part in the quiz game:

> PROGASTARON – [...] An bhfeiceann sibh é seo? (*Mí-Ábha atá i gceist aige.*) An tUasal Uasal Mac Uí Jeaic Ó Rudaí! (*Miongháire mór ó Mí-Ábha. Miongháire mór bréige ó Mhomo.*) [...] B'fhéidir go mbeadh an t-ádh le Jeaic inniu, nó b'fhéidir nach mbeadh. B'fhéidir go mbeadh sé libhse. B'fhéidir go bhfaigheadh sibhse an pota óir ach sciorta an áidh a ardú féachaint cad a nochtfadh sé daoibh. Is é an t-ádh an buachaill i mBaile Ádh an Chluiche!
>
> ESTRAGON – Ambaiste móide, mhuis, by dad!
>
> VLADIMIR – Caithfidh mé a rá nár fhoghlaimíos é sin riamh ar scoil.
>
> ESTRAGON – Nach é seo an saol, a dhuine! (*TG*, 20–1.)

> PROCRASTIGNORE – [...] Vedete costui? (*Riferendosi a Sfighino.*) Vi presento Sua Eccellenza eccellente Sfighino, il Delfino di Cosin de' Cosi. (*Sorriso di Sfighino. Finto sorriso di Mamina.*) [...] Forse la fortuna oggi è col nostro Delfino, o forse no. O forse è con voi. Forse troverete la grolla d'oro solo sollevando la sottana della fortuna e guardandoci sotto. Fortunello sta a Fortunpopoli!
>
> ESTRAGONE – Perdinci! Perbacco! Perdincibacco!
>
> VLADIMIRO – Devo ammettere che a scuola non me l'hanno mai insegnato.
>
> ESTRAGONE – Questa sì è la dolce vita! (*AG*, 34.)

2.

> PROGASTARON – [...] Cad a thabharfá ar chailín álainn i gCo. Longfort? [...]
>
> MÍ-ÁBHA – [...] Caitlín, mo húirín. [...]
>
> ESTRAGON – [...] Cailín álainn i gCo. Longfort, thabharfá turasóir uirthi. (*TG*, 25.)

> PROCRASTIGNORE – [...] Come si definirebbe una bella figliola napoletana? [...]
>
> SFIGHINO. – [...] Caterinella, la puttanella. [...]
>
> ESTRAGONE – [...] Una bella figliola napoletana si chiamerebbe Cicirinella la Pacchianella. (*AG*, 40.)

3.

PROGASTARON – Conas adeirtear 'Dia dhuit' i gConamara?
ESTRAGON – Halób. (*TG*, 27.)

PROCRASTIGNORE – Come si dice 'Buongiorno' in Puglia?
ESTRAGONE – Bongio'. (*AG*, 43.)

4.

PROGASTARON – Cathain a dhéantar cábóg de dhuine uasal?
ESTRAGON – Nuair a fhágann sé an seomra.
PROGASTARON – Ainmnigh triúr afradisiac.
ESTRAGON – Mike Tyson, Jesse Jackson agus Winnie Mandela. (*TG*, 28.)

PROCRASTIGNORE – Quand'è che un signore diventa cafone?
ESTRAGONE – Quando si dà alla coltivazione.
PROCRASTIGNORE – Nomina tre afrodisiaci.
ESTRAGONE – Form A. Gin, Salam Hussin, Cacia Turin. (*AG*, 43.)

5.

PROGASTARON – Tusa i dtosach, a Aibhistín, mar is túisce muc ná scéal (*le Mí- Ábha.*) (*TG*, 21.)

PROCRASTIGNORE – (*a Sfighino*) Tu per primo, Gonfiettino. Prima il bussolotto, poi il tombolotto. (*AG*, 35.)

'Aibhistín' (Little Fat One) is a word play on the Irish saying: 'Is túisce deoch ná scéal' (First a drink and then the story), which an Italian audience would not find funny, let alone being in a position to pick up the resonance of the Irish saying. So, to keep the sense of fun, I translated Prograstaron's cue as: 'Tu per primo, Gonfiettino. Prima il bussolotto, poi il tombolotto.' (*AG*, 35.) Here the expression '... bussolotto ... tombolotto' was chosen both because it contains an easy rhyme based on '... otto' – an ending that suggests a small and chubby size – and because it is in line with the quiz game and, more in particular, with Mí-Ábha's characterization. In fact, 'bussolotto' stands for 'dice-box', 'box from which lotto numbers or quiz numbers are drawn', and 'tombolotto' derives from 'tombolo' (lace-pillow), which can be a funny appellative for somebody clumsy and chubby like Mí-Ábha, who is the first to attempt to solve the quiz proposed by Prograstaron (and Mí-Ábha will be followed by Estragon).

As to the appellative 'Aibhistín' ('Gonfiettino') – one of the various appellatives used for Mí-Ábha –, apart from being the Gaelic for Augustine, it is an invented name in the diminutive form, to be linked with the verb 'aibhsigh', which means 'to enlarge' – hence the Italian appellative 'Gonfiettino'.

The other appellatives for Mí-Ábha are also worth mentioning. They are:

- 'Asailín' ('Ciuchettino'), from 'asal', meaning 'donkey' (*TG*, 24 – *AG*, 38).
- 'Ashóilín' ('Sforatino'), from 'só<i>l, meaning 'sole' (a type of fish), but also an echo of the English word 'hole' (*TG*, p. 25 – *AG*., p. 40).
- 'Aimiltín' ('Amilino'), from 'aimil' (a chemical subsance) (*TG*, p. 26 – *AG*, p. 41).
- 'Abhaichín' ('Bucatino'), which suggests both 'abhac', meaning 'dwarf', and also 'ábhach', meaning 'hole, recess' (*TG*, 28, 40 – *AG*, 40, 44).
- 'Aitléirín' ('Adolfino'), from 'aiteall' (genitive: 'aitill'), which means 'fine spell between showers', is also a pun on the name 'Hitler', hence the Italian 'Adolfino' (from Hitler's first name) (*TG*, 30 – *AG*, 46).

As to the name of the character under scrutiny, Mí-Ábha, various resonances and links may be found there:

- 'Mí-' is a prefix that stands for 'ill-, badly-' (in Italian, 'dis-, mal-' or deprivative 's');
- 'Ábha' plays on various assonances, that is, 'ádh' for 'luck, prosperity', 'abhac' for 'dwarf', ábhach' for 'hole, recess', 'ábhal' for 'big, immense', 'ábhar' for 'matter, cause'.

Because Mí-Ábha is not very lucky in the quiz game and in his fate (he is transformed into a cat, as his onomatopaeic name suggests), I first decided on the Italian name 'Sfortunello', meaning 'Little Unlucky One'; then I opted for the more colloquial and funny one, 'Sfighino', thus discarding two more possibilities I entertained for him, that is, 'Tomino' ('Funny Little Lump'), as he is somewhat dull, blockheaded and funny, and 'Momino', assonant with Momo, the female character, with whom he shares the role of assistant to Prograstaron.

As to Momo, her name is a word-play on the Gaelic term 'Mamó', a familiar appellative for 'Granny'. I translated it as Mamina, that is, 'Little Mam<m>y, which is near to the original Gaelic and also a compromise between the other two possibilities that came to me: 'Nonina' (for 'Nonnina', corresponding to 'Gran<n>y') and 'Coccolina', meaning 'Mother's Pet'; all that in the light of her endearing smiles and gestures, but also as a pun (considering her curvaceous figure), which the Italian audience would easily link with 'Cicciolina', that is,

Ilona Staller, the porno-star provocatively chosen by the Italian Radical Party, some years ago, as their representative in Parliament.

As to Prograstaron, his name plays with the adjective 'gasta', meaning 'fast, quick, quick in the uptake'; but there is also a possible link there with 'grásta', meaning 'grace', and a possible reference to Partalon, a Hannibal or Brennus of Irish proto-history. The possibilities contemplated for his Italian name were: 'Pracutone', 'Procrastirone', 'Procrastarone'. It was finally rendered as 'Procrastignore', which keeps the first syllable of the original name in Gaelic and also plays with the verb 'procrastinare', meaning 'to postpone, to defer' – what he does with his illusionistic quiz game, that is, that of extending only for a while Vladimir's and Estragon's hope in a comfortable and untroubled life. As Prograstaron is a master – at first, taken for Godot – I included the term 'signore' ('sir, master, lord') but with the intrusion of a distorting 't', hence the full name: Procrastignore.

Much more could be written about the 'distortions' in translation and the contorsions of the translator, who prefers to end here with the invitation to the reader to return to the original texts, Samuel Beckett's *Waiting for Godot*, and Alan Titley's *Tagann Godot*, and enjoy them thoroughly.

Italian film culture in the English-speaking world: translations and transpositions

George Talbot

In October 1909, James Joyce returned briefly from Trieste to Dublin, for the second time that year, as a businessman, with the aim of opening a chain of cinemas in Ireland, beginning with the *Volta* on Mary Street, Dublin's first commercial film auditorium. Joyce was acting as a representative for a group of four Triestine entrepreneurs, in search of new market opportunities. His Slovene partners already owned three cinemas: the *Americano* and the *Edison* in Trieste as well as the *Cinematograph Volta* in Bucharest. Joyce's career as a cinema manager never really got off the ground, as he returned to Trieste a couple of months later, leaving the Dublin operation in the charge of Francesco Novak, the most technically-minded of the Triestine entrepreneurs. Novak, the proprietor of a bicycle shop in Trieste, was unable to speak English, and, for reasons that will become apparent, it is no surprise that the *Volta* changed management within a matter of weeks. The venture, short-lived though it was, caused a stir and was praised in the *Evening Telegraph* an as important innovation in Dublin's cultural life:

> Yesterday at 45 Mary Street a most interesting cinematograph exhibition was opened before a large number of invited visitors. The hall in which the display takes place is most admirably equipped for the purpose, and has been admirably laid out. Indeed, no expense would appear to have been spared in making the entertainment one deserving of the patronage of the public. Perhaps its special feature is that it is of Italian origin, and is in that respect somewhat out of the ordinary and more conventional forms of such displays. For an initial experiment it was remarkably good, remembering how difficult it is to produce with absolute completeness a series of pictures at the first stage of their location in new surroundings the occasion may be described as having been particularly successful. [...] An excellent little string orchestra played charmingly during the afternoon. Mr James Joyce, who is in charge of the exhibition, has worked apparently indefatigably in its production and deserves to be congratulated on the success of the inaugural exhibition.[1]

1 Cited in Richard Ellmann, *James Joyce*, rev. edn (New York: Oxford UP, 1982 [1959]),

Indirectly, Joyce's brief career raises some interesting issues in relation to the translation, transformation and reception of Italian culture abroad, and these are issues which I will pursue in this essay as I examine some aspects of the history and theory of screen translation, using some well-known and suitably contrasting examples from the canon of Italian cinema.

Cinema is now a mature global medium and an established academic discipline, but we should be aware that conventions of its consumption tend to be local and culture specific, to differ over time and between different places. Our experience in the English-speaking world of watching movies in public places, that is, not on television, is so familiar as to appear entirely natural, rather than 'constructed' and historically contingent, which of course is what it is. When we go to foreign-language movies, as a rule, we expect to hear foreign dialogue and to see subtitles on the screen. Things are different in Italy, where we expect most foreign films to be dubbed, both in cinemas and on television. From the advent of the talkies in 1927, the Italian film industry has dubbed foreign films. Indeed post-synchronous dubbing was the common practice for domestic Italian movies right into the 1960s (and beyond in notable cases such as that of Sergio Leone), which goes some way to explain why the two main male actors in a film such as *Il Gattopardo* are not native Italian speakers. Conventions differ from country to country. France, Germany, Italy and Spain tend to be dubbing countries; Belgium, Cyprus, Denmark, Finland, Greece, the Netherlands, Norway, Portugal, and Sweden tend to opt for subtitling.[2] We take these differences for granted and they do not affect the cinema's status as a mature medium. But the history of film viewing reveals a changing set of expectations, each regarded in their day, probably, as entirely natural. James Hay cites a story of awe from an early Italian audience dealing with 'intertitles', the blocks of text placed on screen in silent movies to represent dialogue. Whereas nowadays going to the cinema is an informal experience, it was once a place of quasi-religious silence, punctuated by the choral voices of the audience reading the intertitles out loud:

> Ormai ci si entra spensieratamente nelle sale cinematografiche, quasi direi senza respetto [*sic*]: allora no: il silenzio dello schermo imponeva riguardo: il coro delle didascalie lette ad alta voce dagli spettatori faceva venire in mente addirittura un oratorio; e più misterioso di quelli chiesastici.[3]

pp. 302–3. **2** For some wide-ranging discussions on screen translation and minority languages, see the special issue of *Current Issues in Language and Society*, 7 (2000), p. 2. **3** See James Hay, *Popular Film Culture in Fascist Italy: The Passing of the Rex* (Bloomington–Indianapolis: Indiana UP, 1987), p. 261, who cites Arrigo Benedetti, 'Il cieco accompagna il muto', *Cinema* 10 (25 November 1936), p. 370.

Arrigo Benedetti, recalling the days of early cinema in Italy, tells how at his local cinema, a blind pianist used to accompany the silent movies, responding (with popular Italian songs) to the intertitles (often localized Italian versions of American 'dialogue') being read out like a litany by literate members of the audience. This is a form of audience participation which we lost with the coming of sound. Such participation required two conditions to be fulfilled: firstly, at least some members of the audience had to be literate, and secondly, the intertitles had to be written in a language they could understand.

This brings us back to James Joyce, briefly. Recent research has complemented Ellmann's account of which films Joyce brought to English-speaking audiences in Dublin.[4] These included a very early movie adaptation of *Francesca da Rimini*, as well as comedies and condensed versions of opera stories. Many of the films Joyce showed in Dublin were Italian or French. As a general rule, continental movies imported into the United Kingdom came through a clearing house in London. There the foreign intertitles were removed, the text translated, filmed and spliced into the film for national distribution.[5] Joyce and Novak, however, imported their spools of film directly from Trieste, by-passing London, which means that the intertitles remained in Italian or French. Joyce's *modus operandi* was to translate the intertitles himself, type them out, and make copies to distribute to the audience as they entered the cinema. The fact that the audience, once seated comfortably, was plunged into darkness and therefore unable to read his translations, is one of the more serious weaknesses of this procedure. (As it happens, 1909 was also the year in which a technical device was patented for the on-screen translation of these intertitles for different markets, but Joyce does not appear to have been aware of this development.)[6] Matters can only have got worse when Joyce returned to Trieste leaving the operation in the charge of a Novak, a non English-speaking partner.

Essentially there are two modes of screen translation, dubbing and subtitling. As already indicated, different countries adopt distinct policies on whether to subtitle or to dub. Subtitling, originally the expensive option, is now ubiquitous, for film and on television, and there are now recognisably different forms of subtitling, for example (monolingual) subtitling for the deaf and hard of hear-

4 I am grateful to Luke McKernan who sent me a pre-publication copy of his paper 'James Joyce's Cinema', which, to my knowledge, has not yet appeared in print.   5 For details of this procedure see Jan Ivarsson, *Subtitling for the Media* (Stockholm: Transedit HB, 1992), p. 15.   6 See Ivarsson, p. 23: 'The very first "subtitles" saw the light of day during the silent film era. In 1909 M.N. Trop registered a patent for a "device for the rapid showing of titles for moving pictures other than those on the film strip". With this method the projectionist, using a sciopticon (a kind of slide projector), showed the subtitles on the screen below the intertitles. However, this was never much more than a curiosity'.

ing, subtitling for children (who have reading speeds slower than educated adults), subtitling for language learning as well as subtitling for the reception of foreign films).[7] In recent years subtitling has emerged as a research topic within Translation and Interpreting Studies. But although it is a relatively new technique, it grapples with most of the philosophical problems common to older forms of translation. (In what follows, I will be dealing with translating for the cinema, rather than for television, which is a slightly different medium.)

Two pioneers in the field of Translation Studies, Susan Bassnett and the late André Lefevere, have provided a useful overview of how translation models have developed over time.[8] It may be helpful to review some of the models which they have identified before engaging directly with empirical data from the field of subtitling. They begin with what they characterize as the 'Jerome model', after St Jerome, and this model has at its core the idea of textual equivalence. Unique among translation models, it concerns itself with a single text, the Bible, and the driving force behind the model is that here is a text, the written word of God, which needs to be transposed as faithfully as possible into another language, using the best dictionaries available. It is a text-based model, unlikely, on the face of it, to have any serious application within Film Studies, leaving aside the strict literalism provided by the counter-example of Mel Gibson's *The Passion of the Christ* (shot in Macerata and released in 2004).[9] It is a model which deals with translation as purely a linguistic exercise, which implicitly makes a number of important assumptions about the needs and motivations of the audience. It would be applied very rarely in the field of screen translation. Where the model may have some purchase, at least by analogy, is in the practice of film as literary adaptation, something to which we will return below.

The second model Bassnett and Lefevere consider is the 'Horace model' which is based on Horace's *fidus interpres*, who is faithful not to the text, but to his own customers. He is trusted by them because he is a reliable cultural mediator who knows how to negotiate between languages, dealing with many different types of text. The latter is a model of translation which has more relevance to the contemporary world, where the translation and interpreting industries support the spheres of business, science, diplomacy and public administration to a far larger extent than they support the cultural industries or indeed

---

7 See Zoé de Linde and Neil Kay, *The Semiotics of Subtitling* (Manchester: St Jerome Press, 1999) for a detailed account of the different forms of subtitling.   8 See Susan Bassnett and André Lefevere, *Constructing Cultures: Essays on Literary Translation* (Clevedon: Multilingual Matters, 1998), pp. 1–11.   9 The dialogue in this film is a mixture of Aramaic, Hebrew and Latin (including some distinctly Teutonic Latin used by the Roman soldiers, especially the more brutal ones). Subtitles appear on the film screen.

the devotional life. The text types in question are important, but often ephemeral. Examples for the screen might include weather forecasts, soap operas or advertisements. It is an important and influential model, but not one which is going to concern us in this essay to the exclusion of other models.

Bassnett and Lefevere offer a third model, named after the German translator and translation theorist Friedrich Schleiermacher. This is a model which deals with texts that represent cultural capital, and which advocates different strategies to foreignize texts from different languages. Whereas Victorian translators, by and large, translated all foreign texts into standard literary English, the Schleiermacher model would yield English translations of German texts which retained something of their Germanic strangeness, which would be different from the Italian strangeness of a text translated from Italian. This model, it should be stressed, was applied to texts representing cultural capital, a concept which they define as follows:

> These are the texts the bourgeoisie hastened to read from the seventeenth century onwards because the aristocracy had been reading them, indeed claiming them as their own, and because the bourgeoisie did not want to be cut off from the company of the aristocracy, because that company would eventually provide access to the aristocracy's power, often also in exchange for the money of the bourgeoisie.[10]

A little less tendentiously, cultural capital may be regarded as text that has prestige which exceeds its apparent monetary value. Such text is often literary and sometimes filmic, and is often bound up with national identities. Its transposition into foreign contexts is invariably difficult, and that transposition involves concepts now familiar from Translation Studies, such as acculturation, domestication and foreignizing. It will help to define the terms as these are concepts which will inform the discussion which follows. 'Acculturation', which has its terminological roots in anthropology, is defined by the *Oxford English Dictionary* (*OED*) as 'the adoption and assimilation of an alien culture'. Acculturating procedures might include bringing loan words into the target language and culture, for example, the now ubiquitous 'latte', 'panini' (often used as a singular) and 'barista'.[11] In their new surroundings, however, these loan words become neutralized and assimilated, for example, adapted to target-language pronunciation patterns. 'Domestication' involves making a text familiar to a foreign audience, often by

---

10 See Bassnett and Lefevere, p. 7.   **11** This process is to be distinguished from cod acculturation, a cognate phenomenon where, for example, something that looks like an English word turns up in Italian and takes on a semantic life of its own, e.g., 'footing'.

using familiar terms for something cognate but different in the source culture. At a very basic level it means modifying place-names (for example, 'Genoa' for 'Genova', 'Leghorn' for 'Livorno' or 'Florence' for 'Firenze') but can often be much more distorting, for example, 'Chief Constable' for 'Prefetto'. The more or less one culture feels free to domesticate another one is usually tied to perceptions of power and prestige, or their opposites. 'To foreignize' is defined by the *OED* as 'to refashion after foreign models; to give a foreign air to'. It is at the root of Schleiermacher's idea that translations from different languages should read and sound different in the target language. Implicitly the privileged position of the target language is denied. This is a more pointed form of acculturation which has a special role in screen translation.

In one of the few essays dedicated to the translation of film dialogue, Christopher Taylor sets out the task of contemporary subtitlers:

> It is important to deliver the whole semiotic message of the source text (the said and the unsaid, which might be relayed by gestures, by pregnant silences, by accompanying images, etc.), while at the same time creating a target language flavour that will sound convincing to the audience. The translator must try to analyse and fully understand the characters to imagine what they would say in a similar situation or scenario in the target language culture, and yet not divorce it from its origins which might be in a very different cultural milieu. In other words, although a certain domestication or localization may be required to make the discourse sound more natural, the film's original setting and flavour, a large part of which is enshrined in language, also need to be preserved.[12]

What Taylor is describing very effectively is the implicit tension between the Jerome and the Horace models, or fidelity to the source text and culture versus fidelity to the wishes, culture and expectations of the customer, held in check by the Schleiermacher model when dealing with cultural capital. We will best illustrate these tensions by considering some examples, from two films which represent cultural capital.

Luchino Visconti's adaptation of Giuseppe Tomasi di Lampedusa's meditative historical novel *Il Gattopardo* is widely recognized as a masterpiece of Italian cinema, especially outside Italy. Released in 1963, it stars some non-Italian actors (principally Burt Lancaster and Alain Delon) and was therefore dubbed, on the standard Italian post-synchronous fashion.[13] The version released in the English-

---

12 See Christopher Taylor, 'The Translation of Film Dialogue', *Textus*, 12, no. 2 (1999), pp. 443–58 (p. 451). **13** In fact, two parallel versions were made, partly to placate Burt Lancaster, who wanted the film made in English. See Francesco Petrucci, 'La realizzazione de *Il*

speaking world, however, had a post-production soundtrack, recorded in America independently of Visconti's supervision. It is now universally accepted that the American dubbing was very poor. Worse still, Twentieth Century Fox – co-financier with the Italian film company Titanus, and sole US distributor – also mutilated the film by pruning about half an hour from the director's cut (including much of the magnificent ball scene), and printing the English-language version on inferior film stock, to contain costs, as the film had gone far over budget. Visconti's colour effects were destroyed, his film shortened arbitrarily and his Don Fabrizio, in his view, sounded like a drawling cowboy. Burt Lancaster himself was in charge of the American dubbing project. More arbitrarily, other characters spoke with caricatures of British received pronunciation, almost in *Carry On*-mode. Visconti was furious and wrote to *The Times*, dissociating himself from the English-language release.[14] For nearly thirty years, however, this is the version of the film most of us will have seen. In 1991, a restored version was released under the supervision of Visconti's director of photography, Giuseppe Rotunno, with the original Italian dubbing. The DVD released by Medusa Video of Milan in 2001 offers this restored version, with subtitles in English and Italian (the latter for the hard of hearing).

Tomasi di Lampedusa's novel is filtered through the consciousness of Don Fabrizio Corbera, Prince Salina, and it contains a relatively small number of significant conversational exchanges, none more important than those between Don Fabrizio and Chevalley, the representative of the Turin government sent to invite the Prince to join the Senate of the newly united kingdom of Italy. Of the two extracts which follow, the first is part of a conversation taken almost verbatim from the novel; the second is also taken verbatim from the novel but it is not a conversation as such, it is the narrator's description of the thoughts running through the minds of the two characters, as Chevalley is taking his leave:

Chevalley: Dopo la felice annessione, volevo dire dopo la fausta unione della Sicilia al Regno di Sardegna, è intenzione del governo di Torino di procedere alla nomina di alcuni illustri siciliani a Senatori del Regno.

Gattopardo: intervista a Pietro Notarianni', to be found in the very informative booklet which accompanies the DVD release (Milan: Medusa Video, 2001), pp. 5–10 (p. 7): 'Alla fine fu girata una doppia versione (mai montata), una in italiano e un'altra in cui tutti parlavano inglese maccheronicamente'. Notarianni was Visconti's executive producer for the film. **14** On the vicissitudes of the film and on questions of adaptation from the novel see Geoffrey Nowell-Smith, *Luchino Visconti*, 3rd edn (London: British Film Institute, 2003), pp. 79–93; Millicent Marcus, *Filmmaking by the Book: Italian Cinema and Literary Adaptation* (Baltimore and London: Johns Hopkins UP, 1993), pp. 45–66 and Ernest Hampson, 'Visconti's *Il Gattopardo*. Aspects of a Literary Adaptation', *Spunti e ricerche*, 15 (2000), 69–78.

Certo il suo nome è stato fra i primi, un nome illustre per antichità, per il personale prestigio di chi lo porta, per i grandi meriti scientifici, per l'atteggiamento dignitoso e liberale, anche, assunto nei recenti avvenimenti. Prima di far prevenire la lista a Torino i miei superiori hanno ritenuto doveroso informarla e domandarle se le sarebbe gradita. Il Governo spera molto nel suo consenso. Questo è l'oggetto della mia missione qui, missione che per altro mi ha valso l'onore e il piacere di conoscere Lei e la sua famiglia, e questo magnifico palazzo.[15]

This passage illustrates some of the issues we have been discussing. A first step for any cultural mediator of films is to decide on a translation strategy, such as whether to subtitle or to dub. In practical terms, this decision will be taken at a managerial level, rather than by the translator, who will then work within the constraints which flow from the strategic decision. As we saw in the case of *Il Gattopardo*, Twentieth Century Fox decided on dubbing and on substantial cuts for the English-speaking market. In the English-language version, the Prince's voice is the American voice of Burt Lancaster and Chevalley's is that of an English toff. This strategic decision immediately takes us away from the Jerome model and places the focus of mediation unambiguously on the consumer, and Twentieth Century Fox's market research into what an English-speaking mass audience would expect from an Italian art film. A likely summary might be: not too long, with the Hollywood star (Burt Lancaster) sounding like a Hollywood star, that is, speaking in American English. (Expectations regarding Chevalley are infinitely more interesting.) In other words, the US distributor took domestication to what Visconti (and many others) regarded as a vulgar extreme. What is interesting though is that despite this cavalier use of the Horace model on the part of the distributor, we find distinct traces of the Jerome model in the efforts of the subtitler to render the film's dialogue into English for the screen.

The restored 1991 version re-introduces foreignization by using subtitles to complement the Italian dialogue. The DVD subtitler manages to get on to the small screen a large amount of the dialogue between Don Fabrizio and Chevalley, and very few concessions are made to the English-speaking viewer:

Chevalley: Due to the happy annexation … I mean … the unhappy union of
              Sicily and the Kingdom of Sardinia, the Turin Government intends

15 Visconti follows the text of the novel very closely. See Giuseppe Tomasi di Lampedusa, *Il Gattopardo* (Milan: Feltrinelli ['universale economica'], 1986), pp. 118–19. The dubbed version follows closely the published English translation of the novel – *The Leopard*, translated by Archibald Colquhoun (London: William Collins and Sons, 1960).

to elect a number of illustrious Sicilians as Senators of the Kingdom. Yours, of course, was one of the first names to spring to mind, due to its antiquity and prestige, to your great knowledge, and to the dignity you showed during the recent events. Before making the list official, we thought it proper to inform you, and see if you approved this proposal. The Government hopes you would. This is the object of my mission, which also gave me the opportunity to meet you and your family and to see your beautiful palace.

Chevalley's parapraxis, 'annexation' for 'union', is conveyed faithfully and is marred only by an unaccountable '*unhappy*' instead of 'happy' for 'felice', which makes nonsense of the dialogue which follows. Without a quite detailed knowledge of Italian history, the English-speaking viewer who follows these subtitles has just cause to be confused. This should not have passed Quality Control.

Chevalley's speech sounds like a letter rather than spontaneous speech (as the narrator on the novel observes), and this is in keeping with his timid and reserved character. (He has also been kept waiting for a long time, allowing him to prepare and rehearse his speech over and over again.) This level of formality probably helps the translator, who for the most part conveys the speech in the spirit of the Jerome model, and therefore also conforms, mostly, to the requirements set out by Taylor for translators of film dialogue.

The second example is the non-conversation or silent conversation of two minds. The words with which the characters' thoughts are articulated in Lampedusa's novel become dialogue in Visconti's film:

Chevalley: Questo stato di cose non durerà; la nostra amministrazione, nuova, agile, moderna cambierà tutto.

Don Fabrizio: Tutto questo non dovrebbe poter durare; però durerà, sempre; il sempre umano, beninteso, un secolo, due secoli …; e dopo sarà diverso, ma peggiore. Noi fummo i Gattopardi, i Leoni; quelli che ci sostituiranno saranno gli sciacalletti, le iene; e tutti quanti Gattopardi, sciacalli e pecore, continueremo a crederci il sale della terra.

The subtitler's treatment of Don Fabrizio's famous lines raises an interesting question, and suggests a certain lack of co-ordination:

Chevalley: You may not believe it, but the current situation won't last. Our modern administration will change everything.

Don Fabrizio: It shouldn't last, but it will, forever. It's the human 'forever', a couple of centuries. Only then it will be different, but worse. Goodbye, Chevalley.

Chevalley: Goodbye. Thank you for everything.

Don Fabrizio: We were the servals, the lions. Our place will be taken by jack-
                als, by hyenas. We all, the servals, the lions, the jackals and the
                sheep, will keep on believing we're the salt of the earth.

What we have here might be described as inappropriate use of the Jerome
model. A 'gattopardo' refers to an heraldic animal, similar to a leopard: similar
to but not identical with. On the other hand, for good or for bad, both novel
and film are known in English as *The Leopard*. Therefore it is disconcerting to
see the line which gives the book its title translated on screen in such a way as
to present us with 'servals' instead of 'leopards'. The point is lost. 'Serval' may
well be the best dictionary equivalent, and therefore in line with the Jerome
model, but Horace's customers have been short-changed.

My final set of examples comes not from Visconti's formal and literary dia-
logue, but from a more demotic and controversial film, Roberto Benigni's *La vita
è bella*. This film is one of very few Italian movies to achieve mass appeal in the
English-speaking world and to achieve recognition through winning three Oscars.
Unlike *Il Gattopardo* it is not a literary adaptation. In the British Isles it was released
in Italian with English subtitles. The DVD release contains both Italian and
American-English soundtracks, with subtitles in a number of different languages.
The English soundtrack and the English subtitles are very similar, as might be
expected, but not identical, which again is within the horizon of expectation as
subtitles usually have to be more condensed to fit on the screen without obscur-
ing the picture.[16] The VHS release (in Britain and Ireland) uses the combination
of Italian soundtrack and English subtitles, mirroring the cinema release. The
English soundtrack, therefore, has a limited circulation, and in my view this is no
bad thing, given the stereotypical 'stage Italian' accents it includes, which probably cross the border from domestication into patronizing racism.

The dubbed and subtitled translations are identical for the first exchange I want
to look at. *La vita è bella* is a comedy, so unlike in *Il Gattopardo* we find lots of jokes,
some visual (for example, the recurrent hat gags) and some linguistic. These latter
cause difficulties, especially when puns are involved, as is the case in the following,
which is the riddle waiter Guido presents to Dr Lessing in the Grand Hotel in Arezzo:

Riddle: Biancaneve in mezzo ai nani. Resolvi quest'enigma cervellone nel
             tempo che ti dà la soluzione.

Solution: Fra sette minuti.

---

16 This is especially true of subtitles for video and DVD, which are almost always more condensed than versions for the cinema screen.

Faced with a choice between the Jerome and the Horace models, the translator has opted for the latter:

Riddle: The dwarves and Snow White sit down for a bite. How fast can
             you guess what she serves her guests next?
Solution: Seven seconds.

The linguistic solution may be weak, but it is difficult to envisage a better one, and it is vital to retain a unit of duration (whether seven seconds or seven minutes) as the answer to the riddle, because as with the hat gags, this joke returns later in the film, when Dr Lessing next appears and Guido is with Dora, after the opera. To replace the riddle with a completely different one – a more extreme form of domestication – might make good sense, according to the Horace model, but would cause problems in the longer run. Taylor provides a salutary example of what can go wrong when screen translators stray too far towards their customers' expectations. Referring to the Italian subtitling of an episode from the American sitcom *Friends* he writes:

> The three male characters in the series are arguing about going to an ice-hockey match, until one asks the other two if they are prepared to buy him a 'big foam finger'. The scene ends with this request, which is obviously meant to be picked up later. The translator turns this object of sports' fans paraphernalia into 'una birra gigantesca'. A little later the studio audience laughs immediately on seeing the character in question wearing the 'big foam finger', and not drinking beer.[17]

A weak pun, by comparison, is a lesser evil.

My next example from *La vita è bella* has no particular need of the source text, which is rendered accurately by both the dubbed and subtitled versions. Instead I want to look at some of the significant differences between these forms of translation. At this point in the film, Guido the waiter is impersonating the schools inspector from Rome who has been sent to instruct the schoolchildren of Arezzo on the superiority of the Italian race. This incident is set in 1939, the year after the *leggi razziali* were passed. We begin with the Headmistress introducing the inspector to the children:

Dubbed version:
Headmistress: The good inspector has been sent here to explain to you about
                 the proclamation of race which has been signed by the most

17 See Taylor, p. 453.

enlightened Italian scientists. He will, and we're very honoured to have him do it, demonstrate to us that our race is really superior, the best of them all. Sit down now. Go ahead Inspector.

Guido: I'll explain our race …

Headmistress: Is superior …

Guido: Naturally. So … our race is superior. Uhm … In fact I've just come from Rome, right this minute, to tell you so there won't be any confusion my friends, that our race is definitely superior. I was chosen, eh …, to deliver this message, by racist Italian scientists, in order to illustrate to you how superior a race we really are in this world.

Subtitled version:

Headmistress: As you know, the inspector came from Rome to talk to us about the race manifesto, signed by the most well-versed Italian scientists. He will, and we're very honoured, demonstrate to us that our race is a superior race. The best of all. Take your seats. Go ahead Inspector.

Guido: Our race.

Headmistress: Is superior.

Guido: Naturally. Our race is superior. I've just come from Rome, right this minute, to come and tell you in order that you'll know, children, that our race is a superior one, chosen, I was, by racist Italian scientists, in order to demonstrate how superior our race is.

We would expect the subtitled version to be more condensed than the dubbed one, but in fact the word count is roughly equal, although the syllable count is lower and less screen space is taken up. Curiously, the subtitled version makes a better job of conveying Guido's improvisation. He is taking his cues from the Headmistress's introduction, treading water. In the dubbed version she does not say that he has come from Rome, and this translation therefore loses the spontaneity of his performance, where he is clearly playing for time, repeating the information he has been given, while thinking of what he is going to do next. The jarring effect of 'racist Italian scientists' comes across in both versions. It is a good example of how a collocation can change in nuance over time. In the 1930s, 'scienziati razzisti' was not a term of abuse, as it would be today. On balance, the domestication of the dubbed soundtrack underplays Benigni's linguistic deftness.

My final example finds Guido acting as comic interpreter in the concentration camp, to keep the awful truth from his son Giosuè. The guard, a caricature Nazi, is explaining the camp rules, and has asked if there are any German speakers among the Italian prisoners. Guido, who does not know any German, steps forward. No subtitles are offered of the German speech (which is informing the prisoners that they are now forced labourers, working for the good of the greater Germany):

English dubbing:

> [Untranslated German]
>
> Guido: The game starts now. If you're here you're in, if not, you're out.
>
> [Untranslated German]
>
> You have to score a thousand points to win. If you do that you take home a tank.
>
> [Untranslated German]
>
> Lucky dog!
>
> [Untranslated German]
>
> Every day we'll be announcing who's in the lead from the loud-speaker there.
>
> [Untranslated German]
>
> The one with the least points has to wear a sign each day that spells the word 'jackass' right on his back. Yeah?
>
> [Untranslated German]
>
> We get to play the part of the nasty guys who shout all the time. Anyone who's afraid loses points.
>
> [Untranslated German]
>
> There's three ways a person can lose his points. They would be as follows: one, turning into a big cry baby; two, telling everyone you want to see your Mamma; three, if you're hungry and want us to bring you something to eat. Forget about it!
>
> [Untranslated German]
>
> It's very easy to lose points for being hungry. Just yesterday I was penalized 40 points because I was so hungry I had to have a jam sandwich.
>
> [Untranslated German]
>
> Apricot jam!
>
> [Untranslated German]
>
> He wanted strawberry.
>
> [Untranslated German]
>
> And don't ever ask for any lollipops because you won't get any. We eat them all!

English subtitles:

> [Untranslated German]
>
> Guido: The game starts now. Whoever's here is here, whoever's not is not.

[Untranslated German]

The first one to get a thousand points wins. The prize is a tank!

[Untranslated German]

Lucky him!

[Untranslated German]

Each day we'll announce who's in the lead from that loudspeaker.

[Untranslated German]

The one with the least points has to wear a sign saying 'jackass' right here on his back.

[Untranslated German]

We play the part of the real mean guys who yell.
Whoever's scared loses points.

[Untranslated German]

You'll lose your points for three things. One, if you cry. Two, if you want to see your mommy. Three, if you're hungry and you want a snack. Forget about it!

[Untranslated German]

It's easy to lose points for being hungry. Just yesterday I lost 40 points because I absolutely had to have a jam sandwich.

[Untranslated German]

Apricot jam!

[Untranslated German]

He wanted strawberry.

[Untranslated German]

Don't ask for any lollipops. You won't get any.
We eat them all!

This is a fascinating exchange, which taps into a negative stereotypical view of Germans which used to be found quite widely spread in Italian culture, and it has not quite disappeared even to this day. One thinks of Rossellini's fat sexually-deviant Nazis in *Roma città aperta*, Dante's 'Tedeschi lurchi' (*Inferno*, XVII, 21), or indeed Prime Minister Silvio Berlusconi's verbal attack on German deputy Martin Schulz in the European parliament in summer 2003.[18] Conveying national prejudices into other cultures usually requires particular sensitivity. (In dubbing *Fawlty Towers* for Spanish television, the hapless Manuel from Barcelona becomes an Italian waiter.)

It is also a poignant piece of dialogue, where the intention of the interpreter (Benigni's character Guido) is to be *unfaithful* to the message and to protect his

---

18 See the BBC report of the incident, 3 July 2003, http://news.bbc.co.uk/1/hi/world/europe/3039912.stm.

son's innocence from the lethal absurdity of the Nazis' *Endlosung*. This takes the Horace model to a novel extreme, that of the *infidus interpres*: the message must be kept from the client at all costs, and it must be replaced with a different message which uses comedy to undermine the authority of the speaker. Benigni's strategy therefore poses some difficulties for the screen translator.

In the treatment of the exchange we find a predictable pattern. The subtitles are more condensed, and lacking in phatic language, for example, note the continuous present and the redundant 'there' in the dubbed version 'every day we'll be announcing who's in the lead from the loudspeaker there', as opposed to the subtitled one 'each day we'll announce who's in the lead from that loudspeaker'. This pattern is reinforced by the other lines of Guido's speech. The dubbed version offers English-speaking viewers the bizarre prospect of Italian anti-German prejudice domesticated in Marx-Brothers style, heavily inflected Italo-American English. We may pause to wonder exactly what we are laughing at.

The purpose of the foregoing is not to poke fun at the failures of screen translators, who were probably hard-pressed, poorly supervised and poorly rewarded, but to provide some analysis of what happens when Italian films, even very well-known ones representing cultural capital, are received by English-speaking audiences. Remarkably little research has been carried out yet into the reception of foreign films, much less on the subliminal effects of dubbing and subtitling on audience expectations and prejudices. It has been argued that dubbing is a more insidious process than subtitling, wide open to audience manipulation, allowing material to be 'censored with regard to morals or politics without the audience having the least suspicion'.[19] The final example from Benigni's film gives us a comical illustration that there is some truth in this claim, where Guido *mis*interprets the German guard, for his own (benign) reasons.

Bassnett and Lefevere argue that 'rewriters and translators are the people who really construct cultures on the basic level in our day and age'.[20] If that is true – and the evidence from Film Studies seems to support the thesis – then we should be more aware than we are of the processes which are at work in the transposition of cultures. Far more quantitative research needs to be done into the history of post-production processing and distribution of foreign movies before such a claim could be made to stand up. Such research is unlikely to reveal cases as striking as James Joyce's work in Mary Street, but it may suggest that mass cinema audiences which have to rely on different forms of screen translation may be little less in the dark about aspects of Italian cultural capital than were the patrons in the auditorium of the *Volta* a century ago.

19 Ivarsson, p. 17.   **20** Bassnett and Lefevere, p. 10.

Piero Bigongiari and Mario Luzi: the poet as translator: 'Who may yet be read and may be written yet': Piero Bigongiari and Mario Luzi translated

Mark Hutcheson

MARIO LUZI (1914–2005)[1]

Vita? – «Oh come lo era» –

Vita? – «Oh come lo era» –
dirò più tardi
se ne avrò il tempo,
lo so bene. Ma intanto vita non mi pare,
si disfa in sé una stagione irosa,
un anno oscuro
da cui ci si risveglia sì, ma agri
sulla traccia di che,
in fuga da che cosa? –

pensavo adesso tra me. L'Irlanda ebbe
ora cupo ora chiaro-piovosa
la sua vasta domenica erba e ardesia
con pochi uomini nei campi
di golf e cricket, pochi dietro le greggi,
meno ancora sui cavalli,
verde, con cunei smeraldini
fin dentro l'acqua nera
dei suoi laghi a fondovalle.
M'aprì o mi celò qualcosa?
Fu questo, questo perdutamente
dal mare al più lontano menhir.
Eppure erano grani
di fuoco azzurro gli occhi di Tom e David,
i miei amici esperti del luogo, i miei piloti di lì.

---

1 Mario Luzi's texts are taken from Mario Luzi, *Tutte le poesie*, 2 vols (Milan: Garzanti, 2004),

Life? 'Oh, how good it was,'

Life? 'Oh, how good it was,'
I'll say later
if I've time,
I know. But meanwhile life does not seem life to me,
an irate season in itself undoes itself,
a sombre year
from which we're reawakening, sure, but sour
tracking what,
in flight from what? –

I was thinking to myself now. Ireland had
sometimes murky- sometimes sunny-raining
vast her Sunday grass and slate
with few men on the golf links,
cricket grounds, few behind the herds,
fewer still on horses,
green, with emerald wedges
right into black water of
her lakes on valley floor.
She showed me something? Shut it from me?
This she was, this utter loss
from sea to furthest menhir.
Yet grains of azure fire
were Tom and David's eyes,
my friends who knew the place, my pilots there.

pp. 625, 837, 863. My English versions of 'Lavata – *(Belfastina)'* and 'Eresse in lontananza'

Lavata —

Lavata —
  non ancora, non abbastanza
    è lavata la città.
Corre il sangue, corre
verso le chiaviche
flagellato dagli idranti,
incalzato dalle spazzole.
     Ecco, non c'è più sangue
in vista,
   è disceso tra le griglie
    tutto, dentro gli scarichi
pretto o mischiato
con acqua e con fanghiglia
      tutto, tutto verso le tenebre.
     E ora duramente
lo scandalo cristiano si nasconde,
duramente si occulta a se medesimo,
      si calano
nella loro inesistenza
    i testimoni,
     ritrovano
     fino al nuovo blitz
la loro
   clandestinità gli attanti.
    Calma
si offre la città
   alla muta
    ispezione dei gabbiani.
    Calma
l'isola dispensa
   equa
    la sua domenica di pioggia
a tutte le sue parti,
   a tutta la sua erba.
Cresce o muore l'esperienza.
    O, ancora,
     ammassa loglio nella sua riserva.

were published in an earlier form in *Poetry Ireland Review*, 32 (summer, 1991), 53–4. Catherine O'Brien has also translated the three poems by Luzi that appear here: Mario Luzi, *Irlanda:*

Washed —

Washed —
           not yet, not adequately
               is the city washed.
Towards the sewers
flows the blood, it flows
lashed by hydrants,
chased by brushes.
                 Look, there's no more blood
in sight,
           it's gone down through the gratings
           totally, gone into drains
pure or mixed
with water and with sludge
                  totally, totally into darkness.
                  And obdurately now
the Christian scandal hides itself,
and obdurately to itself conceals itself,
                  the witnesses
into their inexistence
           drop,
             the actors
           till their next atrocity
regain their
           clandestinity.
           Calm
the city offers up herself
           to mute
                inspection by the gulls.
                Calm
the island deals out
           equable
            her rainy Sunday
to all her parts,
           to all her grass.
Experience grows or dies.
             Or, yet again,
                amasses darnel in her store.

'quel riconfermato incontro' (Dublin: Italian Cultural Institute, and Bari: Modugno, 1993), pp.
39, 50, 53.

Eresse in lontananza

Eresse in lontananza
l'Irlanda i neri monti;
ed ecco, ancora, s'inverò nei sensi
la Dublino del ricordo,
                               verità
con verità coincise
in quel lucido momento,
immagine su immagine, figura
su figura, non fosse per espatrio
o morte qualche dolorosa assenza.
E con lei presero corpo
nell'erba e nella torba
le ben rammentate lontananze,
i pascoli, i recinti,
i rari uomini, i campi
di golf e polo, gli sperduti dolmen.
Tutta l'isola rinvenne
ed arse sottilmente
nel suo cielo e nei suoi inferni
a quel riconfermato incontro.
E anche io dentro me stesso.
Ritrovandomi, sì, quanto riconoscendomi?

PIERO BIGONGIARI (1914–1997)[2]

Si dice che Dio

Si dice che Dio, che non parla, però respira nel palpito
    mimetizzato della razza in fondo al mare
e che per dissetarsi saltella col passo gentile anche se cauto del
    gerbillo nel deserto
da una pianta a un'altra pianta arida.

---

2 Piero Bigongiari's texts are taken from Piero Bigongiari, *Moses: Frammenti del poema 1971–1977* (Milan: Mondadori, 1979), pp. 27, 34–6. My English version of 'Phoenix Park' appeared in *Translation Ireland*, 15, 1 (spring 2002), 6–7. For other English renderings of

Far off Ireland

Far off Ireland
raised up her black mountains;
and look, once more, the Dublin of my memory
came real in my senses,
                                    truth
with truth coincident
in that bright moment,
image on image, figure
on figure, were it not through death
or exile some distressing absences.
And with her took on flesh
in grass and turf
the well remembered distances,
the pastures, the enclosures,
the infrequent men, the polo
pitches, golf links, isolated dolmens.
The island whole came round
and keenly burned
in her heaven and her hells
at that reconfirmed encounter.
And I too in myself.
Myself recovering, yes, how much recognizing?

PIERO BIGONGIARI (1914–1997)

It's Said that God

It's said that God, who does not speak, breathes though within the camouflaged
    pulsating of the sole upon the seabed
and that to slake his thirst he skips with the graceful if careful step of a
    gerbil in the desert
from one plant to another arid plant.

Bigongiari's 'Glendalough' and 'Phoenix Park', see those by Bruce Merry in *The Dublin Magazine*, 10, 4 (spring–summer, 1974), pp. 31–4, and 'Piero Bigongiari: four recent poems', translated and introduced by T. O'Neill, *Hermathena*, 123 (1977), pp. 34–49.

Così da una radice a una radice
secca balzella, e non è Dio, la parola
e non ha i denti acuti del gerbillo
e meno mimetica della razza sul fondo
se profonda respira si scopre allo strale
che ne fa sanguinare l'agonia.

Così ho visto sanguinare l'amore,
l'amore parlante, l'ho visto bere inequivocabile alla propria sete.
Se Dio non parla, e lo sappiamo che non parla,
forse in agguato ascoltava, già colpita, accostarglisi la preda
mentre il filo di sangue colava, gambo succulento, già sul fondo.

Glendalough

La torba d'Irlanda non porta le orme dei morti
quando incoraggia il fuoco a non distruggere che se stesso.
Qui giunti i fiumi neri sono i più trasparenti
i più gelidi i più sinceri i più precipitosi
a mostrare il fondo, in una pazza rincorsa
dalla leggenda a quello che può leggersi ancora
e ancora scriversi, come qui ora io
che non credo che Dio abbia solo questa gelida fretta

per chi trema sulle sue rive, vivo o morto, vivo o morto?,
se impaziente il Maggior nostro scorre e la minore, l'ultima, la
        creatura nuda rimane sull'Acheronte
scorrendo solo nel segno che insegue un'altra, la più folle,
        seppure coperta, come coperta! impazienza
e così calma, così calma, mare in fusione con qualche bolla
        d'aria invetriata
o il nulla, il nulla che Dio regge come una parete trasparente
e speculare fino al sorriso infreddolito di Glendalough
mentre ti tingevi le labbra del tuo arco voltaico, o mia E,
o mia eternità Evanescente per intingerle nel nostro
più nordico tè, nel nostro più spinto te.

Thus from one root to another parched
root hops the word, and is not God,
and does not have the gerbil's pointed teeth
and not so camouflaged as sole on seabed
if deep it breathes it bares itself to the arrow
that makes from it bleed agony of death.

Thus I've seen love bleed,
love which speaks, have seen it drinking unequivocal from its own thirst.
If God does not – we know he does not – speak,
perhaps in ambush he was listening to the prey, already struck, as it approached
            him
while the thread of blood was trickling, succulent stem, already on the seabed.

Glendalough

It bears no dead men's footprints, Ireland's turf,
when urging fire to burn up but itself.
Arriving here black rivers are the clearest
coldest truest the most precipitate
to show the bottom, in a crazy rush
from legend to that which may yet be read
and may be written yet, as here now I
who don't believe that God has just this ice cold haste

for him who shivers on its shores, alive or dead, alive or dead?,
if our Maggior impatient courses and the lesser, last, nude
      creature on the Acheron remains
coursing only in the sign that hunts another, maddest,
      even if concealed, and how concealed! impatience
and so calm, so calm, a sea in fusion with some bubbles formed
      of glassy air
or the nullity, the nullity God holds up like a wall – transparent,
mirror-like – as far as Glendalough's chill smile
while you were putting lipstick on the lips of your voltaic arc, O my E,
O my eternity, my Evanescent, so to dip them into our
most northern tea, into our most obliging thee.

Le orme dei morti non bruciano – mi assicurano –, volatili, in
    alcun camino,
il vivo morto se non lascia traccia
lungo i camminamenti dove il fuoco geloso dell'ultima prova
separa quanto scalda in questo gelo,
in questo gelido bacio di orizzonte a orizzonte,
di calma serale allo spettro stesso della calma.
Non resta che camminare con un'altra calma, altrettanto
    raccapricciante
qui dove non è riparo se la tempesta scroscia tra i viscidi
megaliti gaelici, compatto alfabeto della morte da non tagliare
    in pani di torba,

da non gettare nel fuoco ad alimentarne l'eterna separazione che
    unisce distruggendo,
ma anzi da strizzare, nere incomprensibili strisce, oscure serpi,
    segni lubrichi tra le lumache della pioggia
sino al secco grido asciutto, schianto geloso, vivente tra le ultime
    dune
dove portare la vita non è altrettanto facile, chiuso lo sportello
    della BMW.
Forse ero io, ero io il tuo ritorno?, la capra belante di lassù,
    l'altura che scendeva neroverde, e non era acqua,
la torre che rotonda sul mare, non ha feritoie, gira immota e
    vertiginosa su se stessa, centro senza raggi,
l'eccesso – senza accesso – più breve di un punto che non può
    essere cieco che sull'ultima baia lattiginosa.

No dead men's footprints burn – they reassure me –, volatile, in
    any hearth,
the live man dead unless he leave some trace
along the trenches where the jealous fire of final testing
separates as much as heats in this harsh cold,
this gelid kiss horizon to horizon,
of evening's calm to the very ghost of calm.
All that's left is walking with another calm as horrifying
here where there's no shelter should a storm pelt down among the slimy
Gaelic megaliths, death's close-packed alphabet that must not be cut up
    in loaves of turf,

must not be thrown into the fire to feed thereof eternal separation which
    unites as it destroys,
but rather be compressed, incomprehensible black stripes, dark snakes,
    lubricious signs among the snails of rain
till comes the clean sharp cry, the jealous crash, that lives amidst the final
    dunes
where bearing life is not as easy, and the car door
    closes.
Maybe it was I, was I your coming back?, the bleating goat up there,
    the height that poured down black and green, and wasn't water,
the tower that rotund on the sea, it has no loopholes, turns immobile and
    vertiginous upon itself, a centre without radii,
excess – without access – shorter than a point that can't
    be blind except out on the final milky bay.

Phoenix Park

Il sorriso adirato di sorridere
nel pulviscolo slitta strato a strato
ma che agita l'anima che indora
nel suo fremito lungo di mandola
ora il plettro del sole?

                    Scaglia a scaglia
il sorriso laggiù trema boscaglia
di rami nudi dove ora il cerbiatto
insegue scatenato tra alti e bassi
prativi sulla Liffey il veltro in traccia.

Ombre di neve vanno sotto le acque
grige di questo inverno, soli: alterno
saliscendi del candido volatile
verso l'incontro dove il cibo guizza
sopra il cupo vassoio della morte.

È l'inferno che porge alla tua sete
un altro paradiso dove stare
è difficile come stare a filo
del proprio piombo: specchio rovesciato,
il gabbiano vi sfugge ab irato.

Phoenix Park

The smile cheesed off with smiling
into fine dust slips layer by layer
but what agitates the soul
the plectrum sun now gilds
in long mandola quavering?

                            Flake by flake
the smile down there is shivering thicket
of naked branches where unchained
the wolfhound on the scent now hunts the fawn
between the Liffey's meadowy crests and troughs.

Snow shadows go beneath this winter's
grey waters, suns: alternate
soaring and swooping the candid bird
towards the meeting where food flashes
above death's gloomy tray.

Hell it is that proffers to your thirst
another heaven to stay in which
is hard as it is hard to stay in line
with one's own plumb: mirror overturned,
off that way the gull flies fierce displeased.

TRANSLATOR'S COMMENTS

Tom O'Neill introduced me to Italian literature: initially, to Leonardo Sciascia, and then to Piero Bigongiari, in 1985, and to Mario Luzi, in 1990, asking me to help translate four of the six poems given here: Luzi's 'Lavata – *(Belfastina)*' and 'Eresse in lontananza', and Bigongiari's 'Glendalough' and 'Phoenix Park'. Bigongiari's two poems arose from a lecture visit sponsored by Trinity College and the Italian Cultural Institute in Dublin in October 1972; it was then that he met Tom for the first time, together they went to Glendalough, and they remained friends until the poet's death in 1997;[3] indeed, Bigongiari makes fleeting mention of his companions in the poem: 'Le orme dei morti non bruciano – mi assicurano –'. Almost five years later, in Spring 1977, Mario Luzi came to Dublin, also to lecture in Trinity, and from this originated his poem 'Vita? – «Oh come lo era» –', the first translated here.[4] This poem refers to Tom by name, and also to David Nolan, professor of Italian at University College Dublin.

> Eppure erano grani
> di fuoco azzurro gli occhi di Tom e David,
> i miei amici esperti del luogo, i miei piloti di lì.

Luzi made a long stay at Queen's University Belfast in autumn 1985, which occasioned the second poem here, 'Lavata – *(Belfastina)*'; in autumn 1987, Luzi returned to Belfast to receive an honorary degree, and hence the poem 'Eresse in lontananza', in which he seems to be looking out – back at and towards – Ireland as he sets off from Florence to Belfast. By that time, however, David Nolan was dead, and Tom had emigrated to Australia. So, while Luzi is glad that 's'inverò nei sensi / la Dublino del ricordo', he also mourns the loss of his two friends. As he gazes hither, he is almost overwhelmed to see

> immagine su immagine, figura
> su figura, non fosse per espatrio
> o morte qualche dolorosa assenza.

---

3 For Tom O'Neill on Bigongiari, and Bigongiari in Ireland, see Tom O'Neill, '*Nessuno in un pub irlandese*: "Paradigmaticità di un testo bigongiariano"' in *Per Piero Bigongiari. Atti della giornata di studio di Firenze, 1994*, ed. by Enza Biagini (Rome: Bulzoni, 1997), pp. 43–73, and 'Piero Bigongiari, 7 ottobre 1997', *Italica*, 76, 2 (summer, 1999), 175–92. 4 For Mario Luzi in Ireland, see Mario Luzi, *Irlanda: 'quel riconfermato incontro'*, ed. by Rosangela Barone and Pádraig Ó Snodaigh (Dublin: Italian Cultural Institute, 1993), passim. See also, with reference to Luzi's poems translated here, Mario Luzi, *L'opera poetica*, ed. by Stefano Verdino (Milan: Mondadori, 2001), pp. 1657, 1710, 1716.

My rule of thumb in translating the six poems here has, in a sense, been provided by Bigongiari himself. In the opening stanza of 'Glendalough', he writes: 'dalla leggenda a quello che può leggersi ancora / e ancora scriversi': 'what may yet be read / and may be written yet'. Translation is the close reading of a text in one language, and the exact – insofar as possible, and that 'possible' may be far greater than one assumes – reproduction of that text in the target language. You have to know the original text well to begin to translate it well, but also the translating – the 'writing' of the text in the target language – furthers the original reading, since exactitude of rendering requires exactitude of understanding.

Two words summarize my approach: music and meaning. 'De la musique avant toute chose', counsels Paul Verlaine in the first line of his 'Art poétique'; I seek to make my poetry translations as musical as possible, trying at the same time not to make them too much so. As for meaning, Dr Johnson, in his *Dictionary of the English Language* (1755), defined the verb 'translate' as 'to change into another language retaining the sense', a definition incorporated even today into the article on the word in *The Oxford English Dictionary*. I have found that the best way to translate is to keep as faithfully as possible to the original; it is when the *traduttore* strays – for whatever reason, be it fear of the 'literal', desire of the 'creative', or just downright sloppiness – from what the Muse has granted in the source language that he becomes really the *traditore*.

A good example of music in translating is the last three lines of Luzi's 'Vita? – «Oh come lo era» –', which we have already quoted in the Italian.

> Yet grains of azure fire
> were Tom and David's eyes,
> my friends who knew the place, my pilots there.

The effects here are quite rich. The sentence turns on the word 'fire', which almost rhymes with 'eyes' at the end of the next line, and half-rhymes with 'there' at the end of the last line. But 'fire' also doubly alliterates with another important word, 'friends', the 'r' of which in the first metrical stress of the line carries over onto 'there', the final stress, and recalls the 'r' in 'grains' and 'were' in the preceding lines. There is as well a string of assonances, running through all three lines, from 'grains' to 'azure' (if pronounced 'ay') to 'David' and finishing on 'place'. Finally, in the closing line, 'place' doubly alliterates, in sense as well as sound, with 'pilot'.

The rhythm too is noteworthy. The first two lines are perfect iambic trimeters, while the last line is also regular, a complete iambic pentameter. But I must confess that I have cheated. Instead of retaining (as Dr Johnson would have me do) the Italian 'i miei amici esperti del luogo', 'my friends [who were] experts in the place', I have opted for 'who knew the place', for three reasons: firstly, the former is long and ungainly; secondly, I am not sure that 'experts in the place' means an awful lot in English; and thirdly, 'who knew the place' gives us our iambic pentameter to bring the poem to a rhythmically satisfying close.

An example of music in translating Bigongiari would be the first two lines of 'Glendalough': 'La torba d'Irlanda non porta le orme dei morti / quando incoraggia il fuoco a non distruggere che se stesso.' Here there are four internal rhymes (the two different 'o' sounds alternate), all metrically accented, in the opening line: 'torba ... porta ... orme ... morti', echoed in the next line in 'incoraggia'. But there is also a triple link with 'l' in line 1, again echoed in line 2, with other lesser notes in 'b', 'p' and 'm'. In line 2, the 'k' sound is strongly present: 'quando ... incoraggia ... fuoco ... che', while the double 'gg' links, aurally and visually, 'incoraggia' and 'distruggere'. I have tried to duplicate some of this in the English: 'It bears no dead men's footprints, Ireland's turf, / when urging fire to burn up but itself.' We have here three internal rhymes: 'turf ... urging ... burn', all accented, and spread over the two lines. There is further multiple linking on 'r' in 'bears ... footprints ... Ireland's ... fire', with again minor notes in 'b' and 'p'. Also, the vowel sound in 'burn' is very close to that in the next two words: 'up but'. To speak of metre, the two lines are both perfect iambic pentameters, for the sake of which I have inverted 'Ireland's turf', and are neatly sewn together by the accented 'f' sound: '... turf / ... itself', at the end of each line.

To turn very briefly to meaning, let us look again at the final line of 'Vita? – «Oh come lo era» –'. The word 'piloti' might seem best rendered as 'guides'; after all, 'pilots' could make us think of airline pilots, or pilots on ships, or even pilot films. Here, as everywhere, it is worth delving into the dictionary. *The Shorter Oxford English Dictionary* gives one definition of 'pilot' as: 'a leader or guide, especially through an unknown area of land'. This clearly fits the role of Tom O'Neill and David Nolan *vis-à-vis* Mario Luzi in Ireland.

To take an example from Bigongiari, let us go to the second stanza of 'Glendalough', where he says: 'se impaziente il Maggior nostro scorre e la minore, l'ultima, la creatura nuda rimane sull'Acheronte'. Who is 'il Maggior nostro'? Virgil, who for Dante was 'lo maggiore nostro poeta' (*Convivio*, IV. xxiv. 8)? Or Dante himself, who to Bigongiari – or Luzi, for that matter – would be the Greater Poet? Or is it some other, obscure 'Maggiore', somehow linked to the Acheron as Virgil and Dante were? Or could it be tied, since Bigongiari is standing by a lake, to Lake Maggiore? There seemed no adequate solution. In the end, regretfully, I decided to leave it as it was in the Italian and 'let the reader understand', as it were; that is, search as we had searched, principally in Dante himself.

I would like now to examine four little cruces I had in Englishing these poems. Luzi asks in 'Vita? – «Oh come lo era» –', 'M'aprì o mi celò qualcosa?' My initial version was: 'Did she [Ireland] open something up to me or hide it from me?' This was much too rambling: a heptameter where the Italian is a tetrameter, fourteen syllables rather than nine. I then went for 'Was something shown or shut to me?' Metrically, this was better, but it had two flaws. First, it changed 'opened' to 'shown' and 'hid' to 'shut', though this was not too serious since, chiastically, 'opened' is in the same semantic field as 'shut', and likewise 'hid' and 'shown'. The second, graver fault was that it was passive and so excluded Ireland as the agent of showing and shutting. Finally, it lit on me: 'She showed me something? Shut it from me?' Here Ireland is definitely the agent, and two other felicities materialized: the triple alliteration of 'She ... showed ... Shut', and the precise reproduction of the rhythm of the line in Italian – an iambic tetrameter with a hypermetrical syllable at the end.

Bigongiari's 'Si dice che Dio' was problematic too. It begins: 'Si dice che Dio, che non parla, però respira nel palpito mimetizzato della razza in fondo al mare.' 'Razza' is the fish 'ray' or 'skate', and so I translated: 'the camouflaged pulsating of the skate upon the seabed'. This was fine, the more as it had the lush repetition of the sibilant in 'speak ... skate ... slake ... skip' (the latter two in the following line), and the close rhyme 'skate ... slake'; and 'skate' appropriately assonated with 'pulsating'. However, Corinna shrewdly pointed out that 'razza (skate)' is a hair's breadth away in terms of pronunciation from 'razza (race)', and that this latter was probably also in Bigongiari's mind: he speaks of God, the Creator of the human race, and of love which bleeds, as Christ bled for the human race. 'Skate', therefore, for all its musicality, had to go. Another conundrum, another *eureka!*: 'It's said that God, who does not speak, breathes though within the camouflaged pulsating of the sole upon the seabed', recalling *Genesis 2:7* (Authorized Version): 'And the Lord God formed man of the dust of the ground, and breathed into his nostrils the breath of life; and man became a living soul.'

The next line reads: 'e che per dissetarsi saltella col passo gentile anche se cauto del gerbillo nel deserto'. Here I chose 'graceful' for 'gentile', and 'careful' for 'cauto', and decided to reduce 'anche se' to 'if', partly to tighten the line up a little (as can be seen, Bigongiari is prone to wander), but also because English 'if' can imply 'even'. And so: 'and that to slake his thirst he skips with the graceful if careful step of a gerbil in the desert'. Nothing too bad with this, but I had one small difficulty. 'With the graceful if careful step of the gerbil' introduces an anapæstic rhythm whereas here and in all these translations I have resolutely followed an iambic pattern. I interrogated this rendering closely but could see no other way out, left it, and then realized it had in fact two significant advantages: the unusual anapæstic rhythm imitates the 'skipping' of the gerbil, and 'graceful if careful' produces a nice feminine near-rhyme with bonding triple 'f' sounds.

Finally, in the last stanza of the poem we have: 'Se Dio non parla, e lo sappiamo che non parla.' My first attempt at this gave: 'If God does not speak, and we know he doesn't speak.' No worries here semantically, but metrically it was a mess with stressed syllables running up against each other – 'God does' or 'not speak' – and the anapæst of 'and we know'. I was unhappy and worried at it a little until again it all seemed to sort itself out: 'If God does not – we know he does not – speak.' Such a parenthesis might not be readily seizable in the hearing of the translation, but in the reading it is fine. And the line is now a nice, neat iambic pentameter.

I have spoken of the *traduttore* who strays from the original text in pursuit of the 'creative'. I myself am guilty of this sin. In the years after Tom O'Neill introduced me to Bigongiari's 'Phoenix Park' in 1985, I wilfully and foolishly dismissed the Italian and endeavoured to extract my own poem from what I had in memory of Bigongiari's. For years I toiled at it and got absolutely nowhere. Consequently my feeling is that this type of translation is really abusive of the first poet, disloyal to the reader, and useless for the practitioner: if the translator wants to write poetry, let him write poetry. To illustrate, I shall quote, piacular poetry though it is, the final version of my disgraceful 'after Bigongiari'. Let the reader compare and judge.

> Deer run through trees. The naked branches are left
> To quiver behind them. There's barking and dogs in pursuit.
> There's the Liffey with snow beneath its idle grey.
>
> You lift your chin and smile. No sooner given,
> That smile is twisted by irritation, dislodges
> And tumbles down your legs to the dew-flecked grass.
>
> The sun on such days is a plectrum plucking chords
> From your soul. It climbs so high it topples, like Icarus,
> Meeting the tide halfway by a moribund wharf.
>
> For some there is another paradise,
> As hard as standing upright, in hell. A seagull
> Is scrambling away irate from a tottering mirror.

I should like to thank Roberto Bertoni, Cormac Ó Cuilleanáin, Daragh O'Connell and Corinna Salvadori Lonergan for their help with these translations, as well as Eoghan Quigley and Piotr Sadowski.

The literary critic: Tom O'Neill and
modern Italian literature*

Brian Moloney

Tom O'Neill seems to have made up his mind at an early stage where his research interests lay, namely in modern poetry and the novel.[1] As an undergraduate, he wrote a dissertation on the poetry of Cesare Pavese during his year abroad (1963–4). Italo Calvino's edition of Pavese's *Poesie edite e inedite* (Turin: Einaudi) had come out only the year before, so he was very up to date with his reading. His career in fact got off to a splendid start, as he won prizes or certificates of distinction in each year as an undergraduate. He went from his degree course at Glasgow to a teaching post at Aberdeen, with no intervening period of full-time research, an experience not uncommon at the time and one which some of his contemporaries found left them at a disadvantage, but which seems to have made him only the more determined to work on his research. It was not long before he started to publish his first articles on Italian poetry, as well as his views on the teaching of literature and the curriculum. While still at Aberdeen in 1975, he wrote for the *Universities Bulletin* of the Society for Italian Studies a thoughtful short piece on the place of modern literature in a university curriculum.[2] His starting-point was the Italian section of the introductory prospectus of the School of Modern Languages at Trinity College Dublin, which he was to join the following year, according to which the study of nineteenth- and twentieth-century literature found its unity in the relationship of modern writers 'to the rich tradition from which they spring and the originality of their innovations *vis-à-vis* it'. He heroically refrained from commenting on the startling inelegance of that concluding phrase, but warmly endorsed the view expressed: it was for him 'immediately obvious' that 'one cannot really appreciate the major poets of the *Otto-* and *Novecento* unless one can see them against the poetic tradition of earlier centuries'. The same was true of the novel, although he maintained that Italian novelists' models had to be looked for abroad, as well as in the tradition

* I am grateful to David Fairservice and Tony Pagliaro for information used in this essay.
1 For a full list of Tom O'Neill's publications, see Roberto Bertoni, 'Some Aspects of Tom O'Neill's Work as a Literary Critic' and 'Publications by Tom O'Neill', in *Spunti e Ricerche*, 17 (2002), 5–7 and 8–14. 2 T. O'Neill, 'The Place of Modern Literature in a University Curriculum: Some observations', *Society for Italian Studies Universities Bulletin* 8 (1975), 18–24.

deriving from Manzoni. There is a sense in which Tom at that stage was for-
mulating not only his approach to teaching but also to research: his whole
research effort was devoted to working out the implications and consequences
of that view, which was the basic premise from which he worked and from
which he encouraged others to work.

This meant that he set himself demanding standards, since on that basis one
had to be a very good generalist in order to become a specialist. In 1968, he had
linked Ungaretti and Foscolo; but by 1974 he was considering the influence on
the modern poet not only of Leopardi but also of Góngora in order to understand 'Tu ti spezzasti'. Given that the roots of the aulic Italian tradition are to
be found in the classical world, his major study of Foscolo's 'Dei sepolcri' set
out to offer a detailed textual analysis of the poem that took into account the
poet's Greek and Latin sources, as well as the Italian tradition from Dante to
Alfieri and Parini.[3] It is different from much that had previously been written
on Foscolo in English, in that it focuses austerely on the text of the poem, with
little or no reference to the details of the poet's stormy personal life. The textual analysis is very sensitively conducted, but makes no concessions to non-
specialists. Tom's argument in favour of the poem's monothematic unity is surprising in view of the way the poet seems to weave together a multiplicity of
themes and could have been set out more cogently at greater length. But to
wish that a book were longer is undoubtedly a tribute, and this study was certainly a milestone in Foscolo studies.

Tom did not write about the great triad of the later nineteenth and early
twentieth century – Carducci, Pascoli, and D'Annunzio – but he did produce
several important articles on Eugenio Montale, Mario Luzi, Piero Bigongiari,
and Vittorio Sereni. He also produced translations of some poems, mainly but
not only by Bigongiari and usually in consultation with the poet himself. His
versions were usually carefully introduced and annotated for the benefit of non-
specialist English-language readers, although again it has to be said that he
expected them to work at their reading, comparing the Italian original and the
English version in order to follow his analysis of the metrical and linguistic tex-
tures of the poems. It is often said that every act of translation supposes a prior
act of interpretation, but in Tom's case I suspect that the act of translating was
one of the ways in which he explored the meanings of the poem and the ways
in which it might be read, and there is no mistaking his sense of delight in discovering echoes, overtones or sources, as when commenting on Zanzotto's 'il
soffrire dove l'offerta fu senz'altro οὐδὲν ἀπελπίζουσα' he translates the New

3 Tom O'Neill, *Of Virgin Muses and of Love: A Study of Foscolo's 'Dei Sepolcri'* (Dublin: Irish
Academic Press, 1981).

Testament Greek in his note and adds: 'The context (of Luke, that is) impera-
tively demands this meaning but the Greek verb is unparalleled'.[4]

Allusiveness of this kind undoubtedly heightened and highlighted for Tom
the richness of poetry, a sensitivity to which made him a careful and subtle reader
of a poet like Montale, who used allusiveness both to protect the intrinsically
private nature of the love experience that inspired so many of his poems and
also to enrich their language. 'Montale's Fishy Petrarchism' is a splendid example of Tom's method of working, which requires him both to situate Montale
in his own complex personal poetic tradition and to situate his own work in
the context of Montale studies.[5] Helen Gardner wrote (in a book Tom had
clearly meditated on) that much modern literary theory, with its dismissal of
the author as the creator of the work and the denial of objective status to the
text often 'makes the study of literature sound like a highly sophisticated war-
game with the object of annihilating the author on the field of battle of the
text'.[6] Tom's concern, like Gardner's, was with authors and their works, the
choices and decisions authors made in the making of their works.

Tom's work on poets and poetry has perhaps overshadowed his studies of
the novel, given the primacy of poetry in the hierarchy of the Italian literary
canon; but in fact he devoted much time to the study of the modern novel.
Although he began by working on Pasolini[7] and Cassola,[8] it was the modern
Sicilian historical novel that caught and kept his imagination. He wrote most
frequently and illuminatingly on Tomasi di Lampedusa,[9] Sciascia,[10] and

---

4 Tom O'Neill, 'Andrea Zanzotto – Poesia', *Journal of Association of Teachers of Italian*, 44 (1985),
68–9 (p. 69). **5** Tom O'Neill, 'Montale's Fishy Petrarchism', *Modern Language Notes*, 106, 1
(1991), 78–116. **6** Helen Gardner, *In Defence of the Imagination: The Charles Eliot Norton Lectures
1979-1980*. (Oxford: Clarendon Press, 1984), p. 3. **7** Tom O'Neill, 'A Problem of Character
Development in Pasolini's "Trilogy"', *Forum for Modern Language Studies*, 5, 1 (1969), 80–4. Tom
O'Neill, 'Pier Paolo Pasolini: *Biciclettone*', *Modern Languages*, 50, 1 (1969), 11–13. **8** Carlo Cassola,
Il taglio del bosco, ed. with introduction, notes and vocabulary by Tom O'Neill (London: Harraps,
1970), reprinted by Thomas Nelson and Sons, 1984. Tom O'Neill, 'Cassola on Realism', *Modern
Languages Review*, 65, 3 (1970), 552–7, and 'Cassola e Hardy: lettura di *Un cuore arido*', *Rivista di
letterature moderne e comparate*, 25, 2 (1972), 140–52. **9** Tom O'Neill, 'Lampedusa and De Roberto',
Italica, 47, 2 (summer 1970), 170–82; 'Un eco della "querelle" gattopardesca', *Lingua Nostra*, 32,
2 (1972), 47–8; 'Giuseppe Tomasi di Lampedusa', *The Fontana Biographical Companion to Modern
Thought* (London: Fontana Paperbacks 1983), p. 251; 'Manzoni, Tomasi di Lampedusa e Bassani:
Affinità elettive?', *Filologia Italiana (Ankara)*, 14, 15 (1987), 163–81; 'The Leopard's Changing
Spots: Which Version of Lampedusa's Novel Should we Read?' in *Renaissance and Other Studies:
Essays presented to Peter M. Brown*, ed. by Eileen Anne Millar (Glasgow: University of Glasgow
Italian Department, 1988), pp. 280–99; 'Ants and Flags: Tomasi di Lampedusa's *Gattopardo*', *The
Italianist* 13 (1993), 180–208; 'Lampedusa', in *Reference Guide to World Literature* (Detroit: St James
Press, 1995), pp. 694–6; 'Lampedusa, Sciascia and Consolo: A Map of Misreading', in 'Italian
Criticism: Literature and Culture', a special issue of *Michigan Romance Studies*, 16 (1996), ed. by

Consolo,[11] and it was a tragedy that he never realized his ambition of writing a book on the subject, placing modern Sicilian novelists in their historical and broad literary context. As Roberto Bertoni has rightly pointed out, Tom attached importance to history and politics, but 'he questioned the excesses of ideological criticism on Cassola and Tomasi di Lampedusa, and adopted a critical approach based on the intrinsic literary value of their work'.[12] As in the case of Tom's writings on poetry, one is impressed by his close reading of the texts he studies, of the texts his authors read, and the work of his fellow critics. At the same time I, at least, cannot help feeling that an exploration of, say, Tomasi di Lampedusa's treatment of the ideas of Gramsci and Guido Dorso on Sicily and the south would have produced rewarding insights into the workings of his irony. But Tom, never a political animal, was content to leave work of that kind to others more politically inclined than himself. I understand, however, that he was completing a commentary on *Il Gattopardo* and that this should be published soon.[13]

There is one other aspect of Tom's work that calls out for some comment here. He delighted in bringing together scholars with common interests. Before he went to Australia he had organized mini-conferences in Britain: in Australia, he felt that distance made such gatherings even more important. He regularly

G. Lucente, 21–36. **10** Tom O'Neill, Review of Leonardo Sciascia, *A ciascuno il suo*, ed. by Iole F. Magri (Boston, 1976), *Italica* 54, 23 (1977), 62–4; Leonardo Sciascia, *Il contesto*, ed. with introduction, notes and vocabulary by Tom O'Neill (Manchester: Manchester UP, 1986); Tom O'Neill, 'Il contesto del *Contesto*', in *Atti del VII Congresso A.I.P.I.* (Verona: Fiorini, 1987), pp. 147–53; 'Literal Insularity Versus Literary Universality: The Case of Sciascia', in *Literature and National Cultures*, ed. by Brian Edwards (Geelong: Centre for Studies in Literary Education, Deakin University, 1988), pp. 66–74; 'Sciascia's *Todo modo*: La vérité en peinture', in *Moving in Measure: Essays in honour of Brian Moloney*, ed. by Judith Bryce and Doug Thompson (Hull: Hull UP, 1989), pp. 215–28; *Leonardo Sciascia. "A futura memoria"*. Atti del convegno. Melbourne, 25–26 aprile 1992, ed. by Tom O'Neill (*Quaderni dell'Istituto italiano di cultura*, Nuova serie, I, 1994); Tom O'Neill, 'A Sicilian in Parma: per la preistoria di Leonardo Sciascia', in *Leonardo Sciascia. "A futura memoria"*, ed. by Tom O'Neill, pp. 3–32; 'Sciascia', in *Reference Guide to World Literature* (Detroit: St James Press, 1995), pp. 1101–103; 'La scoperta dell'America ovvero ipotesi per come componeva Sciascia', *Lettere italiane*, 47, 4 (ottobre-dicembre 1995), 565–97; 'Lampedusa, Sciascia and Consolo'; 'Leonardo Sciascia (8 January 1921–20 November 1989)', in *Dictionary of Literary Biography*, CLXXVII, Italian Novelists since World War II, 1945–1965, ed. by Augustus Pallotta (London: Bruccoli Clark Layman, 1997), pp. 321–33; 'Foscolo, Montale e Sciascia alle soglie del Duemila', in *Da un paese indicibile*, Quaderni Leonardo Sciascia 4 (1999), pp. 9–34. **11** T. O'Neill, 'Lampedusa, Sciascia and Consolo'; 'Vincenzo Consolo (18 February 1933–)', in *Dictionary of Literary Biography*, CXCVI, Italian Novelists since World War II, 1965–1995, edited by Augustus Pallotta (London: Bruccoli Clark Layman, 1998), pp. 86–94. **12** R. Bertoni, 'Some Aspects of Tom O'Neill's Work', pp. 5–6. **13** Tom O'Neill's edition of *Il Gattopardo* has been completed by Patrick Glennan and is due to be published by the UCD Foundation for Italian Studies in its series 'Belfield

attended and contributed to Dante symposia in Australia[14] as well as organizing a number of conferences in Melbourne. The proceedings of two of these have been published (on Sciascia and on Montale).[15] He also organized a conference on modern French and Italian poetry at Melbourne, and he was actively engaged in editing a volume of studies for Brian Nelson, that University's Professor of French, when he died.

Tom's undoubted strength as a critic lay in a form of textual analysis that was the result of close reading and re-reading not only of the texts he studied, but also of the texts from which they, in turn, drew their language and imagery. He was both specialist and generalist, whose formidable memory and broad culture impressed the Italian critics and writers who were his friends. Massimo Onofri justly described him as 'coltissimo, raffinato, con una conoscenza incredibile della cultura italiana'.[16]

Italian Library'. **14** Tom O'Neill, 'From UWA to Kelly's Plains via Armidale', in *Dante Colloquia in Australia (1982–1999)*, ed. by Margaret Baker and Diana Glenn (Adelaide: Australian Humanities Press, 2000), pp. ix–xxv. **15** T. O'Neill, *Leonardo Sciascia. "A futura memoria"*; 'Dante, Montale and Miss Brandeis: A (Partial) Revisitation of Montale's Dantism', in *Montale: Words in Time*, edited by George Talbot and Doug Thompson (Market Harborough: Troubadour Publishing, 1998), pp. 27–42. The bibliography entries list Tom's contributions without specifying that the volumes in which they were published are conference proceedings. **16** Quoted in R. Bertoni, 'Some Aspects of Tom O'Neill's Work', p. 5.

Mitomodernismo: a poetics of art and action

Roberto Bertoni

INTRODUCTION

Mitomodernismo (myth-modernism) is a literary trend which has existed *de facto* in Italy since the 1970s, but was given both its name and a specific theoretical status in 1994 through an act of foundation by Giuseppe Conte, Roberto Carifi, Tomaso Kemeny and Stefano Zecchi.[1] This essay attempts to illustrate some aspects of the poetics of *mitomodernismo* through reference mainly to manifestoes and other critical writings, but also, to some extent, to poems by Giuseppe Conte and Angelo Tonelli.[2]

'MITOMODERNISMO' BETWEEN TRADITION AND MODERNITY

In the development of literary history, in order to find its own space and become established, a new poetics needs to clarify its relationship with the past (where models are identified) and with contemporary literary trends (with which controversy may occur). *Mitomodernismo* is related to pre-nineteenth-century canonical authors, romanticism, early twentieth-century orphism and some aspects of modernism. Its polemic is against the neoavantgarde, a literary movement created in the 1960s, related to the early twentieth-century avantgarde, and represented in particular by Gruppo 63.

The neoavantgarde attaches major importance to language experiments, rationality and the provocation of the reader's expectations, whereas *mitomodernismo* focuses on content, tradition, archetypal symbols and satisfying the reader's expectations. As is often the case with literary innovators, the trends started by the avantgarde and continued by the neo-avantgarde, but also by the school of orphism / *mitomodernismo*, have eventually been included in the general canon of Italian poetry (in literary histories and anthologies) where we find orphic

---

1 E. Grandesco, 'Intervista a Tomaso Kemeny sul mitomodernismo', *Otto/Novecento*,19, nos 3–4 (1995), 209–13 (p. 209); and P. Battista, *Dagospia*, 11–8–2004, also at http://213.215.144.81/public_html/13000–13999 articolo_13686.html.   2 In addition to individual collections, some works by myth-modernists can be found each year in the issues of

Campana, experimental Palazzeschi, myth-modernist Conte and neoexperimental Sanguineti. The present writer believes that it is from pluralism that the multiple possibilities of poetic expression originate, and therefore has no personal preference for either of these two currents. It is however important here to mention the objections of the *mitomodernisti* to the ideas of the Gruppo 63.

The myth-modernist Tomaso Kemeny, while maintaining that Gruppo 63 has a number of merits, is opposed to the concept of the poet as an 'operatore culturale' (cultural operator) as defined by this group,[3] and by contrast he adopts the romantic concept of 'ispirazione' (inspiration),[4] and attaches major importance to the tendency towards subjectivity of the romantic poets who, in his view, anticipated the modern movement by elaborating their own system of symbols.[5] While being against the ironic detachment of the neoavantgarde, he underlines the necessity for literature to express 'pietà e terrore' (pity and terror).[6]

The myth-modernists also argue in favour of a meaningful use of the semantics of language, and against that manipulation of the signifier which prevails among the neoavantgarde. The myth-modernists do not rule out an interpretation of poetry as language, but in Kemeny's words they define it as an existentially far-ranging language.[7]

By contrast with the neoavantgarde which, in Edoardo Sanguineti's words, rejects the grand style,[8] *mitomodernismo* is stylistically open to the sublime.[9] In Kemeny's interpretation, the concept of the sublime can be defined as a semiotic structure applicable both to real life and literary texts.[10] Sublime texts are based on 'artistic and scientific models' created through a process of *mitizzazione*

Le acque di Hermes / The Waters of Hermes, ed. M. Maggiari (Trento: La Finestra, 2002, 2003 and 2004), and *Altramarea*, ed. A. Tonelli, La Spezia, published by Città di Lerici, Associazione culturale Arthena and Provincia di La Spezia, printed by Tipografia E. Canepa (2001, 2002 and 2003). Conte and Tonelli, rather than other equally interesting representatives of the myth-modernist tendency, are the two poets whose creative work is briefly exemplified here because they visited Trinity College Dublin respectively in 2002 and 2003 as part of an exchange of Irish and Italian poets which involved a number of Institutions including the Parco Letterario Eugenio Montale in Liguria, the Italian Cultural Institute, Dublin and Trinity College, Dublin. **3** 'Intervista a Tomaso Kemeny', p. 211. All translations are by the present writer unless otherwise stated. **4** Ibid., p. 210. **5** T. Kemeny, 'Introduzione', in *Dicibilità del sublime*, ed. by T. Kemeny and E. Cotta Ramusino (Udine: Campanotto, 1990), pp. 13–19 (p. 15). **6** 'Intervista a Tomaso Kemeny', p. 210. **7** Ibid., p. 213. In Kemeny's Italian text, more precisely, we find a 'linguaggio-luogo in cui ci sia anche un respiro esistenziale'. **8** E. Sanguineti, 'Per una critica dell'avanguardia poetica in Italia', in E. Sanguineti and J. Burgos, *Per una critica dell'avanguardia poetica in Italia e in Francia* (Turin: Bollati-Boringhieri, 1995), p. 10. **9** 'Intervista a Tomaso Kemeny', p. 213. **10** T. Kemeny, 'Introduzione', in *Dicibilità del sublime*, p.13.

(mythicizing).[11] The literary effect of the sublime is ultimately due to the linguistic features of literary works.[12]

In their polemic against the neoavantgarde, the myth-modernists consider the beauty of traditional art and literature as essential and see it as the expression of truth, in opposition to what they define as the nihilism of modern experimentalism. Stefano Zecchi writes: 'During the twentieth century, beauty was always considered antimodern, and experiments on style [...] prevailed over the cult of form'; and he goes on to say: 'beauty is the antinihilist form *par excellence*'.[13]

In their pursuit of beauty and truth, their context is, partly, romanticism, understood as 'the first avantgarde' by Kemeny. He also refers to surrealism (especially Eluard) and mentions Goethe and Dylan Thomas,[14] whereas Conte and Tonelli relate to Byron, Shelley and Eliot. The Italian tradition is represented mainly by Dante, Petrarch and Leopardi; the Italian Novecento by Onofri, Campana and Montale, but for Conte Ungaretti and Pasolini are also essential.

Campana is viewed by Conte and Tonelli as a positive predecessor because of his cosmic ideals and flowing language. His influence seems rather to be less in terms of precise reference and quotation than in echoes of his fluent rhythms and allusions to nature accompanied by a sentiment of union between human beings and the landscape. Campana and Onofri constitute explicitly admitted predecessors of *mitomodernismo* in the modern Italian tradition.

Leopardi, too, is seen favourably, and this is due especially to his approach to infinity beyond space and time, and to his metaphor of the *ginestra* (broom plant) signifying human fragility and endurance *vis-à-vis* nature. Conte's *ginestra* springs from the arid ground of gravel and of a motorway, 'spaesata, unica, ispida' (bewildered, one on its own, bristly), much like Leopardi's 'fiore del deserto' (flower in the desert).[15] Similarly, Tonelli's broom bushes are, like Leopardi's, 'consapevoli / dell'arsura al fondo della vita' (aware / of the drought at the bottom of life).[16]

In the above examples we are not aware of the 'anxiety of influence' which we find in relation to Montale. Conte and Tonelli, like Montale, are from the region of Liguria, and this is perhaps one of the reasons why Montale is an inevitable source but at the same time a father-figure to be rejected. Montale's

---

11 Ibid.   12 Ibid., p. 18.   13 'Il Festival dei nemici del bello', S. Zecchi in interview with A. Iadicicco, *Il Giornale*, 21–9–2002 (also at http://lgxserver.uniba.it/lei/rassegna/ 020921d.htm). The Italian text says: 'Nel ventesimo secolo il bello è sempre stato ritenuto antimoderno e sul culto della forma prevalgono gli sperimentalismi e le sperimentazioni stilistiche'; and: 'la bellezza è la forma antinichilistica per eccellenza'.   14 'Intervista a Tomaso Kemeny', p. 210.   15 G. Conte, *Le stagioni* (Milan: Rizzoli, 1988), pp. 66–8.   16 A. Tonelli, *Frammenti del perpetuo poema* (Udine: Campanotto, 1998), p. 39.

influence on Conte may be partly seen in the language he uses in his first two collections of poetry, *L'oceano e il ragazzo* and *Le stagioni*. A very visible word from Montale is the rarely used Italian term *botri*, employed in the poem 'L'anguilla' in a context of life versus death:

> l'anguilla, torcia, frusta,
> freccia d'Amore in terra
> che solo i nostri botri o i disseccati
> ruscelli pirenaici riconducono
> a paradisi di fecondazione.

(the eel, torch, whip / arrow of Love on earth / that only our ditches or the dried-up / Pyrenean streams lead back / to paradises of fertilization).[17]

Conte, in 'Le stagioni del fuoco, 1', adopts a similar symbolic context but the water imagery changes into a simile of horses running on earth, and *eel* (*anguilla*) signifying interiority is transformed into *soul* (*anima*), a spiritual and psychological concept which was alien to Montale. What Conte writes is:

> Come cavalli rovani
> in corsa sul confine
> di lunghe sabbie e di botri
> va l'anima, attraversa
> il regno del fuoco.[18]

(Like roan horses / running on the border / of long sands and ditches, / the soul goes, crossing / the kingdom of fire.)[19]

The presence of *botri* in Conte's poem indicates an obvious tribute to his Ligurian predecessor, but the changed context shows that he has also carefully distanced himself from Montale. Similarly the sea, constantly present in Montale's work with a variety of meanings, often appears in Conte, but, unlike the reticent Mediterranean sea of *Ossi di seppia*, Conte's ocean is more personalized.

Italo Calvino rightly notes that *L'oceano e il ragazzo* belongs to a poetic tradition which may be defined as Ligurian because Conte, like other poets from that region, makes constant reference to the landscape in order to express

---

17 E. Montale, *L'opera in versi*, ed. by R. Bettarini and G. Contini (Turin: Einaudi, 1980), p. 254. English translation supplied by C. Ó Cuilleanáin. 18 G. Conte, *Le stagioni*, p. 108. 19 Translation by L. Stortoni-Hager, in G. Conte, *The Seasons / Le stagioni*, ed. L. Stortoni-Hager (Chapel Hill: The University of North Carolina at Chapel Hill, 2001), p. 115.

'ragionamento' (reasoning), but unlike Montale he goes in a direction which is opposed to the earlier author's 'scarnificazione, smorzamento, prosciugamento' (stripped-down writing, dimming and draining).[20]

This observation may be stretched even further in the direction of unstripped and undrained language until we come to D'Annunzio's influence. In *Le stagioni*, a footnote by the author to 'Estate. Poseidone' specifies that the line 'Estate non declinare' (Summer, do not decline) is derived from D'Annunzio's 'Madrigali d'estate': 'Estate, Estate mia, non declinare!'.[21] In *Canti d'Oriente e d'Occidente*, Conte states that he prefers Pascoli and Pasolini to D'Annunzio whose echoes, he admits, can be found in his work.[22] Indeed his approach to the language of nature, while owing something to Montale mediated through D'Annunzio, may be seen as standing between Eliot's and Montale's objective correlative and Pascoli's symbolism. In 'Ai Lari', one of the poems in the collection *Canti d'Oriente e d'Occidente,* the author himself has admitted that Pasolini's contribution is mostly visible in the field of metrics where we find irregular hendecasyllables. Ten to twelve syllable lines, in Conte's work in general, cohabit with other line lengths. What is perhaps most relevant in this respect is Conte's feeling of constraint within twentieth-century free verse, and consequently his attempt to adopt organized and more traditional forms of metrics. On a thematic level, in various works by Conte, where we find a presence of Shelley and Foscolo, there is also Pasolini's theme of life experienced through passion. In *Canti d'Oriente e d'Occidente*, there is an aspiration to asceticism contradicted by involvement with earthly life more specifically related to Pasolini: 'Ho servito i piaceri / e ho servito la Luce' (I have served pleasures / and I have served the Light); 'io sono sempre la carne e sempre l'anima' (I am always flesh and always the soul).[23]

Montale, as mentioned above, is present also in Tonelli's poetry. Tonelli takes on Montale's controversy against pompous poets, and, like Conte, adopts objective-correlative procedures in the literary rendering of coastal landscape in connection with feelings and reflections. In *Frammenti del perpetuo poema*, 'il mare che si frange tra gli scogli / canta al sereno enigmi della vita' (the sea breaking onto the rocks / sings the enigmas of life to the clear sky),[24] and a marine mother is evoked to render a sense of emptiness, the vacuum of death and the impermanence of human life:

---

20 I. Calvino, 'L'oceano e il ragazzo di Giuseppe Conte' (1984), in Italo Calvino, *Saggi*, 2 vols, ed. by M. Barenghi (Milan: Mondadori), 1995, I, pp. 1049–52. **21** G. Conte, *Le stagioni*, p. 39. **22** G. Conte, *Canti d'Oriente e d'Occidente*, p. 124. **23** Conte, *Canti*, pp. 27 and 88. **24** Tonelli, *Frammenti*, p. 85.

> Madre marina da segreti anfratti
> a me ridente immobile – parole -
> nell'ora dell'addio sorgi conducimi
> là dove il tempo è vuoto labirinto
> e la vita istanti impercettibili
> d'oblio guizzanti d'uno ad altro cuore.[25]

(Marine mother smiling at me / motionless from secret ravines – words – / at the time of farewell rise, lead me / where time is an empty labyrinth / and life is imperceptible instants / of oblivion darting from one heart to the next.)

However, Tonelli moves away from Montale's secular views when he portrays nature as pervaded by a spiritual essence and even by the presence of gods and angels. In the following short text, for instance, we observe a respectful quotation of a key-concept, Montale's 'varco' ('Il varco è qui?' Is the opening here?) from 'La casa dei doganieri',[26] situated within the landscape and metaphorically indicating a search for a way out of an existential block, but we also note that Tonelli's philosophical context is metaphysical and therefore different from Montale's:

> è tale il nostro andare assorto, vigile
> di goccia in goccia limpida di vita
> o torbida. E il cerchio che s'irradia
> al nostro profondare è cosa breve
>
> ma non piccola cosa: si apre un varco
> e ciò che era forma nel disperdersi
> diviene eternità, nasce ad un Essere
> più fermo e impenetrabile, più vasto.[27]

(such is our going, absorbed, watchful, / drop by drop of life, clear / or unclear. And the circle that radiates / out from our sinking down is a brief // but not a little thing; a pathway opens / and that which was form in the scattering / becomes eternity, born of a Being / more fixed and impenetrable, more vast.)[28]

---

25 Tonelli, *Frammenti*, p. 93. **26** E. Montale, *L'opera in versi*, p. 161. **27** Tonelli, *Frammenti*, p. 104. In 'La casa dei doganeri', Montale writes: 'Il varco è qui?' (E. Montale, *L'opera in versi*, p. 161). **28** Translation by B. Lynch, in A. Tonelli, *Parole sul dorso di serpente del mare / Words on the Serpent-shaped Back of the Sea, Chapbook for a poetry reading*, ed. R. Bertoni,

This leads to a first conclusion. With regard to the literary tradition from the middle ages onwards, the critical canon formulated by the myth-modernists gives renewed value to classical and modern authors characterized by ideological depth and communicative language; these are two literary features employed by the myth-modernists in their own creative writing. Despite this, they see themselves as a modern movement. According to Kemeny, *mitomodernismo* can be in fact 'imagined as the latest avantgarde' in the twentieth century.[29]

SACRALITY, MYTH, ARCHAISM, SYMBOLS

In the creation of its poetic code, *mitomodernismo* values positively myth, symbols, and spirituality, in a constellation of concepts which will now be briefly examined. While doing so, archaic sources from Greek, Oriental and other traditions will be mentioned in addition to the literary models indicated in the previous section of this essay. The mystic aspect of *mitomodernismo* consists in attributing a sacral significance to poetry and life.

In a manifesto written in verse, Conte states that *mitomodernismo* 'del cosmo celebra il segreto divino' (celebrates the divine secret of the cosmos).[30] Life and death are linked to archetypes, as in the following lines:

> Acqua della fine
> Acqua del principio
> l'anima ti attraversa
> forse su nave o naufraga
> tra venti immani, o forse
> a nuoto, a nuoto
> e lenta, come un loto,
> una zattera.[31]

(Water of the end / Water of the beginning – / the soul crosses you / perhaps on a ship, or it shipwrecks / among powerful winds, or maybe / swimming, swimming / slowly, like a lotus, / like a raft.)[32]

Italian Department, Trinity College Dublin, 2003, p. 8. (Other translators in the same volume: V. Benzoni, L.S. Gatta, C. Ó Cuilleanáin, C. O'Brien and one translation revised by C. Salvadori Lonergan.) **29** 'È immaginabile come l'ultima delle avanguardie' – 'Intervista a Tomaso Kemeny', p. 211. **30** G. Conte, *Mitomodernismo*, <http://www.maschiselvatici. it/pensieroselvatico/conte.htm>. **31** G. Conte, *Le stagioni*, p. 92. **32** Translation by L. Stortoni-Hager, in G. Conte, *The Seasons / Le stagioni*, p. 95.

Within this context, we note spiritual and religious symbols:

> Staremo allora nella luce, nella
> verità
> e ciascuno di noi conoscerà
> il suo Dio.[33]

(we shall then be in the light, in the / truth / and each of us will know / his God.)

In 'Oh Omero, Oh Whitman', Conte defines the meaning of poetry as salvation by alluding to the Hindu religious tradition (Shiva, the destroyer and giver of life) with Jungian motifs: 'io sono il poeta, il distruttore, io sono il poeta, colui che salva' (I am the poet, the destroyer, I am the poet, he who saves).[34] Such a peculiar type of religiousness is confirmed later in this poem through an allusion to Shiva's cosmic dance: 'questo linguaggio, eredità di Dio e dei poeti, è ancora preghiera e danza' (this language, a legacy from God and the poets, is still prayer and dance).[35]

In the aforementioned dialectic of flesh and spirit, even the aim of Conte's carnal knowledge is an approach to the divine:

> La meta del desiderio è la fine del desiderio, la meta del piacere è la fine
>   del piacere.
> L'anima non ha altra meta che essere, la pienezza dell'essere – se l'essere
>   è Dio –
> e la Parola, la pienezza della Parola, – se è vero che abita all'inizio presso
>   Dio ed è Dio –.[36]

(The aim of desire is the end of desire, the aim of pleasure is the end of pleasure. / The soul has no other aim than being, the fullness of being – if being is God – / and the Word, the fullness of the Word – if it is true that it dwells in the beginning with God and is God –.)

In Conte's aesthetics, poetry, like nature and the whole universe, is pervaded by a sense of the sacred: 'Sacra, sacra, sacra la Parola, la Terra, la mano che scrive e che carezza, la nuvola, la volta del cielo' (Sacred, sacred, sacred is the Word, the earth, the hand which writes and caresses, the cloud, the vault of the sky).[37]

The sacred assumes similar, though distinct, connotations in Tonelli's work.

---

33 Ibid., p. 109. 34 G. Conte, *Canti d'Oriente e d'Occidente*, p. 88. 35 Ibid., p. 92. 36 Ibid., p. 105. 37 Ibid.

Distancing himself somewhat from *mitomodernismo* in a strict sense, he has recently started a literary current called 'rite-modernism', *ritomodernismo*, and in its manifesto he states: 'the rite-modernist poet and artist recreate the link with the sacred. [...] The sacred should not be confused with religion – I define as *sacred* the sense of absolute which dwells at the root of all things, even the most secular'.[38] Thus in his poetry we find the constant presence of immortal entities and symbols called 'gods' which indicate aspects of nature and the interiority while they are the givers of the gift of poetry to human beings. According to Tonelli, the language of poetry is a 'riverbero di luce / l'Immortale che pulsa alla radice' (it is rapid reflection of light / the Immortal that pulses at the root).[39] The voice of the poet is compared to a bow which releases musical notes ('così tende le note l'arco mio') that permeate an environment inhabited by pale gods ('pallidi dèi').[40]

In Tonelli's poetics Montale's opening (or 'varco') is changed in such a way as to become the space and time hinge between the world of the secular and the world of mysterious and immaterial entities. Such a 'varco' will open up again at some stage, and through it the gods will return to earth: 'si aprirà il varco / torneranno gli dèi' (there will be an opening again / and the gods will come back).[41]

This sacral aspect in *mitomodernismo* cohabits with myth, understood as the source of poetry, associated with dreams and filled with mysterious connotations. As Kemeny puts it, 'dream and myth are defined in an enigma'.[42] Common to Conte and Tonelli is reference to Greek classical myth. Tonelli communicates messages which he sees as conveyed in a dreamy way from the gods Apollo and Dionysus – these messages assign him the mission of expressing the harmony of the cosmos.[43] Conte, in *Le stagioni*, receives poetical mes-

---

38 A. Tonelli, *Per un manifesto del ritomodernismo*, leaflet distributed by hand and electronically from Lerici, November 2004. (Italian text: 'Il Poeta, l'Artista Ritomodernista ricompone il legame con il sacro [...]. Il *sacro* non va confuso con il religioso: definisco *sacro* il senso dell'Assoluto che dimora alla radice di tutte le cose, anche le più laiche'). **39** Tonelli, *Frammenti*, p. 105. Translation by B. Lynch, in A. Tonelli, *Parole sul dorso di serpente del mare / Words on the Serpent-shaped Back of the Sea*, Chapbook for a poetry reading, cit., p. 11. **40** Ibid., p. 92. **41** Ibid., p. 226. **42** 'Il sogno e il mito si definiscono in un enigma' – 'Intervista a Tomaso Kemeny', p. 209. **43** 'In my early youth I went to Greece. My project was to reconstruct the Orphic-Dionysiac Mysteries and render their spirit through poetry without mimicking them in a neoclassical way. Traces of this can be found in my *Canti del tempo* (1988) as well as in *Poemi dal Golfo degli Dei* (2003). I was fortunate to see the gods – Apollo on Parnassus, and Dionysus in Crete. I asked for a sign from them, and in a starry night a meteorite crossed the sky. A dimension which combines life and magic constitutes the true essence of poetry' (A. Tonelli, *Poetry, knowledge and the sacred in the classical Greek lyrical poets, Empedocles and Eliot*, lecture given at Trinity College Dublin, 24 October 2003).

sages from Hermes, and visits both the areas of Hades and the Empyrean.[44] However, each poet develops references to myth in his own distinctive way. Tonelli, moving towards a magical direction, gives his own interpretation of early alchemists (Zosimus of Panopolis in particular) and pre-Socratic philosophers (especially Empedocles) as being shamans and wizards. In his manifesto of rite-modernism he brings together writers and thinkers, both eastern and western, ancient and modern: 'Buddha and Breton, Nagarjuna and Neruda, Empedocles and Gozzano, Parmenides and Montale'.[45] Conte initially combines Greek myth with northern myths, namely the Celtic tradition of Ireland, as can been seen in *L'oceano e il ragazzo*, while in *Il sonno degli dèi* he addresses mythical worlds from Egypt, America and the Far East.[46]

This interest in a variety of unusual myths, systems of thought and cultures constitutes an enlargement of the system of intertextual references to classical Greek, Latin and Italian sources normally found in the traditional Italian canon. There are other Italian writers who have shown similar interests in the twentieth century, but they have remained a minority until recent years.[47]

This leads to a second conclusion. The relationship of *mitomodernismo* with the canon of antiquity does not appear to be a routine reference of a neoclassical type – it does not intend merely to imitate the past, but rather to recapture myth as a source of literary inspiration and collective ritual. At the beginning of a theatrical performance directed by Tonelli and based on Sophocles, the Chorus recites an alchemical formula while holding flaming torches, the fire of which is a symbol of regeneration.[48] Barbara Ferullo, an actress in the myth-modernist theatrical company Vertex, states that the work of her company is something sacred, like an ancient Greek invocation to the gods.[49] As already noted, despite its tribute to tradition, *mitomodernismo* projects itself towards modernity. Of this double link with antiquity and the present, Tonelli writes that 'the rite-modernist poet is situated within the tradition of poetry and art as an avantgarde dated 2500 years before Christ and

---

[44] G. Conte, *Le stagioni*. [45] A. Tonelli, *Per un manifesto del ritomodernismo*. [46] G. Conte, *L'oceano e il ragazzo* (Milan: Rizzoli, 1983); *Il sonno degli dèi. La fine dei tempi nei miti delle grandi civiltà* (Milan: Rizzoli, 1998). [47] See in particular P.P. Pasolini and G. Bonaviri, who refer ideologically and intertextually both to Italian folklore and international archaic cultures. [48] *Vitriolum. Alchimia per Edipo Re*, played by Compagnia Teatro Iniziatico Athanor, a theatrical company founded and directed by Angelo Tonelli. (Actors: Luigi Armelloni, Alberto Fiorito, Simona Menicagli, Sara Montefiori, Susy Polgatti, Susanna Salvi, Angelo Tonelli, Iride Varese.) The performance was given on 30 July 2004 at Castello San Giorgio, La Spezia. [49] 'Per noi è, come per gli antichi greci, compiere qualcosa di sacro, un'invocazione agli dei' – Interview with Barbara Ferullo, <http://www.perimetro.com/vertex.htm>.

more than 2000 years after'.[50] Kemeny explains more concisely that the modern is 'eternal'.[51]

One eternal aspect of myth-modernist poetics is constituted by archetypes. Conte and Tonelli interpret psychological symbolism according to the theories of Jung and Hillman, and in particular they adopt the concept of 'anima', briefly mentioned above, which, it should now be specified, indicates the subconscious.[52] This term is important since it already figured in the 1994 manifesto, where a wish was expressed that myth might bring back the 'anima' to humankind.[53] The task assigned to *mitomodernismo* by Giampiero Marano is a 'transgressive [...] revolt [...] in the name of a forgotten prehistoric, [...] prophetic [...] and visionary soul'.[54] Conte's approach is clearly found in the second part of *Le stagioni*, a sequel of poems subdivided into four sections: water, earth, air and fire. Fire is the element which indicates a passage towards transcendence. Both water and fire are symbols of the 'anima', while the whole sequence may be considered an allegory of a spiritual initiation rite, a Jungian individuation-process open to all human beings.

A third possible conclusion is therefore that in *mitomodernismo* enigmatic archetypes and symbols are expressed with pathos and without euphemism because they are seen both as manifestations of a spiritual type of interiority, and as essential components of the individual and collective psyche.

POETRY AS EXISTENTIAL AND POLITICAL ACTION

An important feature of *mitomodernismo* is the vital and practical side of reflection on beauty, an active intervention in reality which consists of existential action, social ethics and political engagement. Some of these pragmatic aspects of myth-modernist poetics warrant brief illustration.

The importance of action is often highlighted by the *mitomodernisti*. According to Zecchi, beauty has 'great Utopian force'.[55] The 1994 manifesto

50 'Il Poeta, l'Artista Ritomodernista si collocano nella tradizione poetica-artistica come una avanguardia datata duemilacinquecento anni avanti Cristo e più di duemila dopo.' – A. Tonelli, *Per un manifesto del ritomodernismo*. 51 *Intervista a Tomaso Kemeny sul mitomodernismo*, p. 209. 52 See C. G. Jung, *Anima e morte* (1934) and *Sul rinascere* (1940/1950), first published in Italian in 1978 (Turin: Bollati Boringhieri, 2002); and J. Hillman, *The Soul's Code: In search of Character and Calling* (New York: Random House, 1996), Italian translation *Il codice dell'anima* (Milan: Adelphi, 1997). 53 The Italian version of the manifesto says 'Il mito riporti tra noi anima, natura, eroe, destino', quoted in G. Marano, *La democrazia e l'arcaico. Il destino poetico dell'uomo contemporaneo* (Casalecchio, Bologna: Arianna, 1999), p. 43. 54 'Rivolta [...] trasgressiva [...] in nome della dimenticata anima preistorica, [...] profetica [...] e visionaria' – G. Marano, *La democrazia e l'arcaico*, p. 8. 55 'Il Festival dei nemici del bello'.

exhorts: 'Let us create action from art'.[56] In Conte's manifesto in verse, poetry is defined as 'action'. In Tonelli's manifesto, 'rite-modernism is a declension of artistic action in a radical, wise, revolutionary, mystical and operational key'.[57] Within poetry, Conte identifies 'un'energia che smuove' (an energy creating movement);[58] and Tonelli expresses 'a concept of art as energy and as a written, oral or enacted event'.[59] In both cases we note an irrational non-conformism integrated with the lucid power of reason – in Conte's manifesto, *mitomodernismo* is 'un gesto maturato fuori dalla ragione / eppure più razionale di quelli dei potenti' (a gesture grown outside reason / and yet more rational than those of the powerful).[60]

Conte values positively both the asceticism of Arab mystics,[61] and the passion of nineteenth-century European writers. He states: 'il mitomodernismo è etica e piacere. / Sesso ascesi virtù sfrenatezza rigore' (*mitomodernismo* is ethics and pleasure, / sex, asceticism, virtue, unbridledness and rigour); he hopes that the poet may be motivated by 'rivolta e destino, [...] sogno e [...] avventura' (revolt and destiny, dream and adventure).[62] In brief, he proposes existential liberation, coherent with the fact that the ethical mission of art, for the myth-modernists, consists in awakening the individual, thus giving meaning to life; more precisely, as stated in the verse manifesto:

> il mitomodernismo è [...]
> dire: questo io sono, dire: questo io voglio.
> Dare un senso alla vita per assurda che sia.[63]

(myth-modernism is [...] / to say: this is what I am, and this is what I want. / To attach a meaning to life, as absurd as it may be.)

Kemeny highlights the relationship between the individual and society by observing that the 'lotta per la bellezza' (struggle for beauty) is conducted by individuals both in solitude and through solidarity with one another.[64] In Kemeny's view, poetry, as in the humanist and Renaissance traditions, has the

---

56 The Italian phrase in the manifesto is 'Facciamo dell'arte azione', quoted in G. Marano, *La democrazia e l'arcaico*, p. 43. **57** 'Il Ritomodernismo è una declinazione dell'agire artistico in chiave radicale, sapienziale, rivoluzionaria, mistica, operativa' – A. Tonelli, *Per un manifesto del ritomodernismo*. **58** G. Conte, *Mitomodernismo*. **59** 'Una concezione dell'arte come energia/evento scritto orale o agito' – A. Tonelli, *Per un manifesto del ritomodernismo*. **60** Ibid. **61** See G. Conte, 'Canti di Yusuf Abdel Nur', in *Canti d'Oriente e d'Occidente* (Milan: Mondadori, 1997), pp. 9–64. **62** G. Conte, *Mitomodernismo*. **63** Note in passing the polemic with Montale's 'Codesto solo oggi possiamo dirti, / ciò che *non* siamo, ciò che *non* vogliamo' (E. Montale, 'Non chiederci la parola', *L'opera in versi*, p. 27). **64** 'Intervista a Tomaso Kemeny', p. 210.

task of directing the 'energia spirituale dell'epoca' towards 'la sopravvivenza, la dignità, la cortesia, la bellezza' (survival, dignity, courtesy and beauty);[65] contemporary poets should rediscover positive values even in an era characterized by technology, and therefore rediscover 'valori umani' (human values) in opposition to the present consumerist world.[66]

The questioning of contemporary chaos by a number of myth-modernists includes a critique of the reduction of human beings to economic, consumer entities. They see art as a vehicle for salvation. In a wider political sense, as stated in the 1994 manifesto, in order to offer some salvation, they wish that 'politics may have supremacy over economics, and poetry may have supremacy over politics'.[67] Zecchi maintains that the defence of beauty stands in opposition to left-wing cultural policies. However, Conte and Tonelli explicitly support freedom and civil rights, denounce the environmental and social deterioration of the planet Earth, and engage with social issues in ways which would appear to be oriented towards the left (even though within the contemporary so-called post-ideological political panorama). Conte writes that *mitomodernismo* 'è innanzi tutto azione […], inventa una politica' (is primarily action […], invents a type of politics), and he clarifies: 'il poeta […] fa del canto ribellione / contro il tiranno ingiusto, contro ogni oppressione' (the poet makes his song into rebellion / against the unjust tyrant, against any oppression).[68]

The particular type of awakening proposed by Tonelli is a non-violent struggle based on a transformation of individual consciousness. Such a change should stimulate individuals to fight against what he calls the three 'demons' of contemporary society, namely ignorance, greed and violence, which, combined with ecological carelessness and the lack of scruple among politicians, are bringing the planet to the verge of an apocalypse. Tonelli has even attempted to found a political association based on such ideals. In his poetry, these political propositions assume overtones of invective and prophecy:

> scuotiti da cima a fondo, immensa chiavica
> umana, fatti colma
> di una purezza immacolata, nevica
> candore di rinascita, orma su orma
> di luce riscattata dalle tenebre.
> liberati dal dominio dei tre dèmoni
> e del diodenaro, che ti involgono

---

65 Ibid., p. 211.   66 Ibid., p. 212.   67 'La politica abbia il primato sull'economia, la poesia abbia il primato sulla politica' – in G. Marano, *La democrazia e l'arcaico*, p. 43.   68 G. Conte, *Mitomodernismo*.

> in una nube nera che degli uomini
> farà insetti nocivi.[69]

(shake from top to bottom, immense human / sewer, become full of / immaculate purity, pour a candid / snow of rebirth, footprint on footprint / of light rescued from the darkness. / free yourself from the rule of the three demons / and the money-god, which wrap you / in a dark cloud that will change men / into harmful insects.)

And:

> […] lacero la maschera
> di preti papi capi e presidenti,
> scherani dei tre dèmoni
> e del diodenaro.[70]

([…] I tear the mask / of priests popes leaders and presidents, / bandits of the three demons / and of the money-god.)

For Conte, too, the world around us is pervaded by negative passions, corruption and fraud:

> La fame dell'oro è contagiosa
> e incurabile, ben più di un colera.
> Hanno vinto ogni guerra frode e usura.[71]

(Greed for gold is far more / contagious and incurable than cholera. / Fraud and usury have won every war.)

He suggests that salvation from this may take place through Utopia (or 'sogno', dream).[72] This Utopian dream is created by individuals who are capable of being authentically free. The poet in fact defines himself as born from democratic energy ('figlio dell'energia democratica'), while adding that he does not belong to any specific form of affiliation ('non appartengo a nessuna casta o dinastia, a niente mi inchino').[73]

Ultimately, according to Conte, it is the task of poetry to express a holistic and cosmopolitan position, sympathy for the oppressed, and an ideal of freedom

---

69 A. Tonelli, *Alphaomega (variazioni per violino e voce)* (Lerici, La Spezia: Abraxas-Keraunós, 2000). **70** Ibid. **71** G. Conte, *Canti d'Oriente e d'Occidente*, p. 109. **72** 'Essere / fedele sino in fondo al sogno' – ibid., p. 81. **73** Ibid., p. 101.

punctuated with romantic and religious connotations, or, as he puts it in 'La poesia apre il fuoco (monito zoroastriano ai Potenti della Terra dal Mar Ligure)':

> La poesia apre il fuoco
> – il fuoco del mondo è Amore –
> è suo l'urlo ai Potenti della Terra
> 'adoratela la Madre Terra
> inchinatevi, inchinatevi
> inchinatevi al Santo Mississippi
> inchinatevi al Santo Oceano Atlantico
> inchinatevi alle Sante Montagne Rocciose
> inchinatevi al Santo Fuoco'
> – il fuoco del mondo è Amore –.
> La poesia apre il fuoco.
> E' sole, legno, rami, germogli, foglie, fiori, frutti
> è fuoco
> – il fuoco del mondo è Amore –
> è mare, nuvola, vapore, pioggia, sorgente, fiume, flutti
> è nave, veliero, rimorchiatore
> Energia & Libertà, Lavoro & Piacere.
>
> Inchinatevi, Potenti, al Santo Golfo di Genova
> inchinatevi al Santo Guglielmo Embriaco
> inchinatevi al Santo Golfo dei Poeti
> inchinatevi al Santo Shelley
> inchinatevi al Santo Fuoco
> – il fuoco del mondo è Amore –.
>
> La poesia apre il fuoco
> è indiana, tamil, maghrebina
> palestinese, albanese, colombiana
> è tutti quelli che soffrono
> è 25 milioni di bambini schiavi
> che lavorano per te e tu non lo sai
> e muoiono per te e tu non lo sai.
>
> La poesia prega per la terra, i mari,
> gli alberi, i campi di grano, i fiori,
> i giardini, i pianeti, i cieli stellati,
> le città, i porti, i naviganti,
> tra le onde e nella rete

per chi ha fame, per chi ha sete,
per i randagi, gli schiavi, i senza lavoro,
per gli dèi di tutte le religioni
per la Santa Libertà che illumina
per l'Anima che si espande infinita
per la Vita, lo spirito della Vita.

Signore pietà
Krishna pietà
Ahriman pietà
Signore pietà
Fuoco pietà.

Il mondo deve rinascere nel fuoco
– il fuoco del mondo è Amore –.

(Poetry opens fire / – the fire of the world is Love – / She will scream to the / Powerful Kings of the Earth / 'worship Mother Earth / bow, bow / bow to the / Holy Mississippi / bow to the Holy Atlantic Ocean / bow to the Holy Rocky Mountains / bow to the Holy Fire' / – the fire of the world is Love –. // Poetry opens fire. / It is sun, wood, branches, buds, leaves, flowers, fruits / it is a fire / – the fire of the world is Love – / it is a sea, a cloud, mist, rain, springs, river, waves / it is a ship, a sailing ship, a tugboat / Energy & Freedom & Work & Pleasure. // Bow, Powerful Kings, to the Holy gulf of Genoa / bow to the Holy Guglielmo Embriaco / bow to the Holy Gulf of the Poets / bow to the Holy Shelley / bow to the Holy Fire / – the fire of the world is Love. // Poetry opens fire / poetry is Indian, Tamil, North African, Palestinian, Albanian, Colombian, / poetry is all those who suffer / poetry is 25 million enslaved children / who work for you and you don't know it / who die for you and you don't know it. // But poetry prays for the land, the seas, / the trees, the fields of grain, the flowers, / the gardens, the planets, the starry skies, / the cities, the ports, the sailors / among the waves and in the net / poetry prays for whoever is hungry and thirsty / poetry prays for the homeless, the slaves, the unemployed / for the gods of all religions / for the Holy Freedom that awakens / for the Soul that grows in infinite ways / for Life and the spirit of Life. // Lord have mercy / Krishna have mercy / Ahriman have mercy / Lord have mercy / Fire have mercy. // The world must be reborn in fire / the fire of the world is Love.)[74]

74 *Le acque di Hermes / The Waters of Hermes*, 3, 2004 (trans. by M. Maggiari, rev. by C. Ó

In conclusion it would appear that a number of myth–modernist poets are inspired by the cultural and pragmatic tradition of social ideologies, and by the ethics of secular and religious philosophies. If, on the one hand, *mitomodernismo* works within the classical literary and modern canons and stimulates them towards new directions, on the other hand it promotes a type of literature which is linked to life, it is not merely a paper product but rather a socially committed project, even though this type of idealistic commitment does not always coincide with previous forms of commitment as they were experienced in recent Italian literary history.

Cuilleanáin), pp. 11–15.

Contributors

RICHARD ANDREWS is emeritus professor of Italian at the University of Leeds. He is the author of *Scripts and Scenarios: the Performance of Comedy in Renaissance Italy* (1993), and of other writings on early modern theatre and opera in Italy, France and England. He has also written on Ariosto, on Calvino, and on the long-standing community theatre project of Monticchiello, Tuscany.

PETER ARMOUR (died 2002), formerly professor of Italian at Royal Holloway, was an eminent Dantist, whose publications include *The Door of Purgatory: A Study of Multiple Symbolism in Dante's 'Purgatorio'* (1983), *Dante's Griffin and the History of the World: A Study of the Earthly Paradise* (1989), and a reassessment of 'Dante's Contrapasso: Context and Texts', *Italian Studies* (2000). Among his many articles, he intended to gather into a volume those on Michelangelo's *Moses*.

ROSANGELA BARONE, literary critic and formerly associate professor at the University of Bari, and Director of the Italian Cultural Institute, Dublin, has published on Hardy, Woolf, Beckett, O'Casey and Friel; she has translated into Italian from English and Gaelic. Her most recent publication (with graphic artist Franco Ferrovecchio) is a bilingual edition of Eoghan Ó Tuairisc, *Aifreann na Marbh, Messa dei defunti* (2005).

ROBERTO BERTONI is senior lecturer in Italian at Trinity College Dublin. He has written *Int'abrigu int'ubagu: Discorso su alcuni aspetti dell'opera di Italo Calvino* (1993), *Calvino ludico* (with Bruno Ferraro, 2003), and articles on modern Italian literature, including Leopardi's influence on recent Italian authors. He edits *Quaderni di cultura italiana*. Translations: poems by Carson, Heaney, Lynch, Mahon, Ní Chuilleanáin and others.

JOSEPH FARRELL is professor of Italian Studies at the University of Strathclyde. He is author of *Leonardo Sciascia* (1995) and *Dario Fo and Franca Rame: Harlequins of the Revolution* (2001). Co-editor of a forthcoming *History of Italian Theatre*, he has edited works on the mafia, on Goldoni, on Primo Levi as well as plays by Pirandello and Fo. Translations: works by Sciascia, Consolo, Fo, Goldoni, and Del Giudice.

MARK HUTCHESON read Russian and French at Trinity College Dublin, where he subsequently taught in the Department of French and the School of English. He is a poet and a poetry translator who has published widely in Ireland and abroad. He works as a teacher of English Language in Dublin.

BRIAN MOLONEY, emeritus professor of Italian at the Universities of Hull and Wollongong, has written mainly on Italo Svevo and other nineteenth- and twentieth-century novelists. His recent books include *Italo Svevo narratore: lezioni triestine* (1998), *'This England Is So Different …': Italo Svevo's London Writings* (with John Gatt-Rutter, 2003) and *Italian Novels of Peasant Crisis: Bonfires in the Night* (2005).

EILÉAN NÍ CHUILLEANÁIN is associate professor of English at Trinity College Dublin. She is editor of *The Wilde Legacy* (2003), has published articles on Thomas More and on translation, and has translated poetry from Irish, French, Italian and Romanian, most recently *After the Raising of Lazarus*, from the Romanian of Ileana Mălăncioiu (2005). Her latest book of poetry is *The Girl Who Married the Reindeer* (2001).

DARAGH O'CONNELL is a graduate of the Italian Department in Trinity College Dublin, where he also lectured for two years. He is currently lecturing in University College Dublin. His main field of interest is nineteenth- and twentieth-century Sicilian literature, and the narrative works of Vincenzo Consolo in particular. He has also published on Giambattista Vico and Joyce.

CORMAC Ó CUILLEANÁIN is senior lecturer in Italian at Trinity College Dublin. His publications include *Religion and the Clergy in Boccaccio's Decameron* (1984) and a new version of Boccaccio's *Decameron* based on John Payne's Victorian translation (2004). He is joint editor of *Italian Storytellers* (1989), *The Languages of Ireland* (2004) and *Patterns in Dante* (2005). As Cormac Millar, his crime novels are published by Penguin.

CAROL O'SULLIVAN is senior lecturer in Italian Language and Translation Theory at the University of Portsmouth. She has published articles on the work and reception of Raymond Queneau, on translations of Blasket Island autobiography and on contemporary Italian genre fiction in translation. Her current research is on the writer as translator. She is a practising translator from Italian.

CORINNA SALVADORI is emeritus Fellow at Trinity College Dublin and Cavaliere all'Ordine della Repubblica. Author of *Yeats and Castiglione: Poet and*

Courtier (1965), editor and translator of Lorenzo de' Medici, *Selected Writings* (1992), and an editor, since 1990, of *Civiltà Italiana*. She has written on Dante, Ariosto, Beckett, and verse translation (Lorenzo de' Medici and Poliziano).

JOHN SCATTERGOOD has been professor of Medieval and Renaissance Literature at Trinity College Dublin since 1980. Among his many books are editions of *The Works of Sir John Clanvowe* (1976) and *John Skelton: The Complete English Poems* (1983). His latest critical books are *Reading the Past: Essays on Medieval and Renaissance Literature* (1996) and *The Lost Tradition: Essays on Middle English Alliterative Poetry* (2000).

GEORGE TALBOT is senior lecturer in Italian at the University of Hull. He has written *Montale's 'mestiere vile'* (1995), edited a volume of Montale's *Selected Poems* (2000), *Lord Charlemont's History of Italian Poetry from Dante to Metastasio* (2000), and several collections of essays, as well as publishing articles on Italian literature and history (Montale, Moravia, Sebastiano Vassalli, and others).

DOUG THOMPSON is emeritus professor of Italian at the University of Hull. His books include *Cesare Pavese: A Study of the Major Novels and Poems* (1982), *State Control in Fascist Italy* (1991) and *Reconsidering Pavese: 'Onde di questo mare'* (with Rossella Riccobono, 2003). Translations: works by Duranti, Capriolo and Marinetti. Author of a novel, *The Lych Gate* (2000), he also paints and has held exhibitions in England and Germany.

Index

This is essentially an index of names, mostly of people, places, works of literature and films, though a number of more general categories have been included. It does not include the names of characters in literary texts or films. It includes the names of scholars mentioned in the main text of the essays but not those referred to only in the footnotes. The arrangement is alphabetical, as generally is the arrangement within items, except in the case of the Bible where the arrangement follows the Authorized Version order of books. There are several general entries – films and television, mythological figures and places, political events, saints – where the arrangement is again alphabetical.